BT 7/16

Cousin Joseph

Cousin Joseph

A Graphic Novel

Jules Feiffer

Liveright Publishing Corporation
A Division of W. W. Norton & Company
Independent Publishers Since 1923
New York   London

For information about permission to reproduce selections from this book,
write to Permissions, Liveright Publishing Corporation,
a division of W. W. Norton & Company, Inc.,
500 Fifth Avenue, New York, NY 10110

For information about special discounts for bulk purchases, please contact
W. W. Norton Special Sales at specialsales@wwnorton.com or 800-233-4830

Manufacturing by Toppan Leefung
Production manager: Anna Oler

Library of Congress Cataloging-in-Publication Data

Names: Feiffer, Jules, author, illustrator.
Title: Cousin Joseph : a graphic novel / Jules Feiffer.
Description: First edition. | New York : Liveright Publishing Corporation, [2016]
Identifiers: LCCN 2016003857 | ISBN 9781631490651 (hardcover)
Subjects: LCSH: Graphic novels. | Noir fiction. | Comic books, strips, etc.
Classification: LCC PN6727.F4 C68 2016 | DDC 741.5/973—dc23
LC record available at http://lccn.loc.gov/2016003857

Liveright Publishing Corporation
500 Fifth Avenue, New York, N.Y. 10110
www.wwnorton.com

W. W. Norton & Company Ltd.
Castle House, 75/76 Wells Street, London W1T 3QT

1 2 3 4 5 6 7 8 9 0

To Roger Rosenblatt, Private Eye

and

To JZH, the Brains of the Operation

Cousin Joseph

1931

PROLOGUE

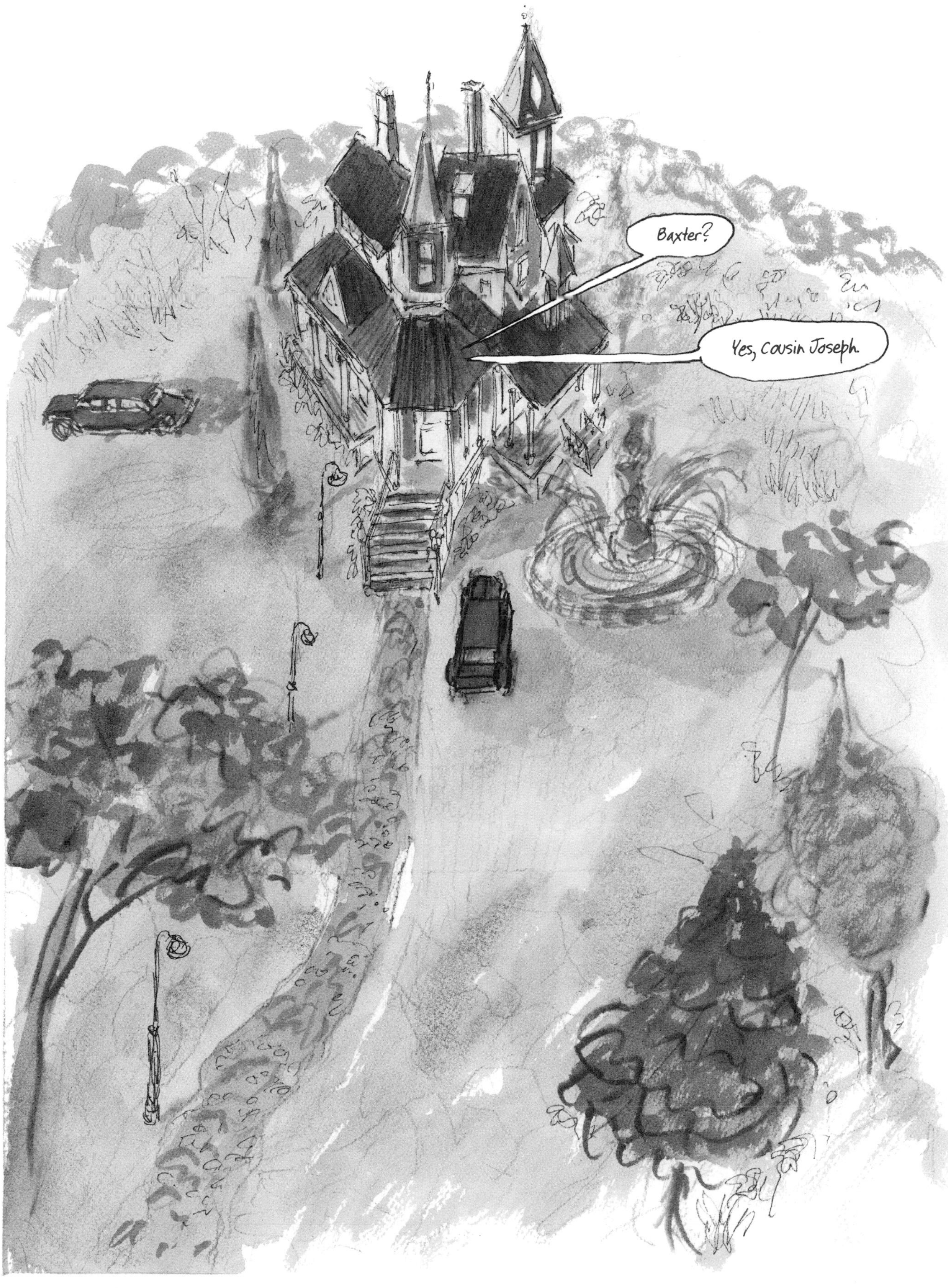

Baxter?
Yes, Cousin Joseph.

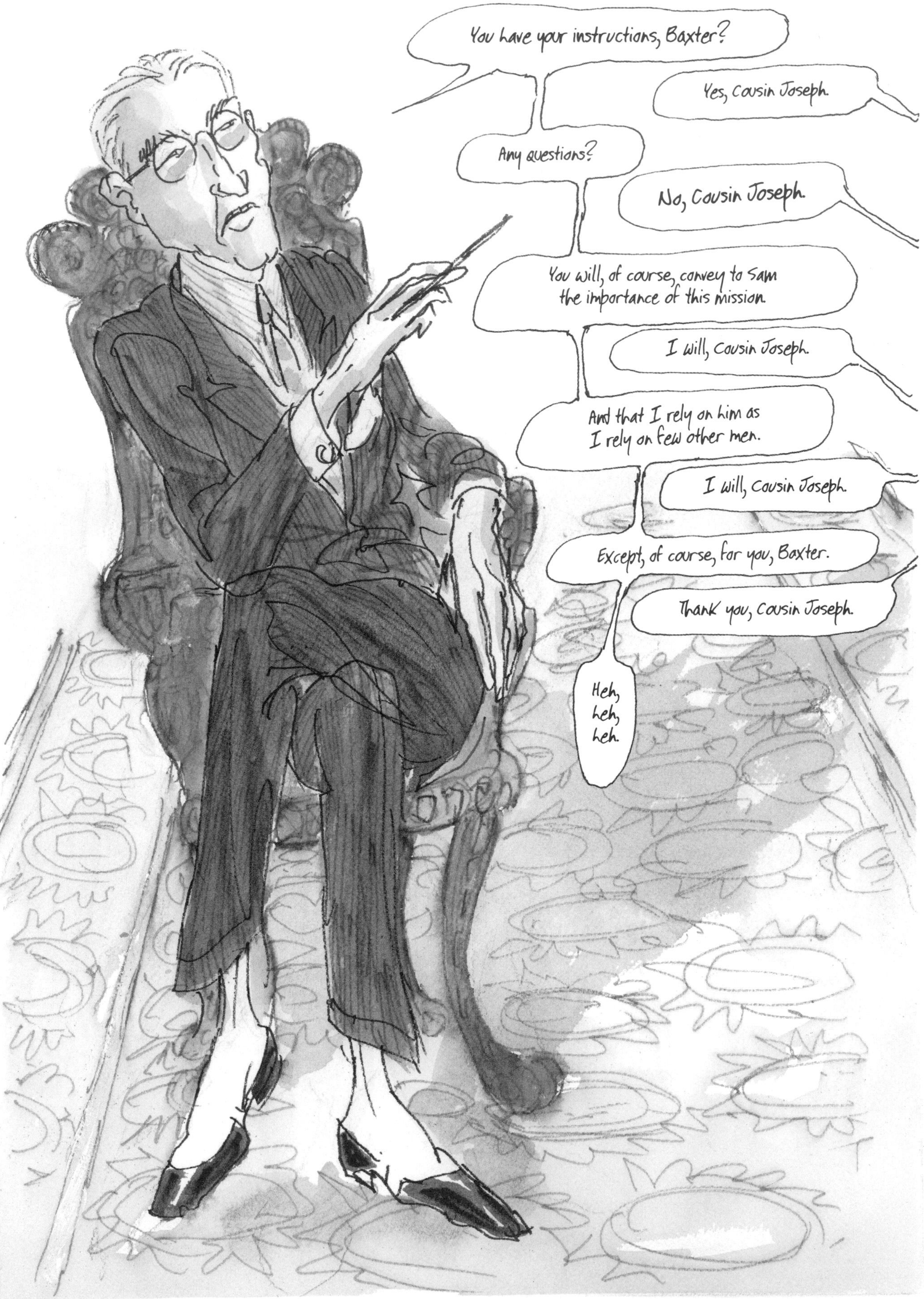
You have your instructions, Baxter?
Yes, Cousin Joseph.
Any questions?
No, Cousin Joseph.
You will, of course, convey to Sam the importance of this mission.
I will, Cousin Joseph.
And that I rely on him as I rely on few other men.
I will, Cousin Joseph.
Except, of course, for you, Baxter.
Thank you, Cousin Joseph.
Heh, heh, heh.

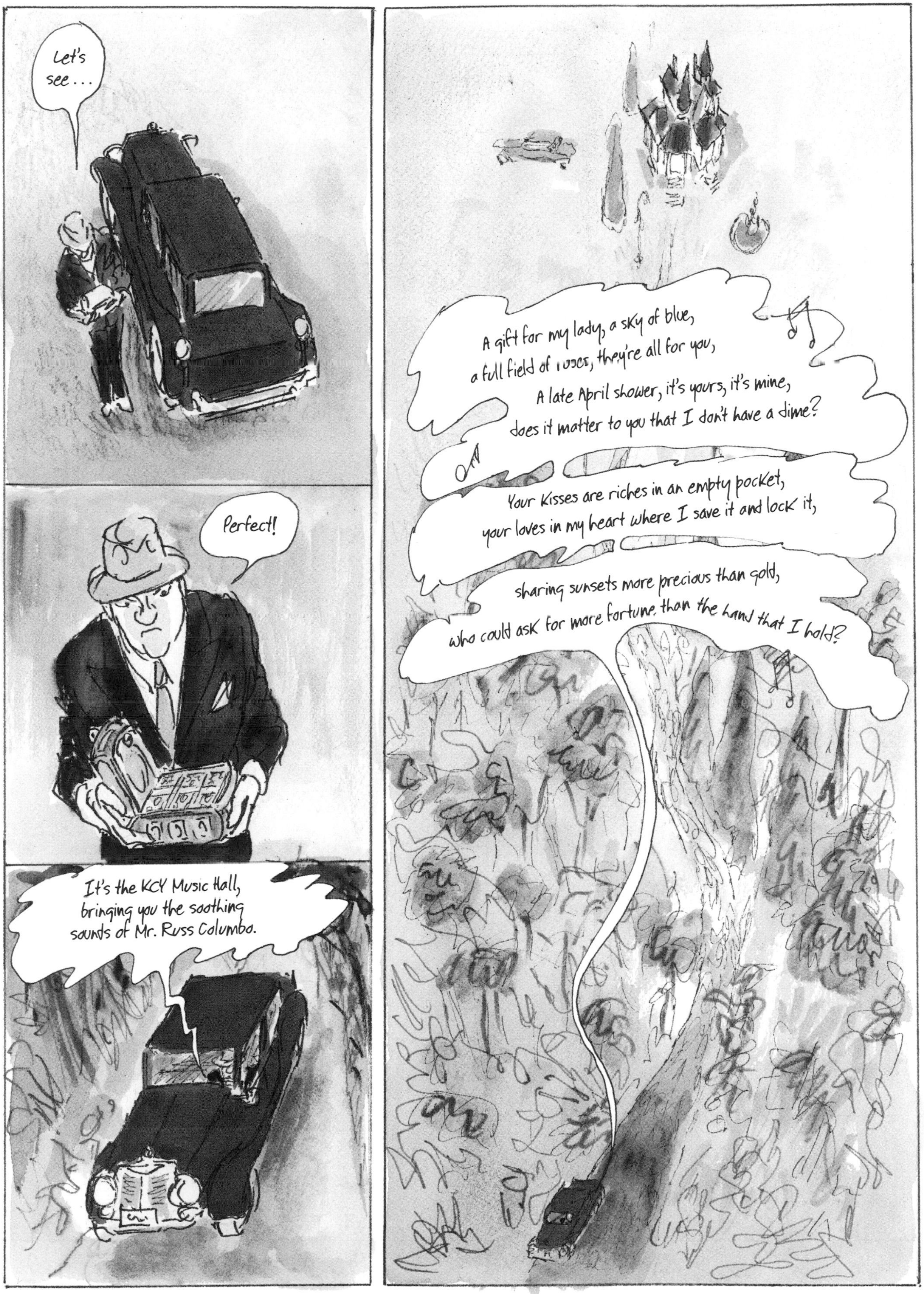
Let's see . . .
Perfect!
It's the KCY Music Hall, bringing you the soothing sounds of Mr. Russ Columbo.
A gift for my lady, a sky of blue, a full field of roses, they're all for you, A late April shower, it's yours, it's mine, does it matter to you that I don't have a dime?
Your kisses are riches in an empty pocket, your loves in my heart where I save it and lock it,
sharing sunsets more precious than gold, who could ask for more fortune than the hand that I hold?

Chapter One: How It Begins

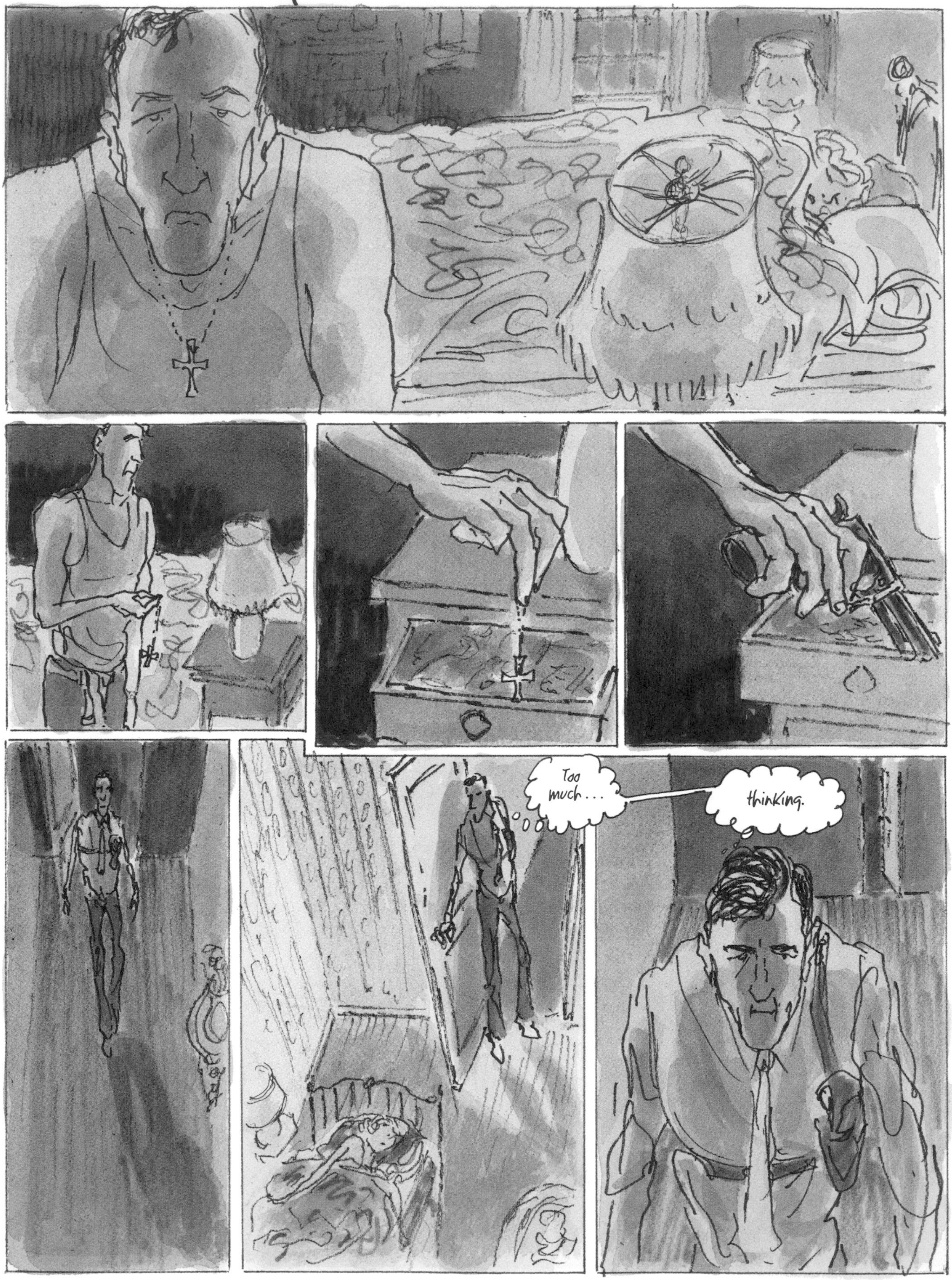
Too much...
thinking.

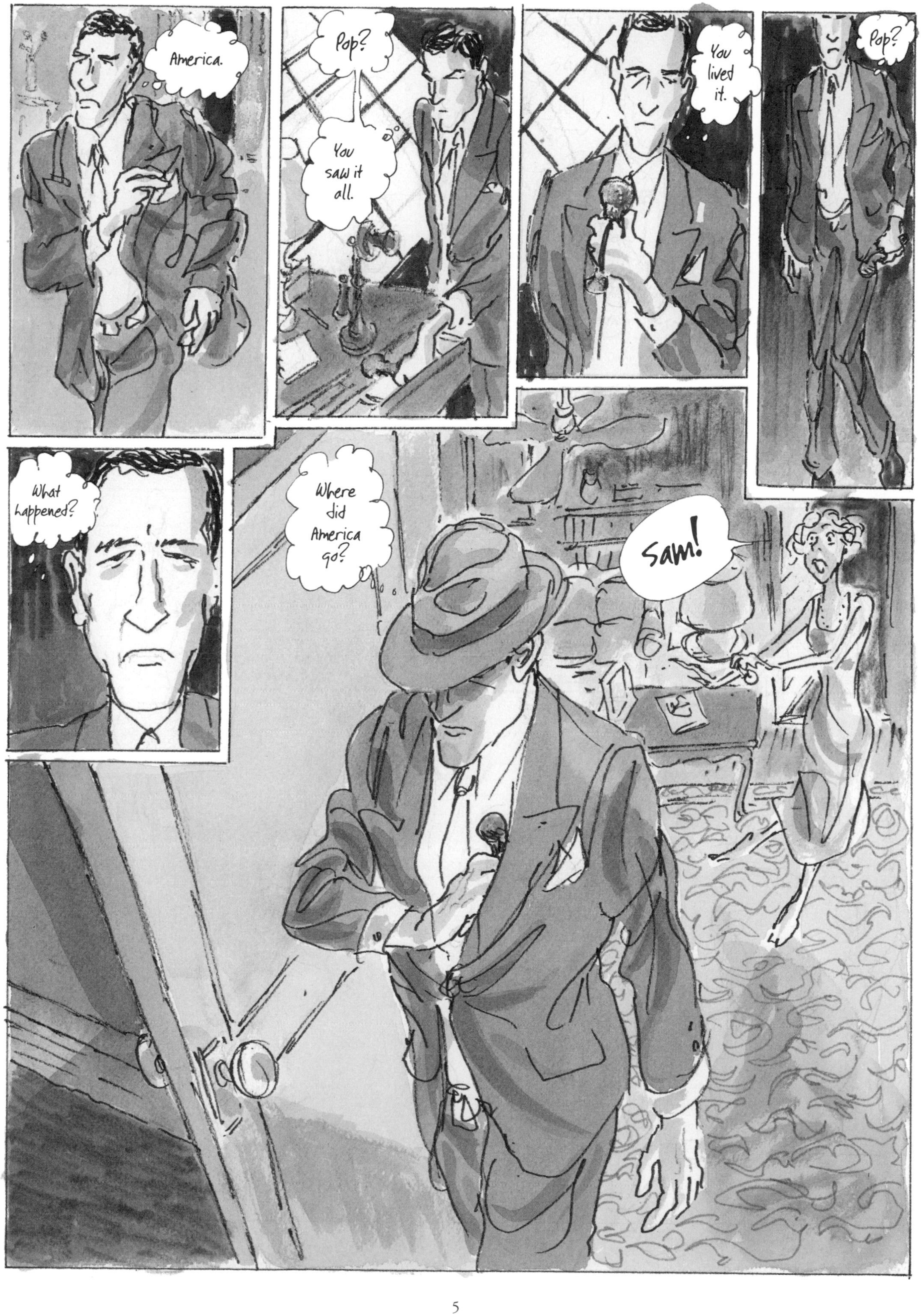
America.
Pop?
You saw it all.
You lived it.
Pop?
What happened?
Where did America go?
Sam!

Chapter Two: Departure

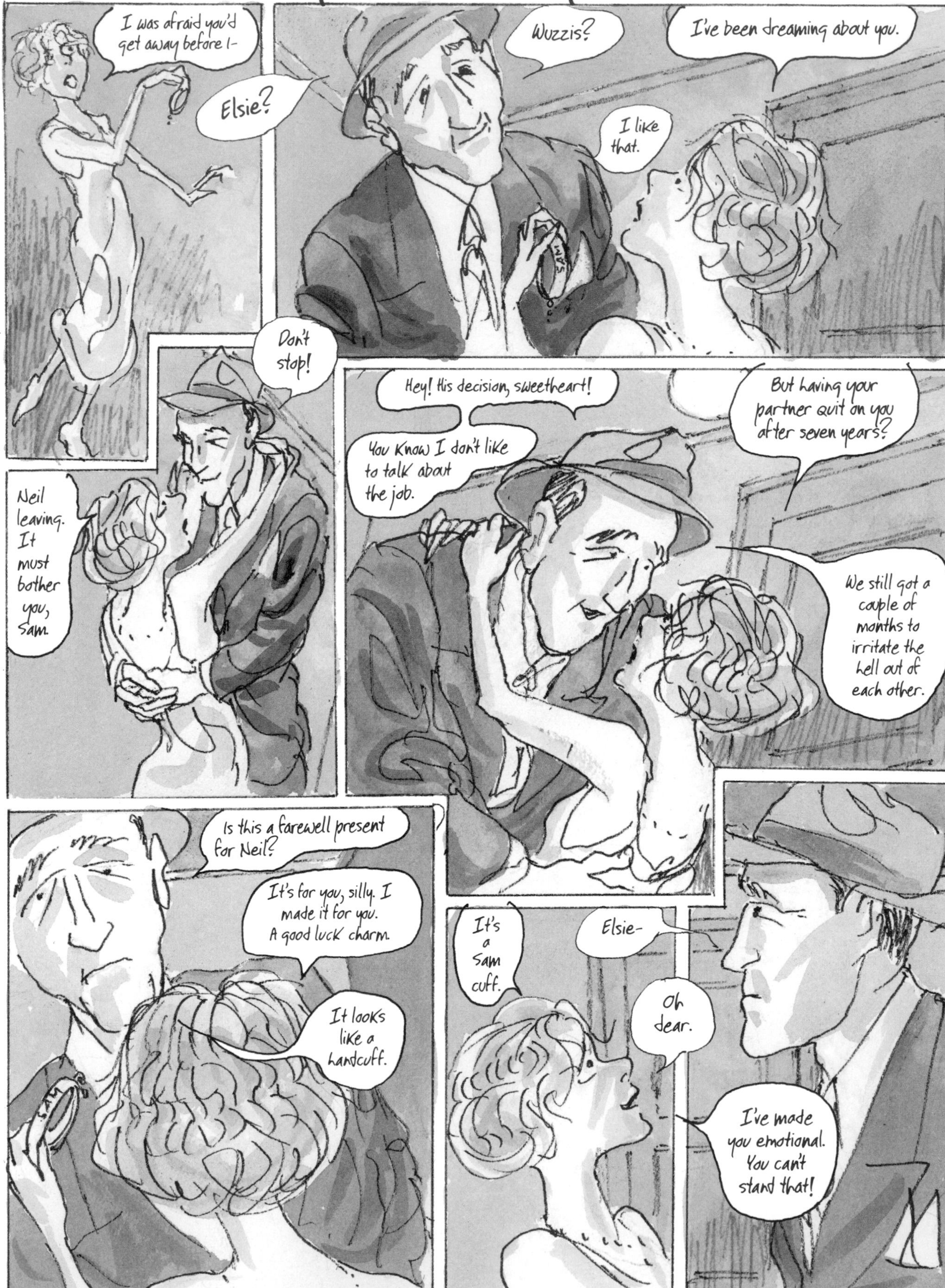
I was afraid you'd get away before I-
Elsie?
Wuzzis?
I've been dreaming about you.
I like that.
Don't stop!
Neil leaving. It must bother you, Sam.
Hey! His decision, sweetheart!
You know I don't like to talk about the job.
But having your partner quit on you after seven years?
We still got a couple of months to irritate the hell out of each other.
Is this a farewell present for Neil?
It's for you, silly. I made it for you. A good luck charm.
It looks like a handcuff.
It's a Sam cuff.
Elsie-
Oh dear.
I've made you emotional. You can't stand that!

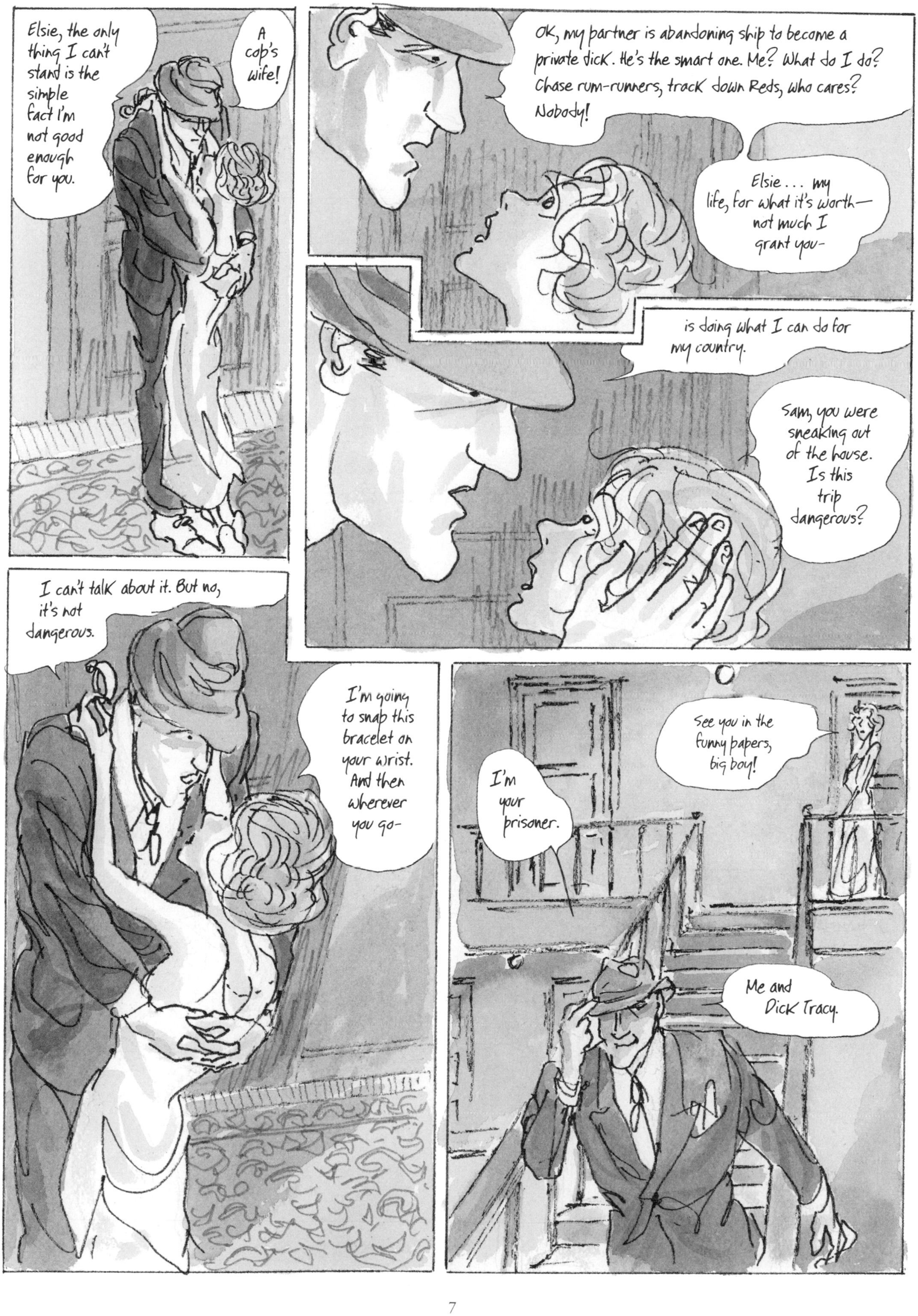
Elsie, the only thing I can't stand is the simple fact I'm not good enough for you.
A cop's wife!
OK, my partner is abandoning ship to become a private dick. He's the smart one. Me? What do I do? Chase rum-runners, track down Reds, who cares? Nobody!
Elsie . . . my life, for what it's worth— not much I grant you-
is doing what I can do for my country.
Sam, you were sneaking out of the house. Is this trip dangerous?
I can't talk about it. But no, it's not dangerous.
I'm going to snap this bracelet on your wrist. And then wherever you go-
I'm your prisoner.
See you in the funny papers, big boy!
Me and Dick Tracy.

Chapter Three: The Mission

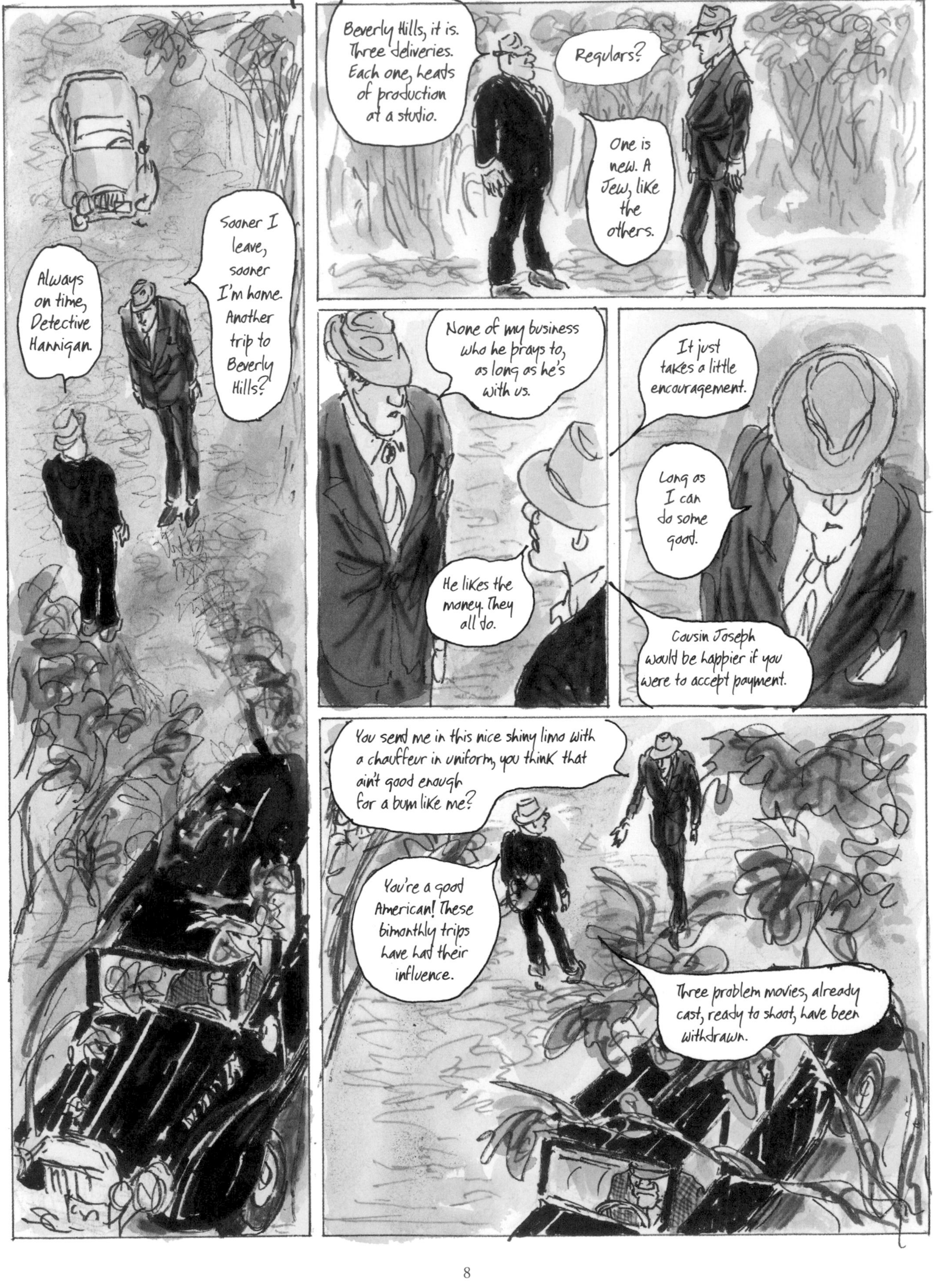
Always on time, Detective Hannigan.
Sooner I leave, sooner I'm home. Another trip to Beverly Hills?
Beverly Hills, it is. Three deliveries. Each one, heads of production at a studio.
Regulars?
One is new. A Jew, like the others.
None of my business who he prays to, as long as he's with us.
He likes the money. They all do.
It just takes a little encouragement.
Long as I can do some good.
Cousin Joseph would be happier if you were to accept payment.
You send me in this nice shiny limo with a chauffeur in uniform, you think that ain't good enough for a bum like me?
You're a good American! These bimonthly trips have had their influence.
Three problem movies, already cast, ready to shoot, have been withdrawn.

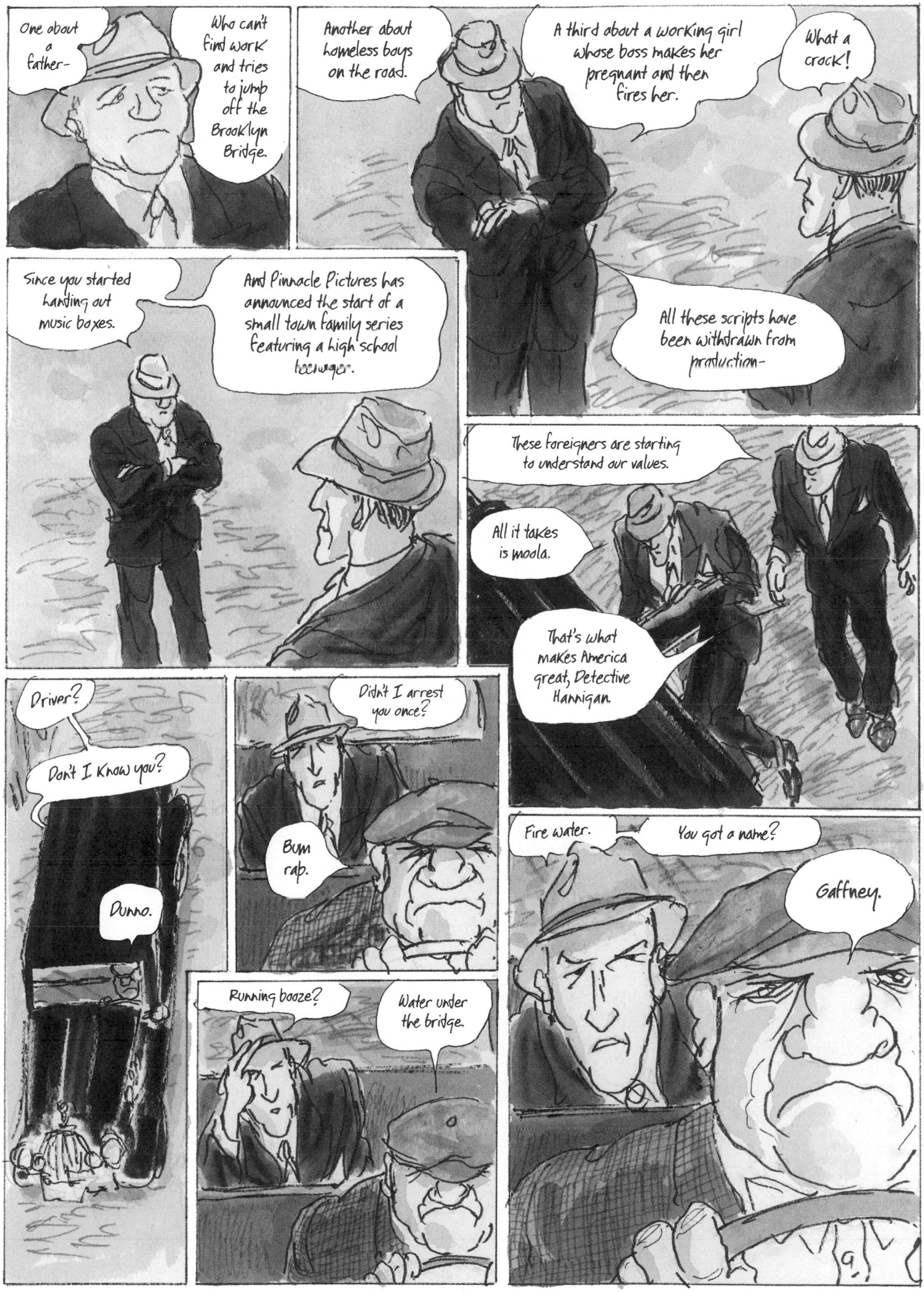

One about a father-
Who can't find work and tries to jump off the Brooklyn Bridge.
Another about homeless boys on the road.
A third about a working girl whose boss makes her pregnant and then fires her.
What a crock!
All these scripts have been withdrawn from production-
Since you started handing out music boxes.
And Pinnacle Pictures has announced the start of a small town family series featuring a high school teenager.
These foreigners are starting to understand our values.
All it takes is moola.
That's what makes America great, Detective Hannigan.
Driver?
Don't I know you?
Dunno.
Didn't I arrest you once?
Bum rap.
Running booze?
Water under the bridge.
Fire water.
You got a name?
Gaffney.

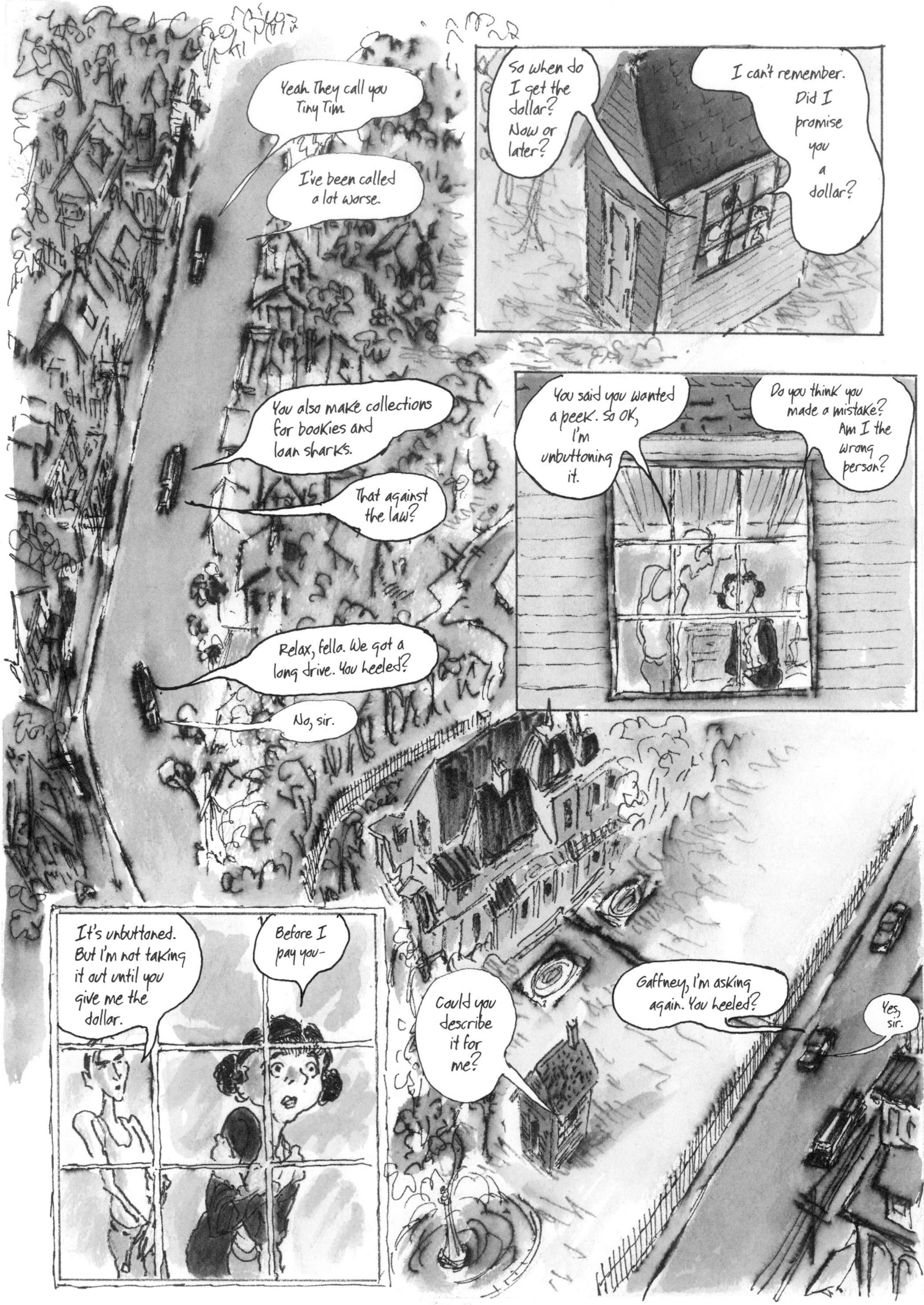
Yeah. They call you Tiny Tim.
I've been called a lot worse.
So when do I get the dollar? Now or later?
I can't remember. Did I promise you a dollar?
You also make collections for bookies and loan sharks.
That against the law?
You said you wanted a peek. So OK, I'm unbuttoning it.
Do you think you made a mistake? Am I the wrong person?
Relax, fella. We got a long drive. You heeled?
No, sir.
It's unbuttoned. But I'm not taking it out until you give me the dollar.
Before I pay you-
Could you describe it for me?
Gaffney, I'm asking again. You heeled?
Yes, sir.

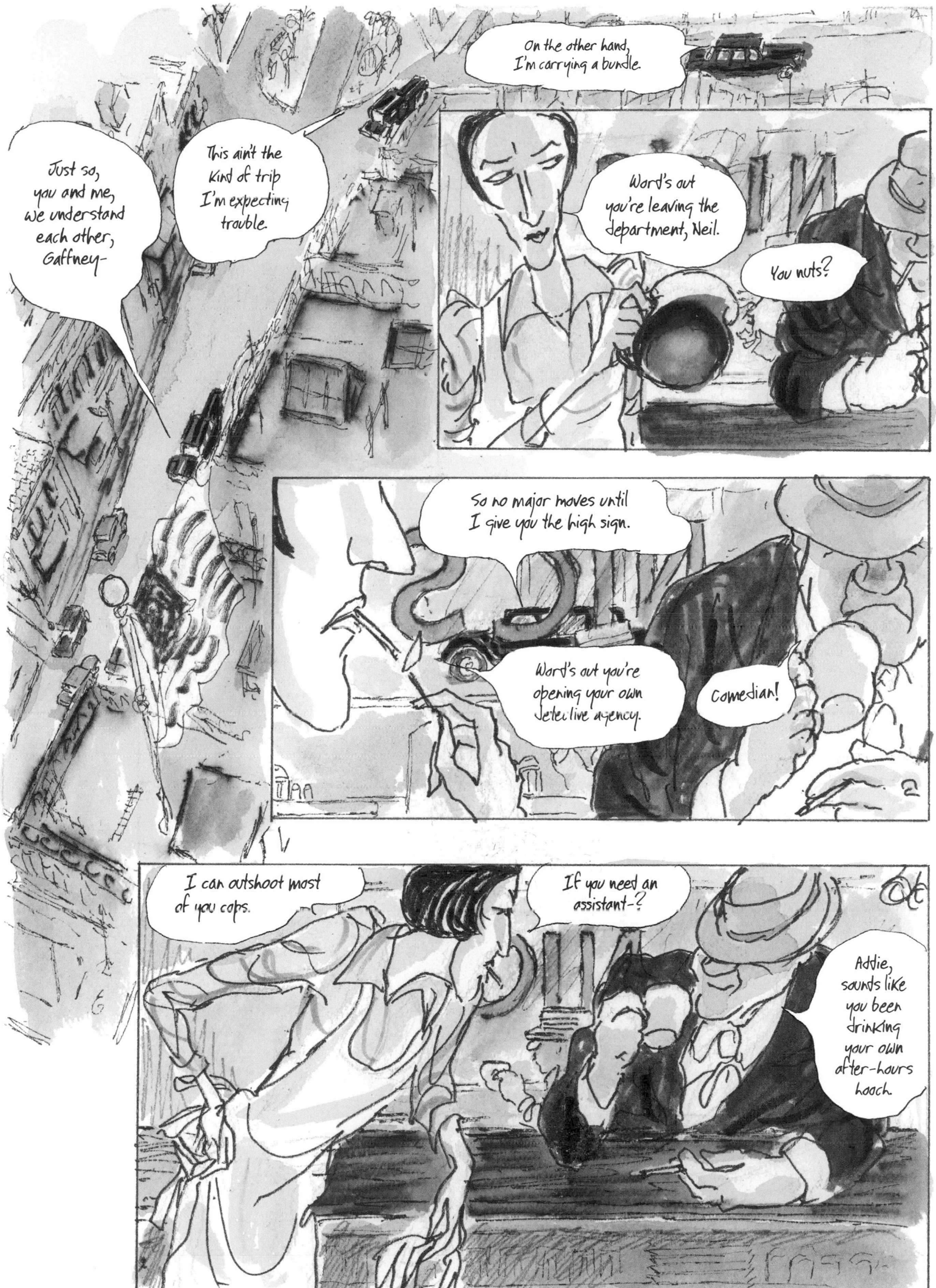
On the other hand, I'm carrying a bundle.
This ain't the kind of trip I'm expecting trouble.
Just so, you and me, we understand each other, Gaffney-
Ward's out you're leaving the department, Neil.
You nuts?
So no major moves until I give you the high sign.
Ward's out you're opening your own detective agency.
Comedian!
I can outshoot most of you cops.
If you need an assistant-?
Addie, sounds like you been drinking your own after-hours hooch.

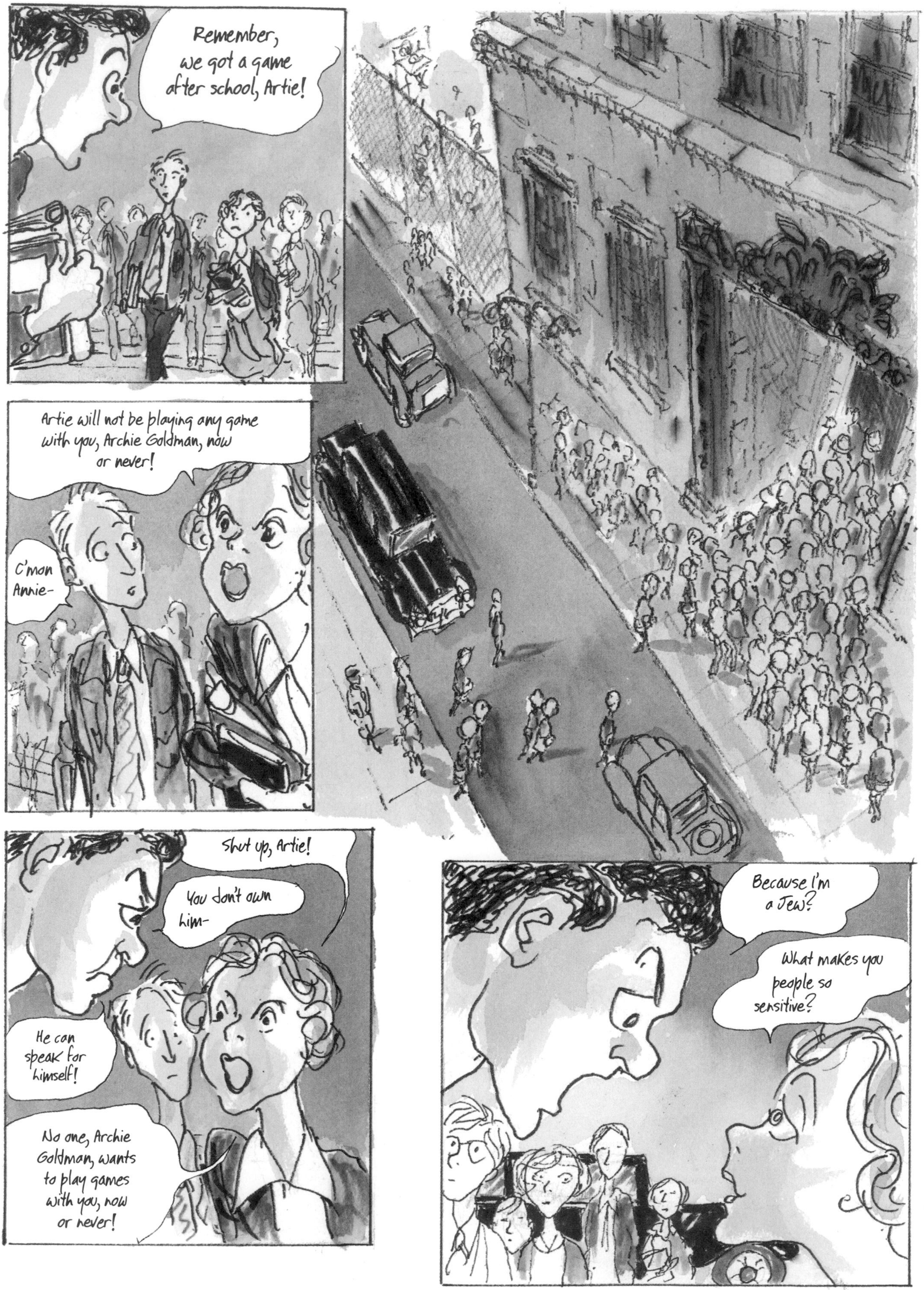
Remember, we got a game after school, Artie!
Artie will not be playing any game with you, Archie Goldman, now or never!
C'mon Annie-
Shut up, Artie!
You don't own him-
He can speak for himself!
No one, Archie Goldman, wants to play games with you, now or never!
Because I'm a Jew?
What makes you people so sensitive?

Chapter Four: Knoxworks

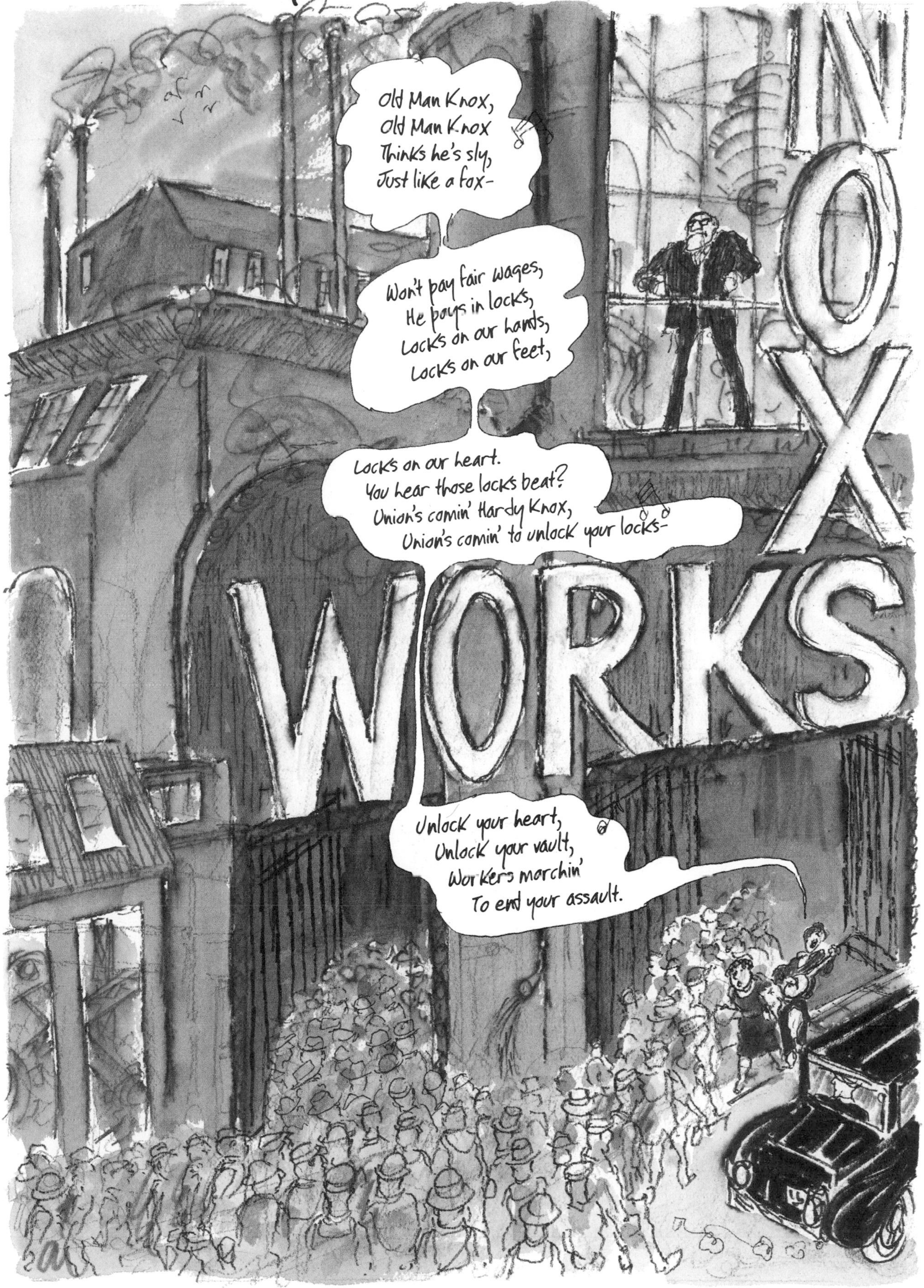

Old Man Knox, Old Man Knox Thinks he's sly, Just like a fox-
Won't pay fair wages, He pays in locks, Locks on our hands, Locks on our feet,
Locks on our heart. You hear those locks beat? Union's comin' Hardy Knox, Union's comin' to unlock your locks-
KNOX
WORKS
Unlock your heart, Unlock your vault, Workers marchin' To end your assault.

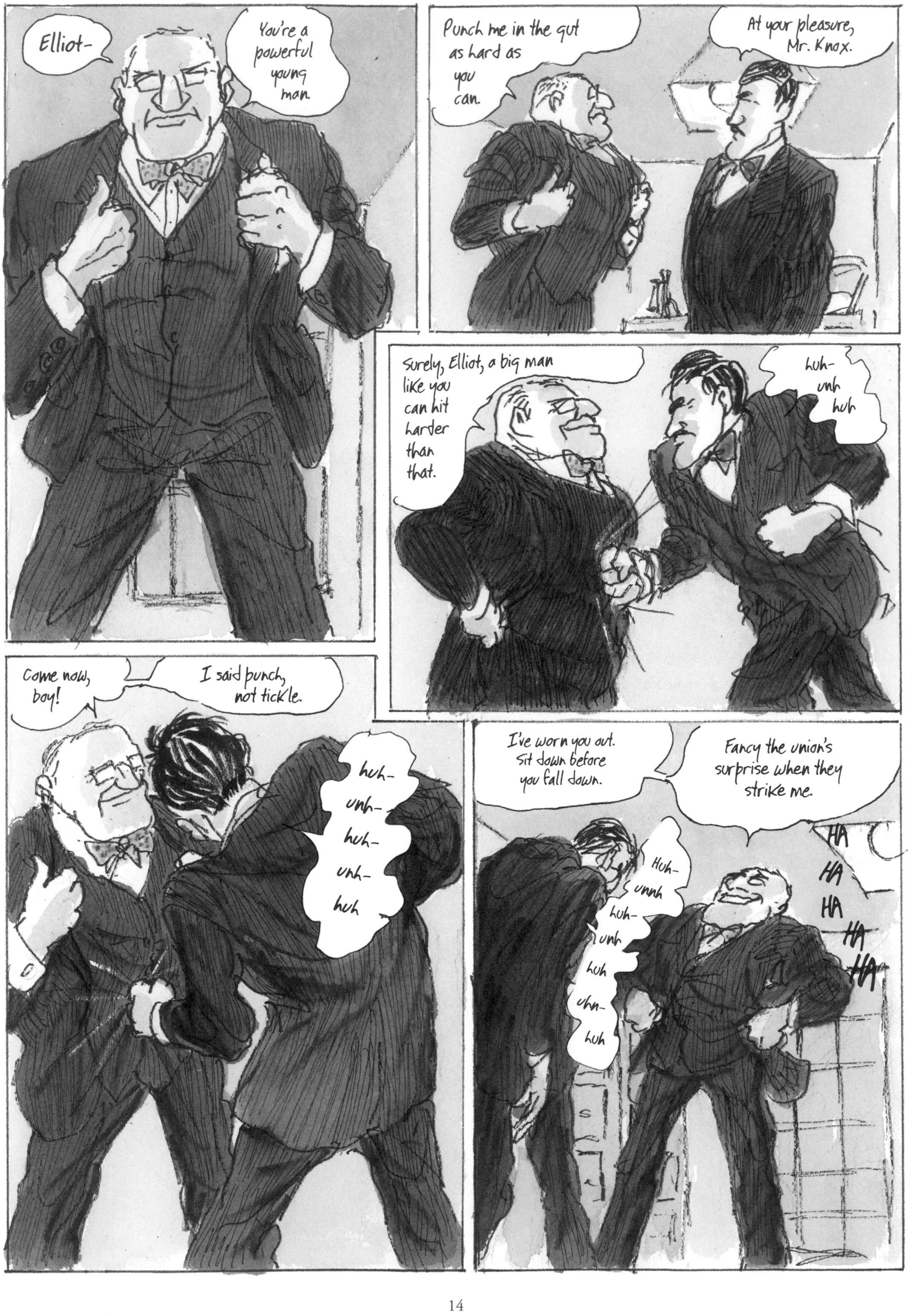
Elliot-
You're a powerful young man.
Punch me in the gut as hard as you can.
At your pleasure, Mr. Knox.
Surely, Elliot, a big man like you can hit harder than that.
huh-unh-huh
Come now, boy!
I said punch, not tickle.
huh-unh-huh-unh-huh
I've worn you out. Sit down before you fall down.
Fancy the union's surprise when they strike me.
Huh-unnh-huh-unh-huh-uhn-huh
HA HA HA HA HA

Chapter Five: The Music Box Caper

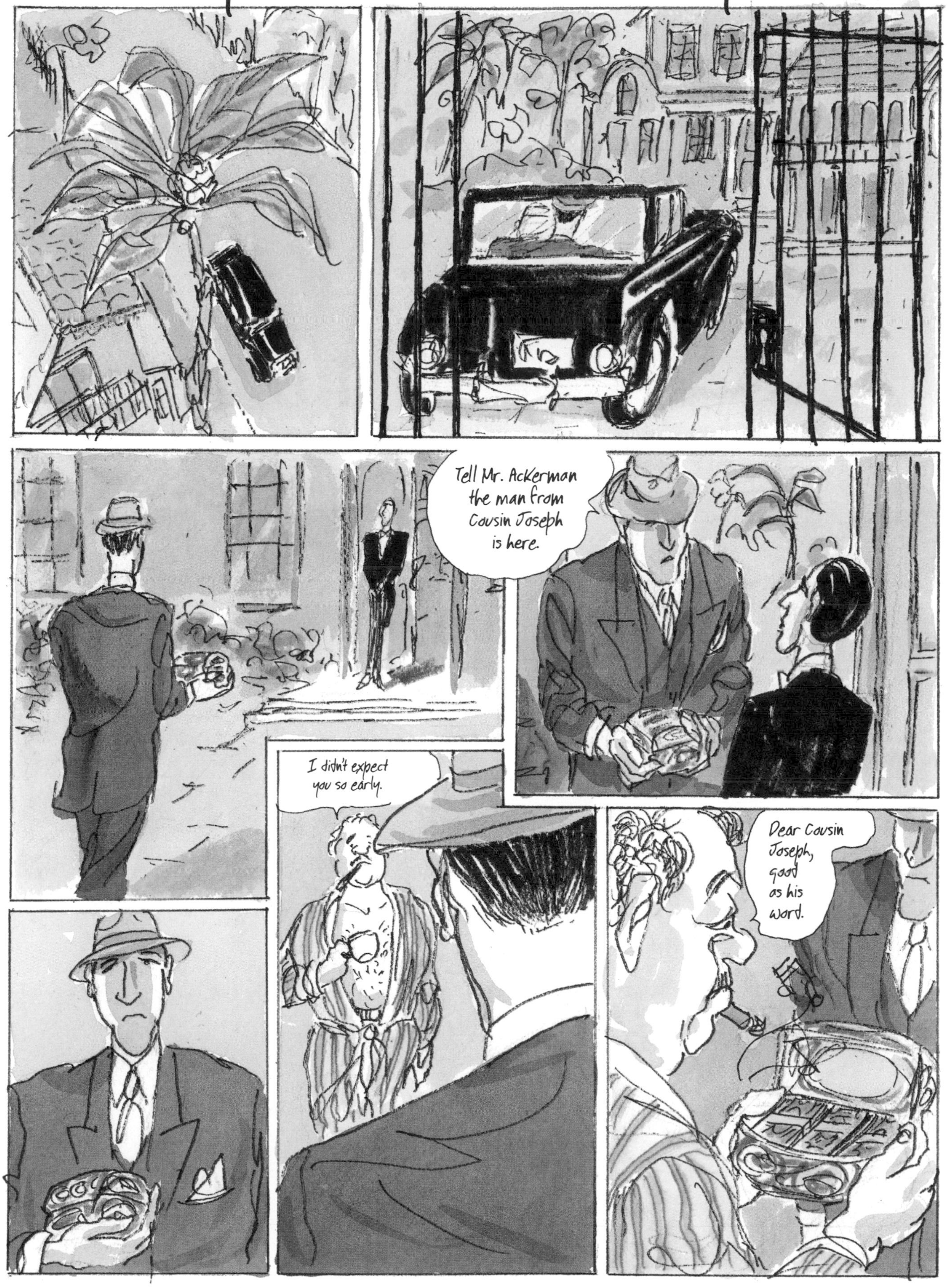
Tell Mr. Ackerman the man from Cousin Joseph is here.
I didn't expect you so early.
Dear Cousin Joseph, good as his word.

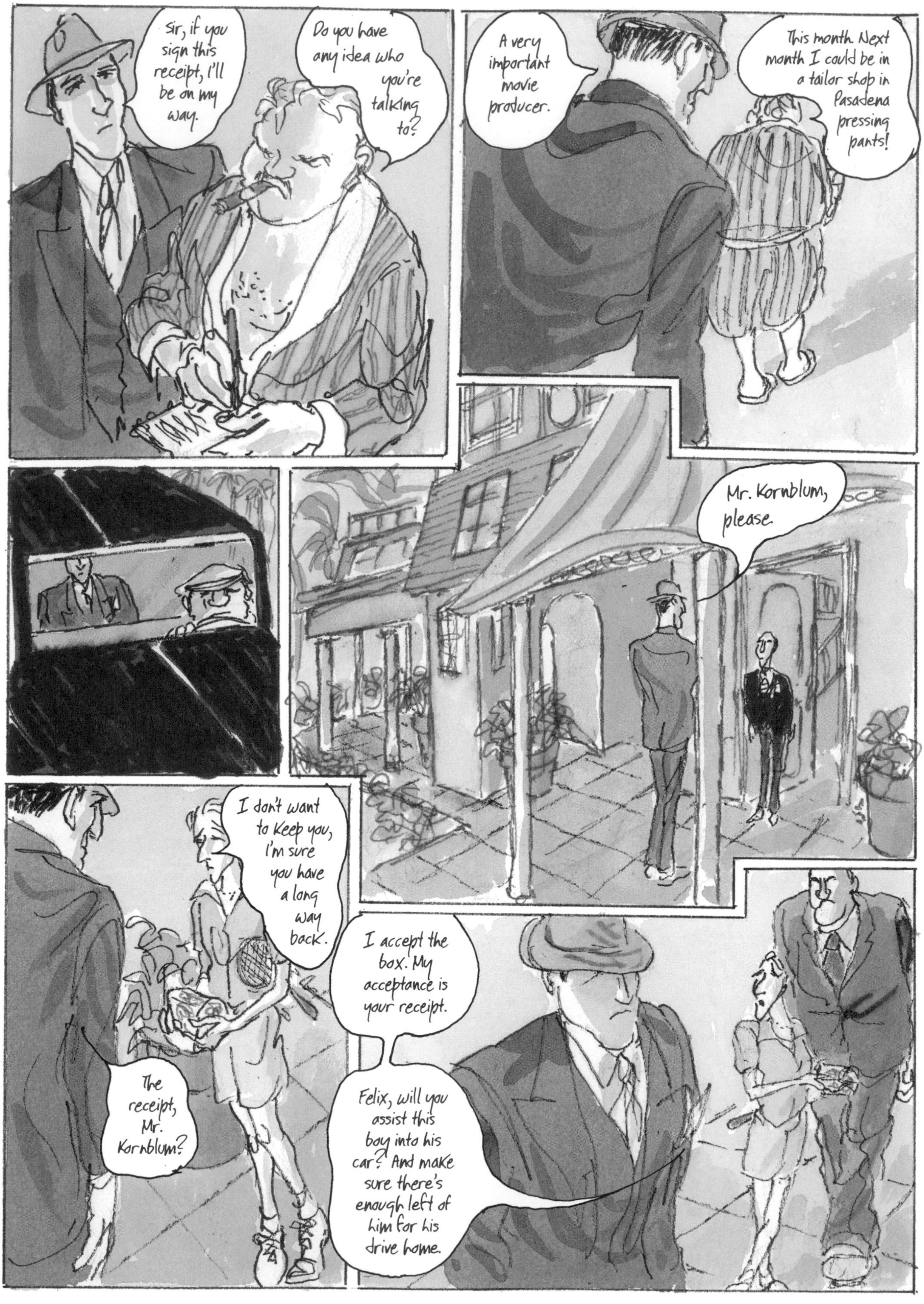

Sir, if you sign this receipt, I'll be on my way.
Do you have any idea who you're talking to?
A very important movie producer.
This month. Next month I could be in a tailor shop in Pasadena pressing pants!
Mr. Kornblum, please.
I don't want to keep you, I'm sure you have a long way back.
The receipt, Mr. Kornblum?
I accept the box. My acceptance is your receipt.
Felix, will you assist this boy into his car? And make sure there's enough left of him for his drive home.

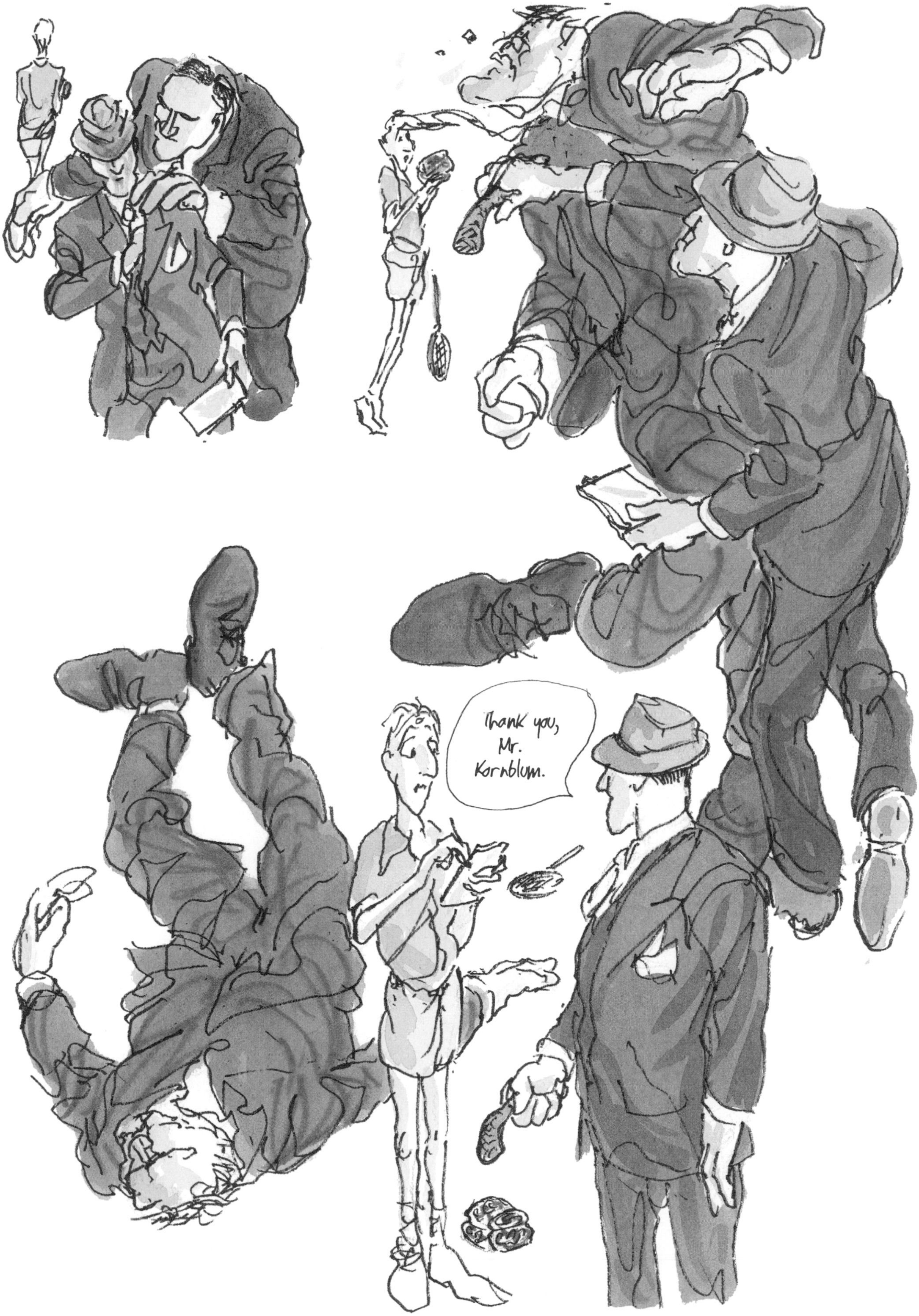
Thank you, Mr. Kornblum.

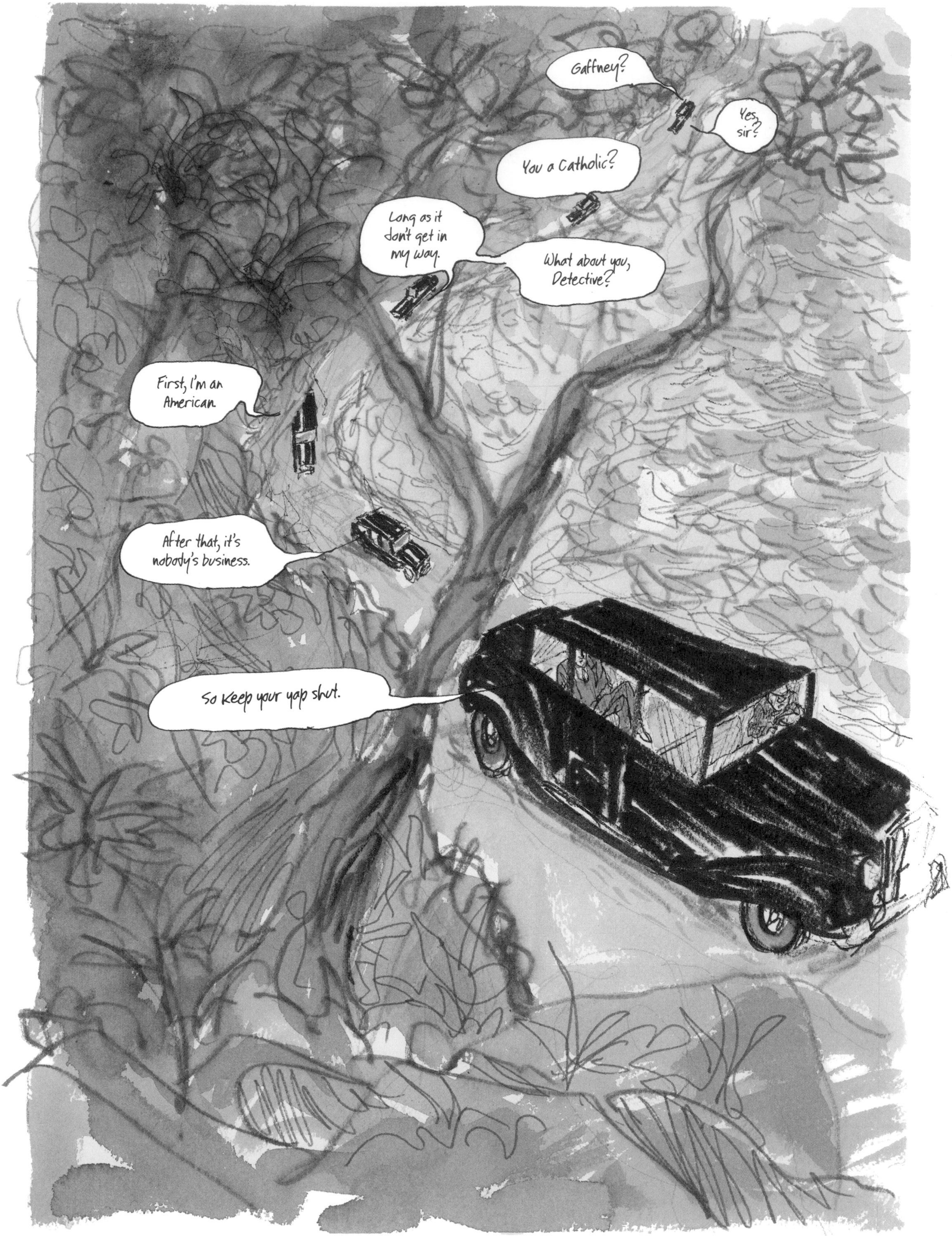
Gaffney?
Yes, sir?
You a Catholic?
Long as it don't get in my way.
What about you, Detective?
First, I'm an American.
After that, it's nobody's business.
So keep your yap shut.

Chapter Six: Valerie

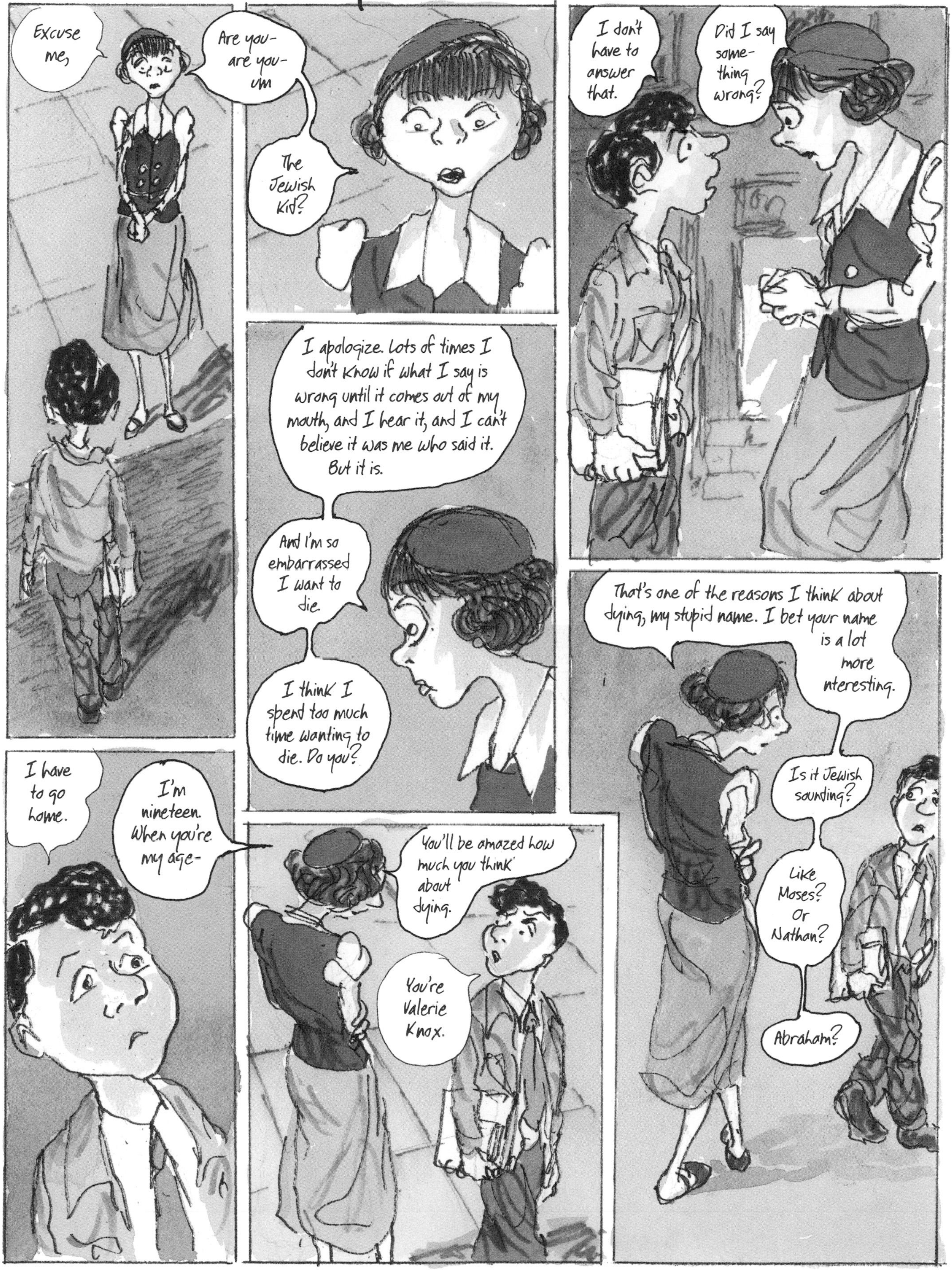

Excuse me,
Are you- are you- um
The Jewish kid?
I don't have to answer that.
Did I say some-thing wrong?
I apologize. Lots of times I don't know if what I say is wrong until it comes out of my mouth, and I hear it, and I can't believe it was me who said it. But it is.
And I'm so embarrassed I want to die.
I think I spend too much time wanting to die. Do you?
I have to go home.
I'm nineteen. When you're my age-
You'll be amazed how much you think about dying.
You're Valerie Knox.
That's one of the reasons I think about dying, my stupid name. I bet your name is a lot more interesting.
Is it Jewish sounding?
Like Moses? Or Nathan?
Abraham?

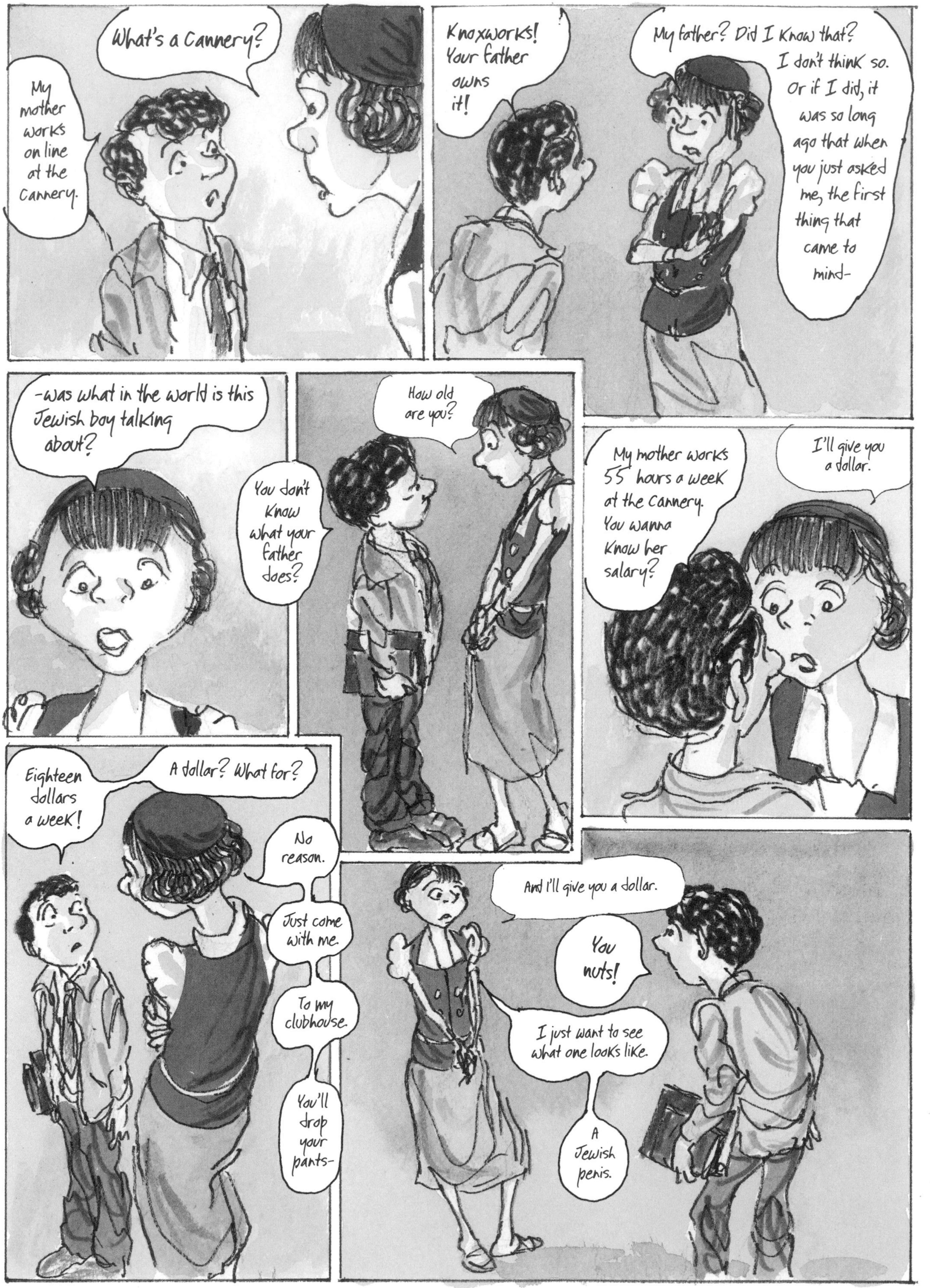
What's a cannery?
My mother works on line at the cannery.
Knoxworks! Your father owns it!
My father? Did I know that? I don't think so. Or if I did, it was so long ago that when you just asked me, the first thing that came to mind-
-was what in the world is this Jewish boy talking about?
How old are you?
You don't know what your father does?
My mother works 55 hours a week at the cannery. You wanna know her salary?
I'll give you a dollar.
Eighteen dollars a week!
A dollar? What for?
No reason.
Just come with me.
To my clubhouse.
You'll drop your pants-
And I'll give you a dollar.
You nuts!
I just want to see what one looks like.
A Jewish penis.

Chapter Seven: Pop!

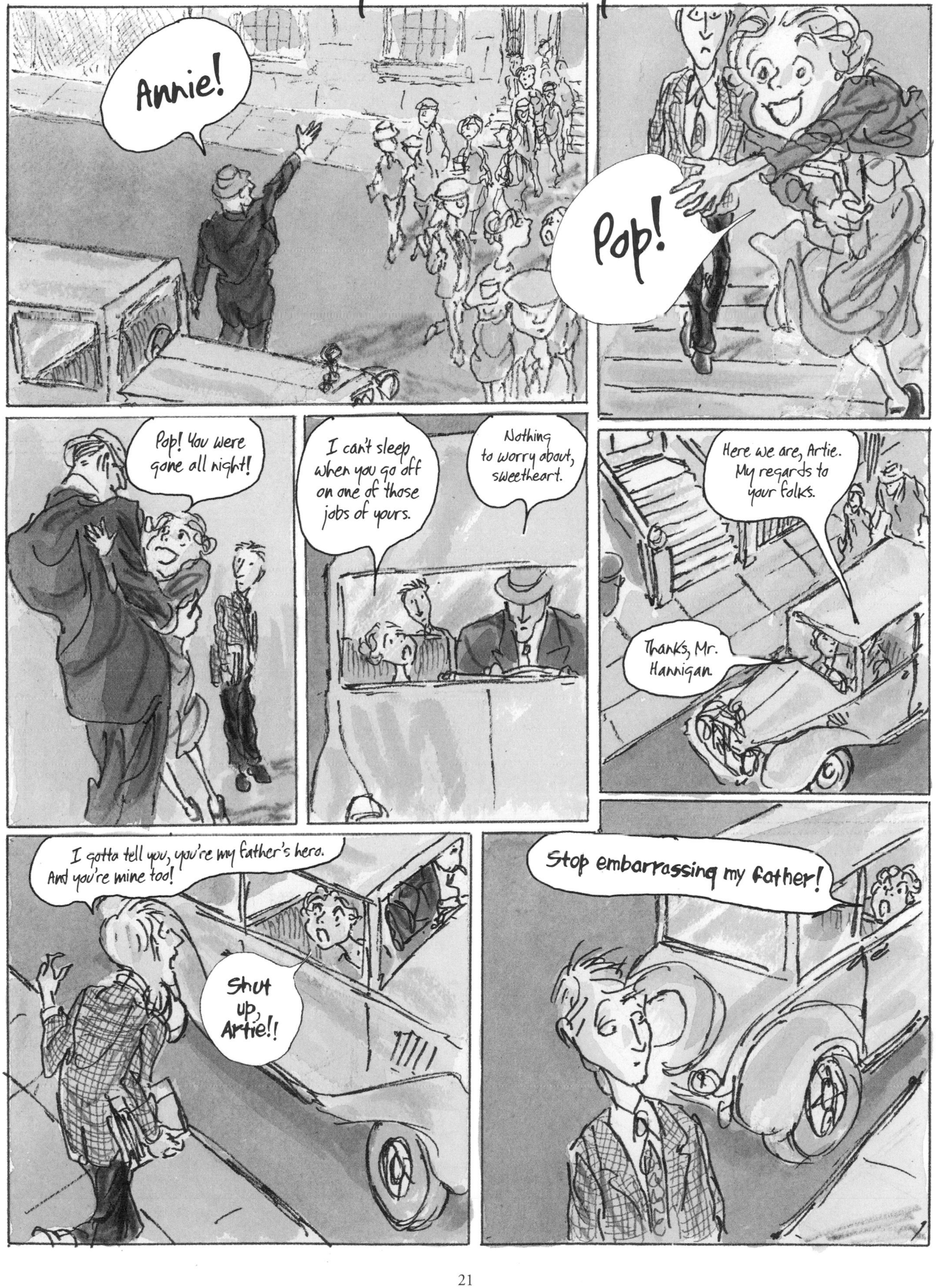
Annie!
Pop!
Pop! You were gone all night!
I can't sleep when you go off on one of those jobs of yours.
Nothing to worry about, sweetheart.
Here we are, Artie. My regards to your folks.
Thanks, Mr. Hannigan.
I gotta tell you, you're my father's hero. And you're mine too!
Shut up, Artie!!
Stop embarrassing my father!

Chapter Eight: Biology

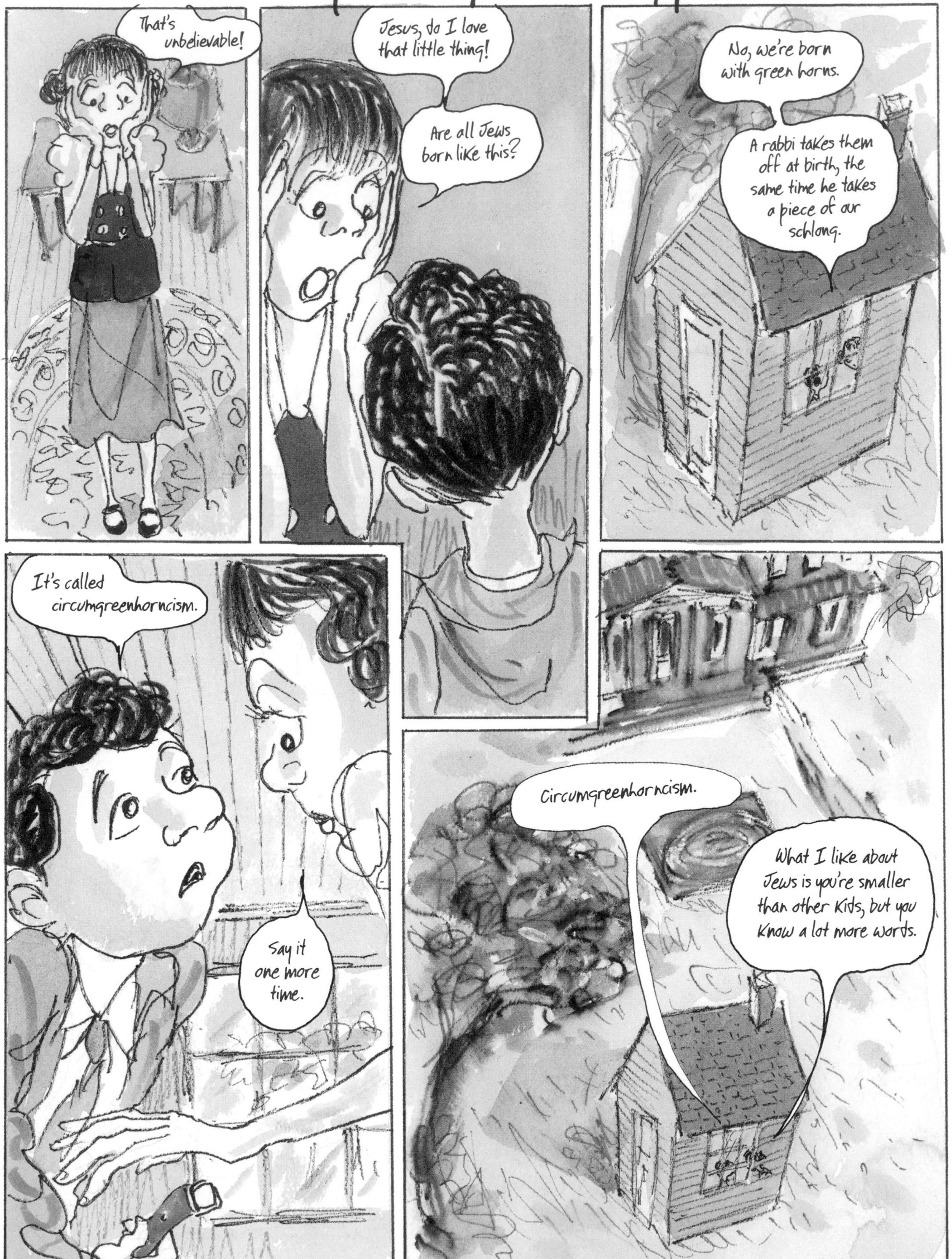

That's unbelievable!
Jesus, do I love that little thing!
Are all Jews born like this?
No, we're born with green horns.
A rabbi takes them off at birth, the same time he takes a piece of our schlong.
It's called circumgreenhorncism.
Say it one more time.
Circumgreenhorncism.
What I like about Jews is you're smaller than other kids, but you know a lot more words.

Chapter Nine: The Red Squad

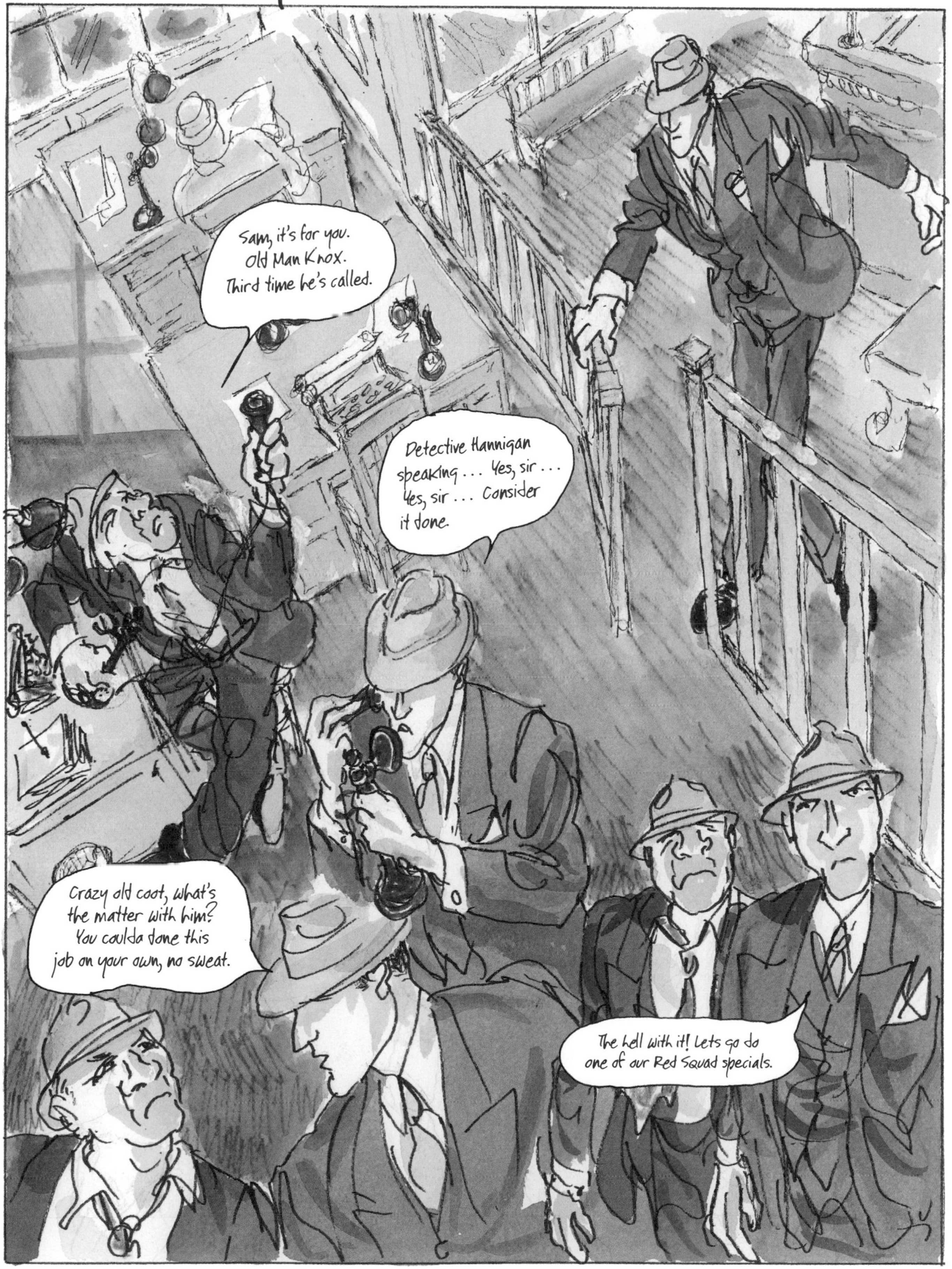
Sam, it's for you. Old Man Knox. Third time he's called.
Detective Hannigan speaking . . . Yes, sir . . . Yes, sir . . . Consider it done.
Crazy old coot, what's the matter with him? You coulda done this job on your own, no sweat.
The hell with it! Lets go do one of our Red Squad specials.

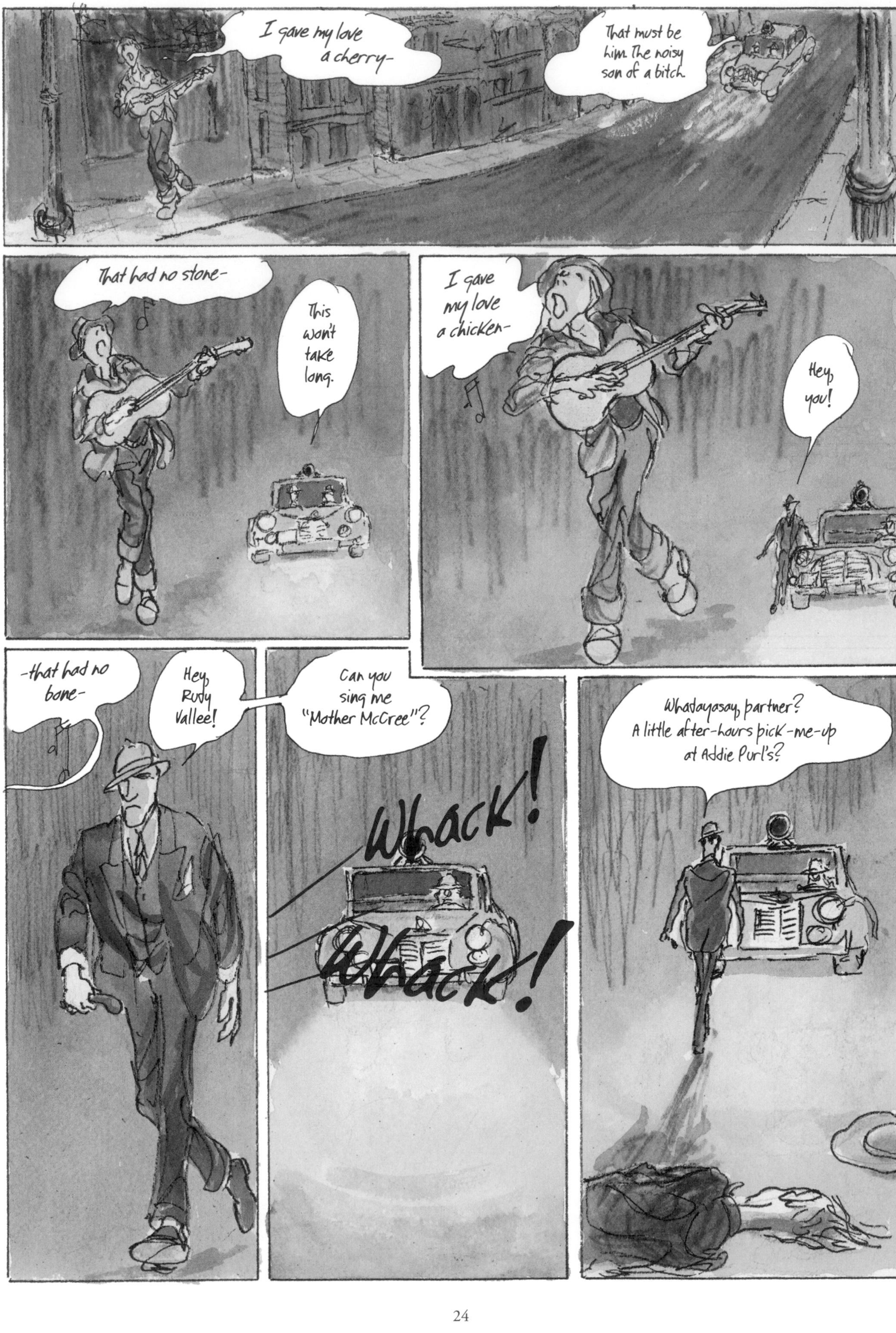
I gave my love a cherry-
That must be him. The noisy son of a bitch.
That had no stone-
This won't take long.
I gave my love a chicken-
Hey, you!
-that had no bone-
Hey, Rudy Vallee!
Can you sing me "Mother McCree"?
Whack!
Whack!
Whadayasay, partner? A little after-hours pick-me-up at Addie Purl's?

Chapter Ten: Not so Hard Knox

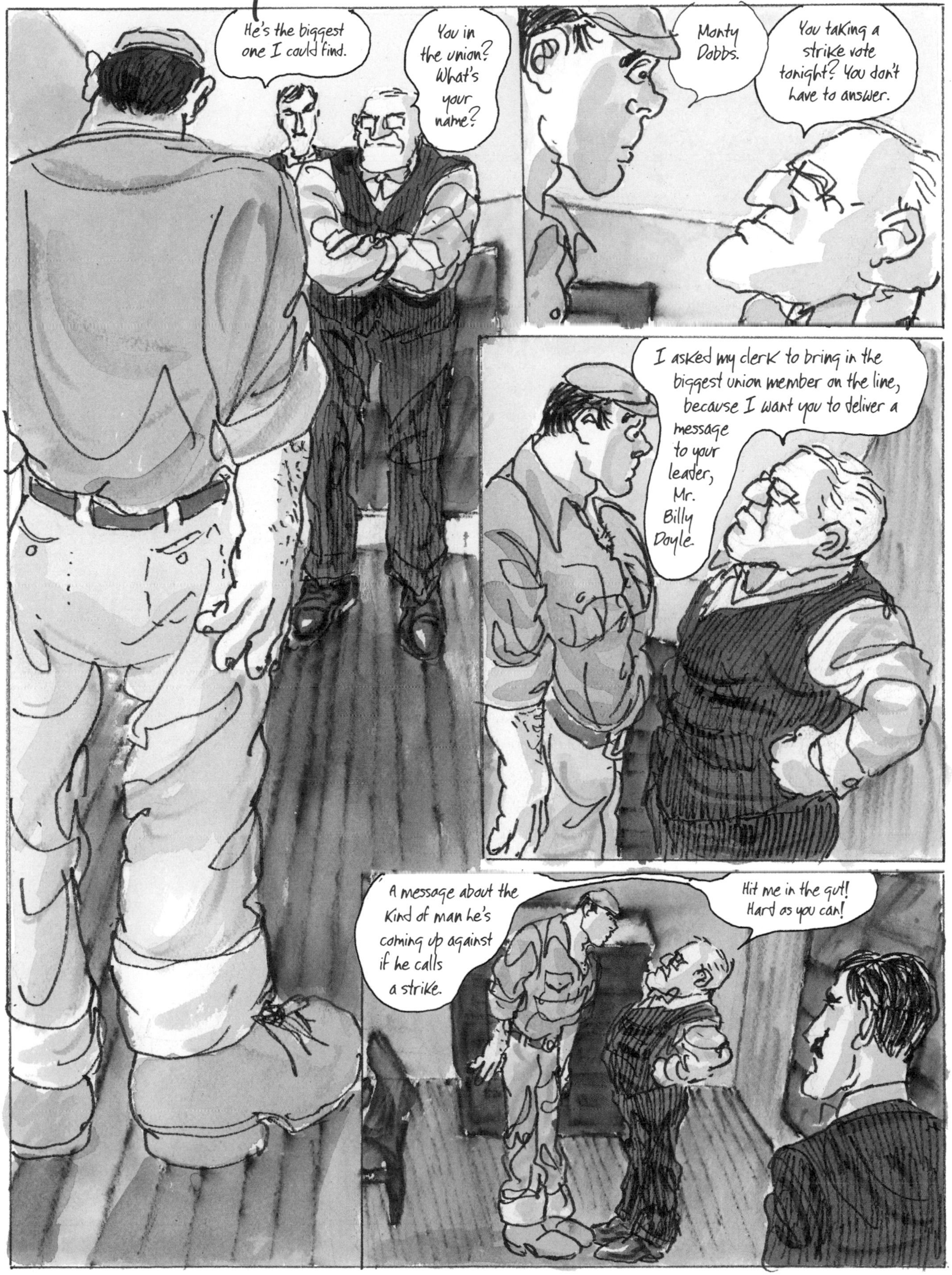
He's the biggest one I could find.
You in the union? What's your name?
Monty Dobbs.
You taking a strike vote tonight? You don't have to answer.
I asked my clerk to bring in the biggest union member on the line, because I want you to deliver a message to your leader, Mr. Billy Doyle.
A message about the kind of man he's coming up against if he calls a strike.
Hit me in the gut! Hard as you can!

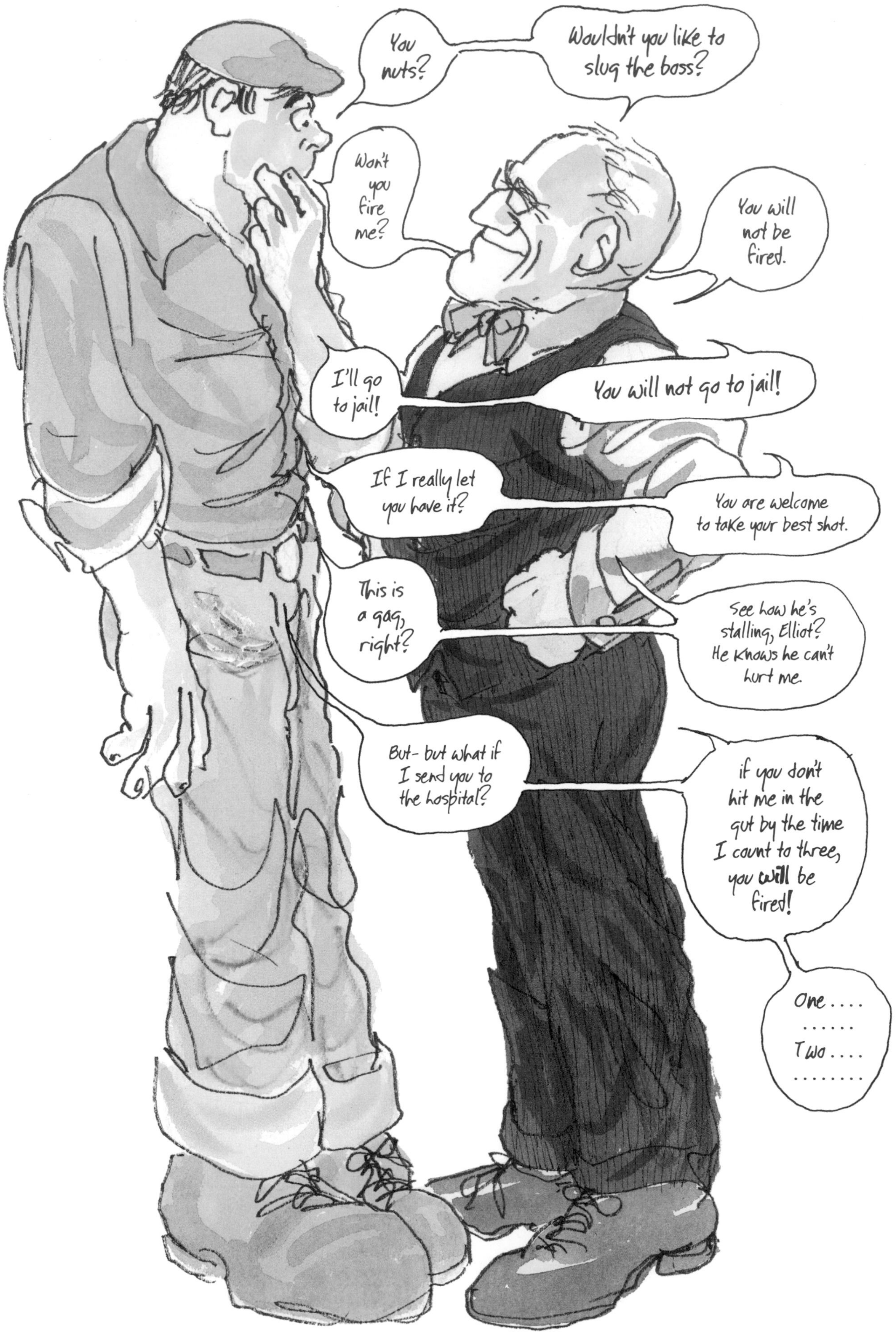
Wouldn't you like to slug the boss?
You nuts?
Won't you fire me?
You will not be fired.
I'll go to jail!
You will not go to jail!
If I really let you have it?
You are welcome to take your best shot.
This is a gag, right?
See how he's stalling, Elliot? He knows he can't hurt me.
But- but what if I send you to the hospital?
if you don't hit me in the gut by the time I count to three, you **will** be fired!
One.... ...... Two.... ....

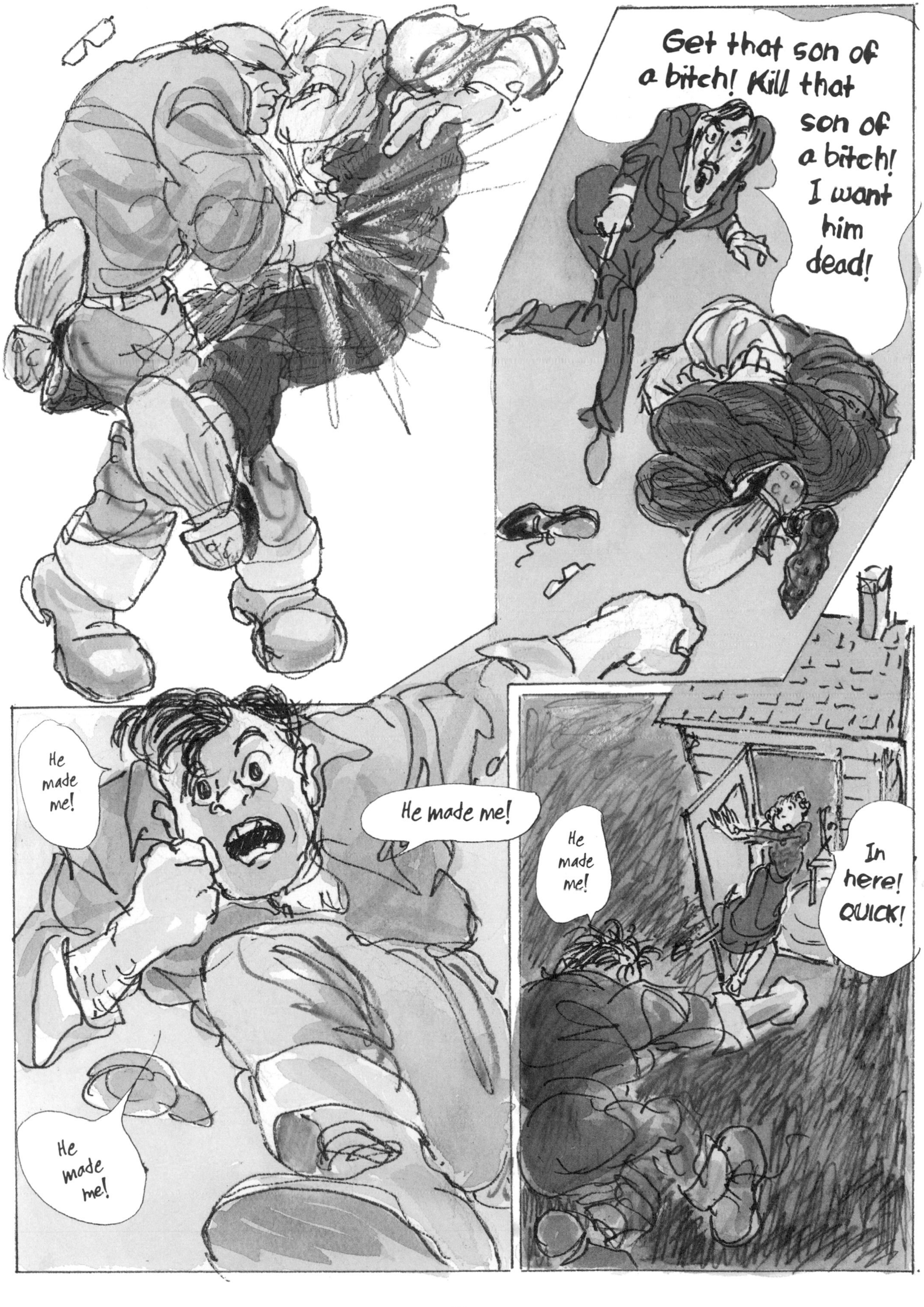
Get that son of a bitch! Kill that son of a bitch! I want him dead!
He made me!
He made me!
He made me!
He made me!
In here! QUICK!

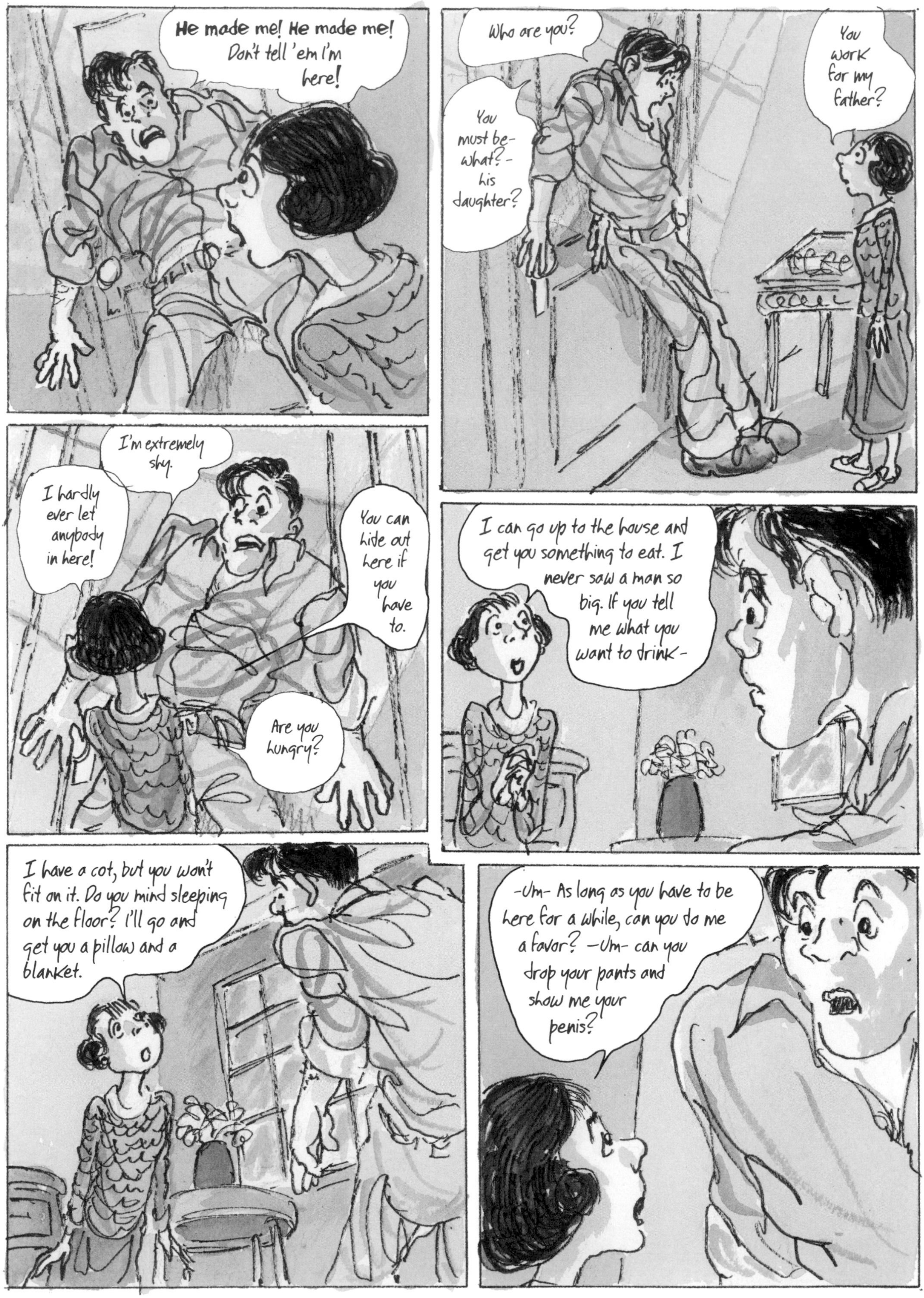
He made me! He made me! Don't tell 'em I'm here!
Who are you?
You must be- what?- his daughter?
You work for my father?
I'm extremely shy.
I hardly ever let anybody in here!
You can hide out here if you have to.
Are you hungry?
I can go up to the house and get you something to eat. I never saw a man so big. If you tell me what you want to drink-
I have a cot, but you won't fit on it. Do you mind sleeping on the floor? I'll go and get you a pillow and a blanket.
-Um- As long as you have to be here for a while, can you do me a favor? -Um- can you drop your pants and show me your penis?

Chapter Eleven: After Hours at Addie's

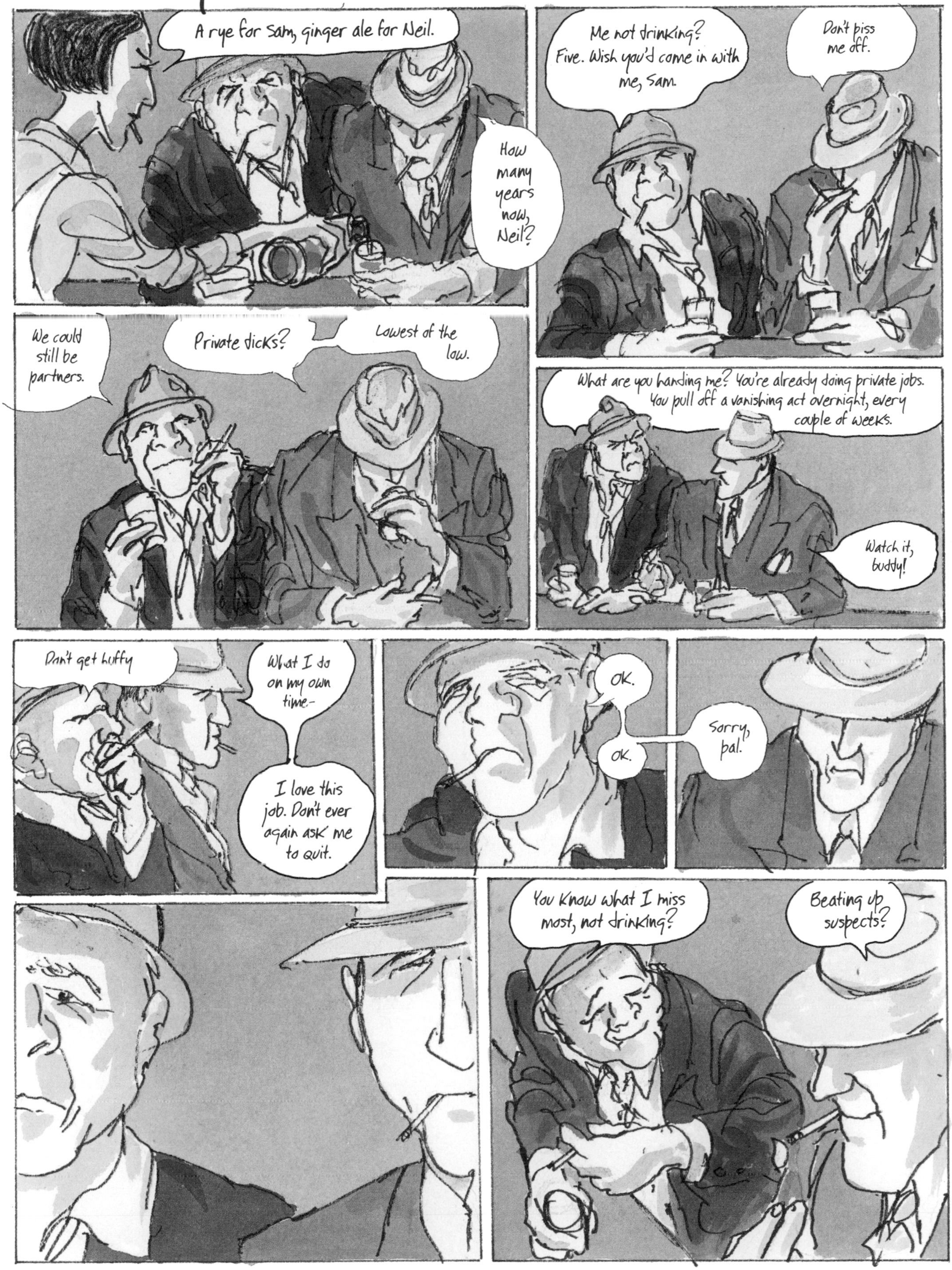
A rye for Sam, ginger ale for Neil.
How many years now, Neil?
Me not drinking? Five. Wish you'd come in with me, Sam.
Don't piss me off.
We could still be partners.
Private dicks?
Lowest of the low.
What are you handing me? You're already doing private jobs. You pull off a vanishing act overnight, every couple of weeks.
Watch it, buddy!
Don't get huffy
What I do on my own time-
I love this job. Don't ever again ask me to quit.
OK.
Sorry, pal.
OK.
You know what I miss most, not drinking?
Beating up suspects?

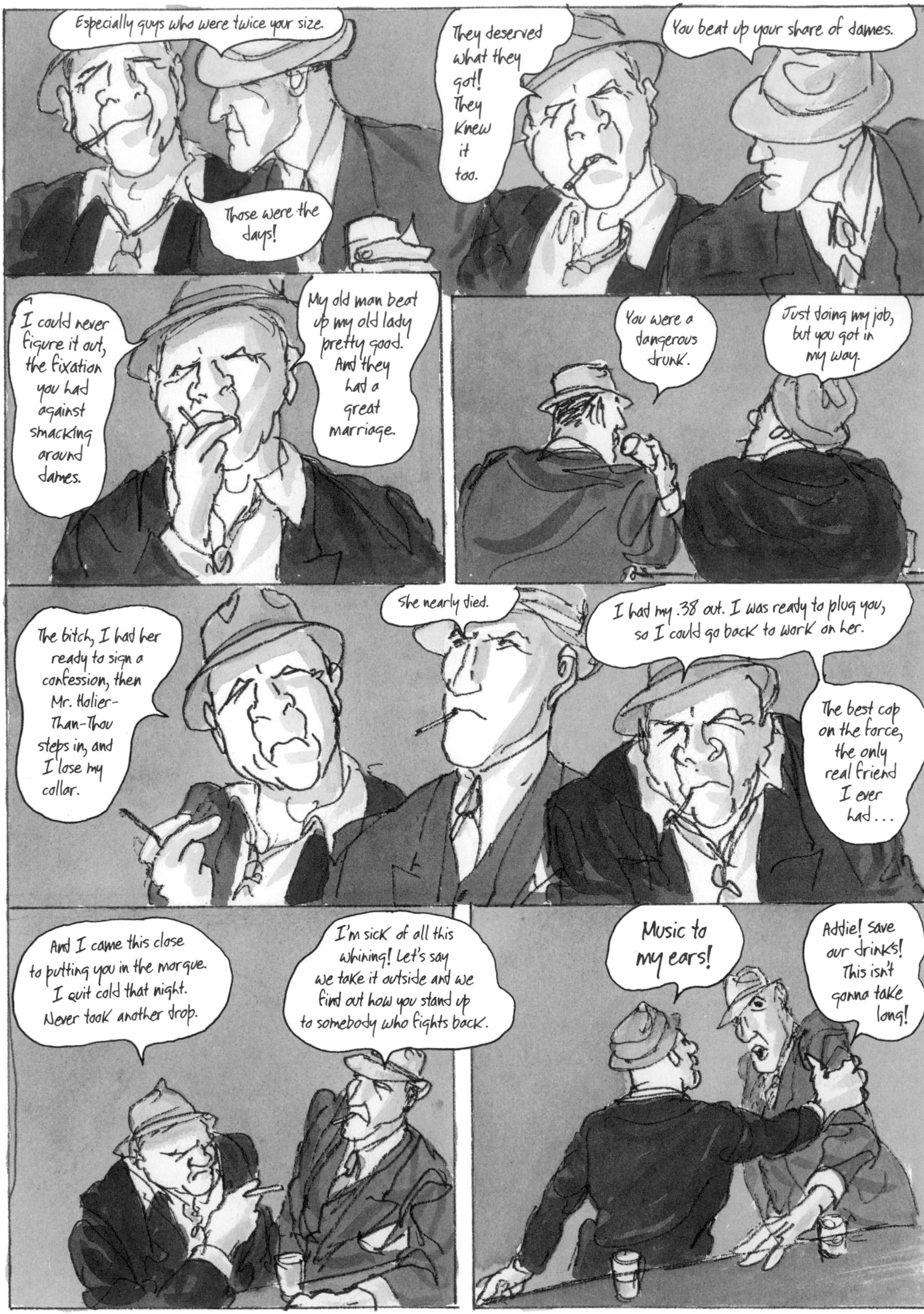
Especially guys who were twice your size.
Those were the days!
They deserved what they got! They knew it too.
You beat up your share of dames.
I could never figure it out, the fixation you had against smacking around dames.
My old man beat up my old lady pretty good. And they had a great marriage.
You were a dangerous drunk.
Just doing my job, but you got in my way.
The bitch, I had her ready to sign a confession, then Mr. Holier-Than-Thou steps in, and I lose my collar.
She nearly died.
I had my .38 out. I was ready to plug you, so I could go back to work on her.
The best cop on the force, the only real friend I ever had...
And I came this close to putting you in the morgue. I quit cold that night. Never took another drop.
I'm sick of all this whining! Let's say we take it outside and we find out how you stand up to somebody who fights back.
Music to my ears!
Addie! Save our drinks! This isn't gonna take long!

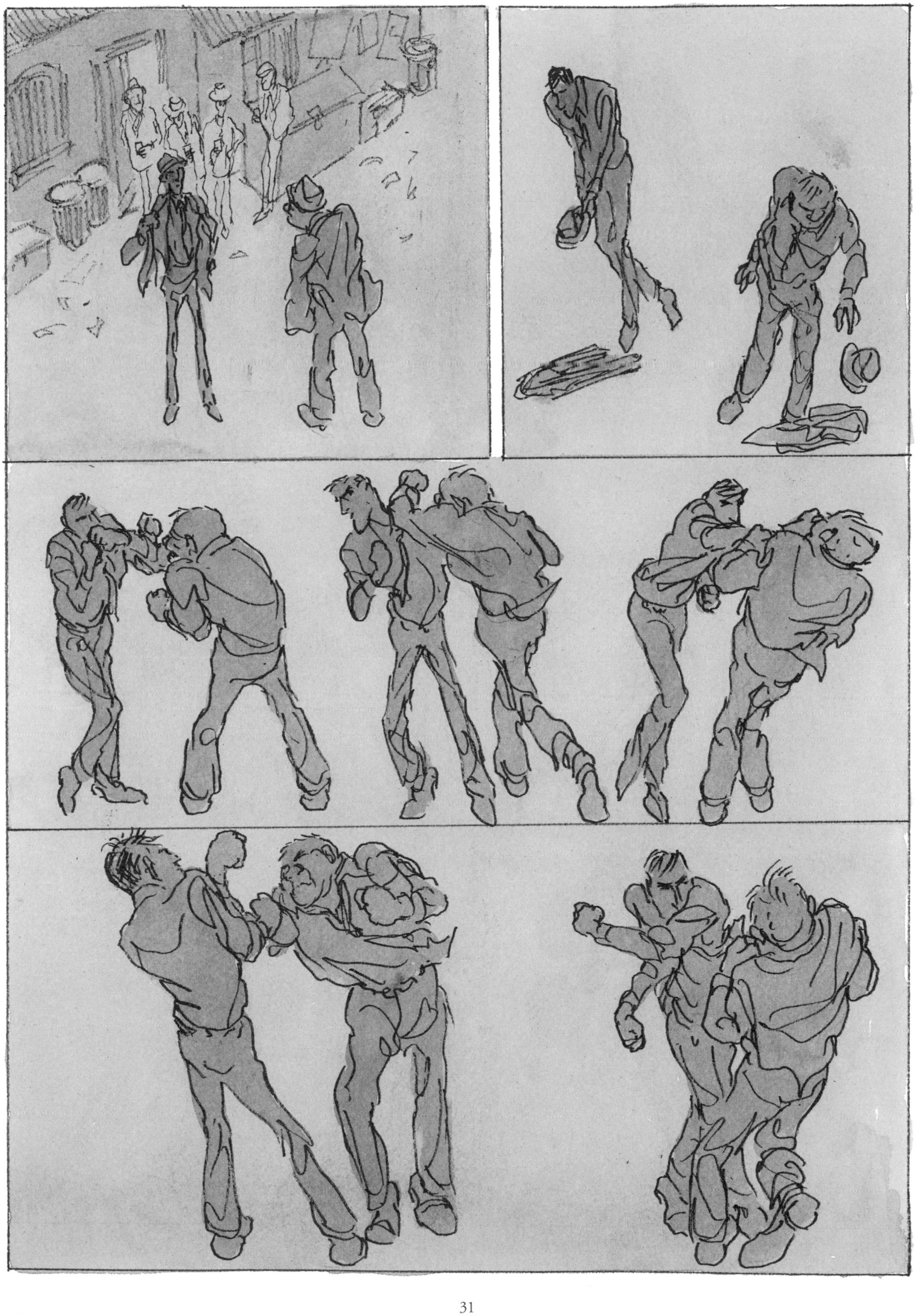

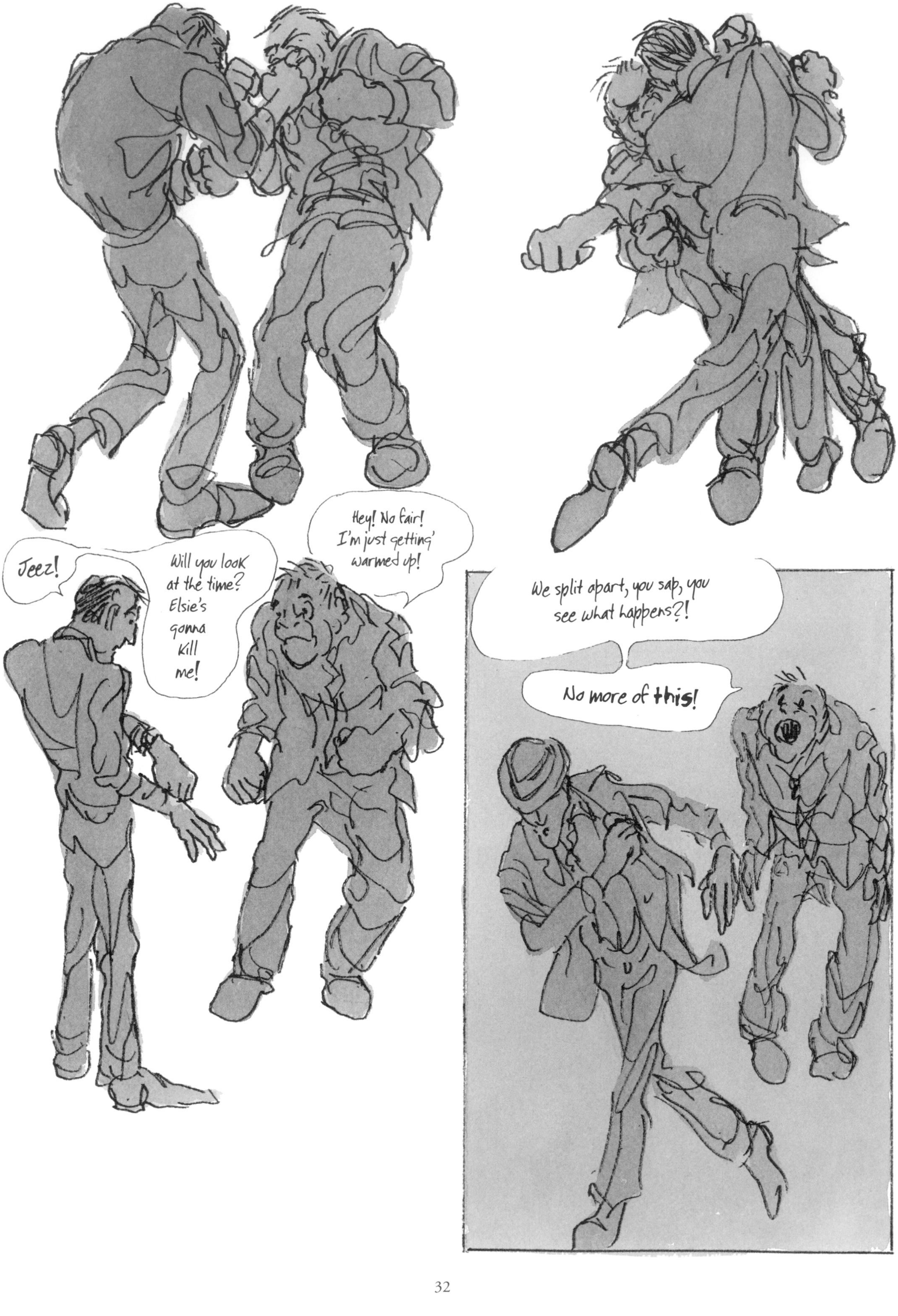
Jeez!
Will you look at the time? Elsie's gonna kill me!
Hey! No fair! I'm just getting' warmed up!
We split apart, you sap, you see what happens?!
No more of this!

Chapter Twelve: The Missing Diary

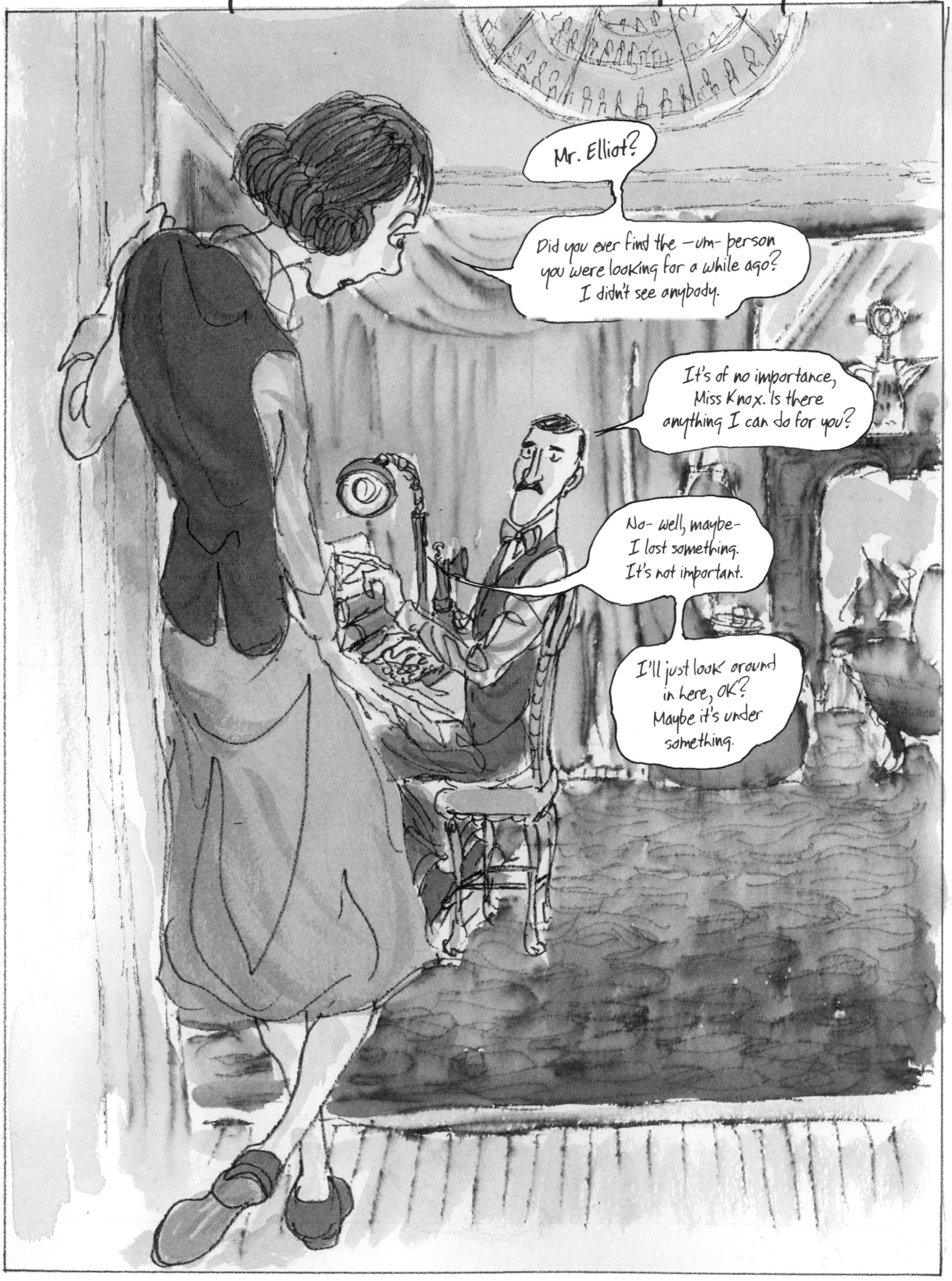
Mr. Elliot?
Did you ever find the —um— person you were looking for a while ago? I didn't see anybody.
It's of no importance, Miss Knox. Is there anything I can do for you?
No- well, maybe- I lost something. It's not important.
I'll just look around in here, OK? Maybe it's under something.

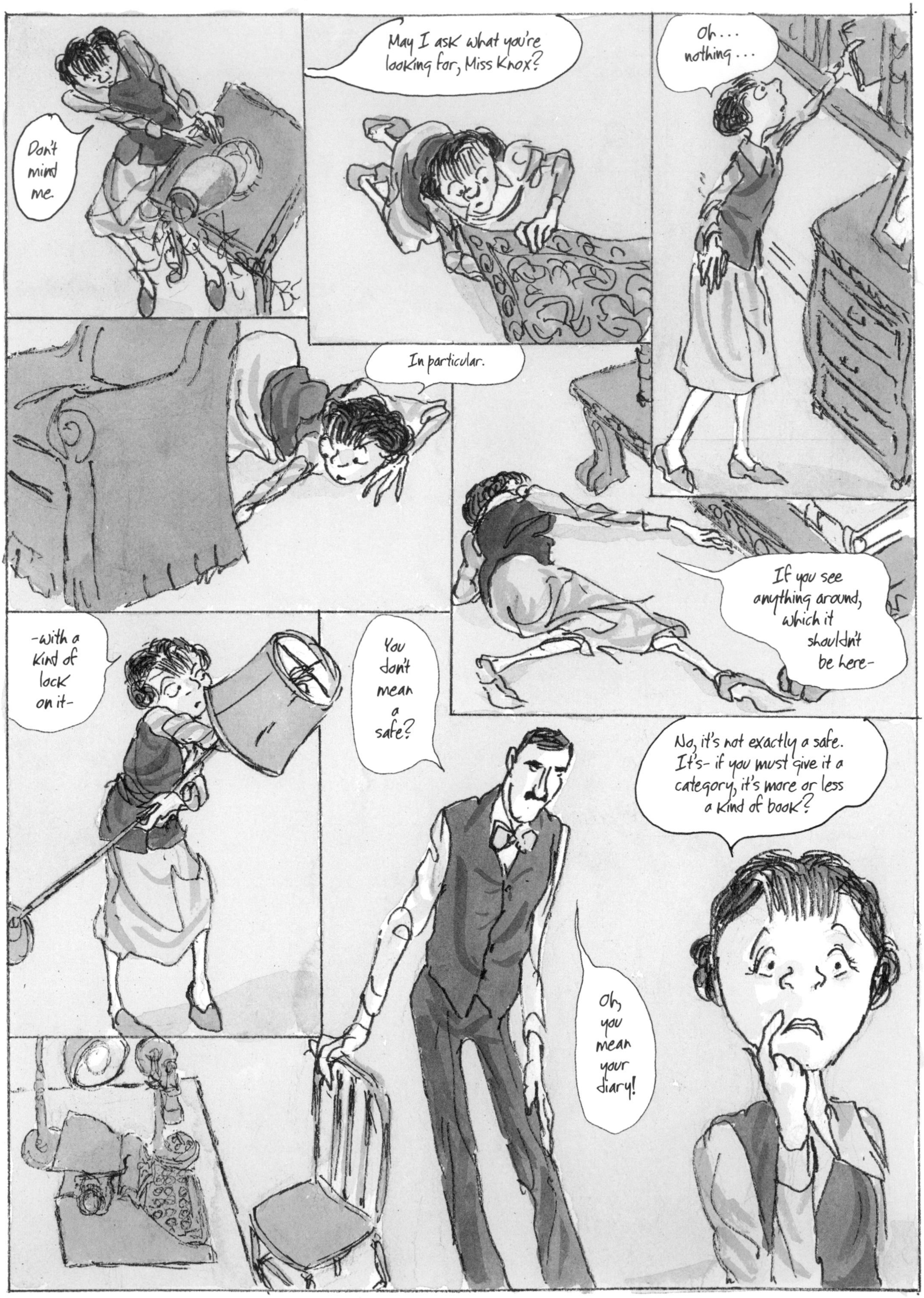
Don't mind me.
May I ask what you're looking for, Miss Knox?
Oh... nothing...
In particular.
If you see anything around, which it shouldn't be here-
-with a kind of lock on it-
You don't mean a safe?
No, it's not exactly a safe. It's- if you must give it a category, it's more or less a kind of book?
Oh, you mean your diary!

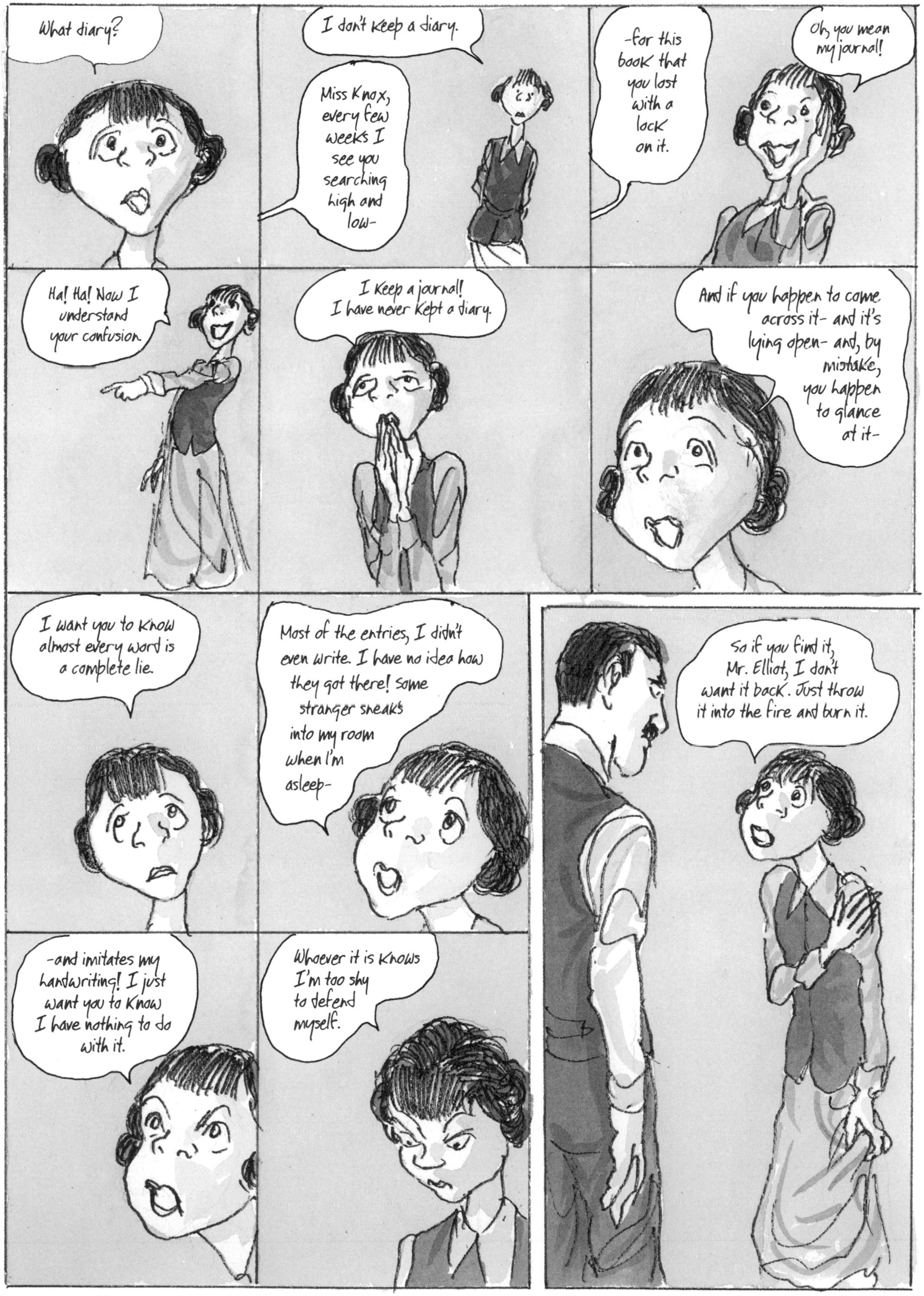
What diary?
I don't keep a diary.
Miss Knox, every few weeks I see you searching high and low-
-for this book that you lost with a lock on it.
Oh, you mean my journal!
Ha! Ha! Now I understand your confusion.
I keep a journal! I have never kept a diary.
And if you happen to come across it- and it's lying open- and, by mistake, you happen to glance at it-
I want you to know almost every word is a complete lie.
Most of the entries, I didn't even write. I have no idea how they got there! Some stranger sneaks into my room when I'm asleep-
So if you find it, Mr. Elliot, I don't want it back. Just throw it into the fire and burn it.
-and imitates my handwriting! I just want you to know I have nothing to do with it.
Whoever it is knows I'm too shy to defend myself.

Chapter Thirteen: Lights Out

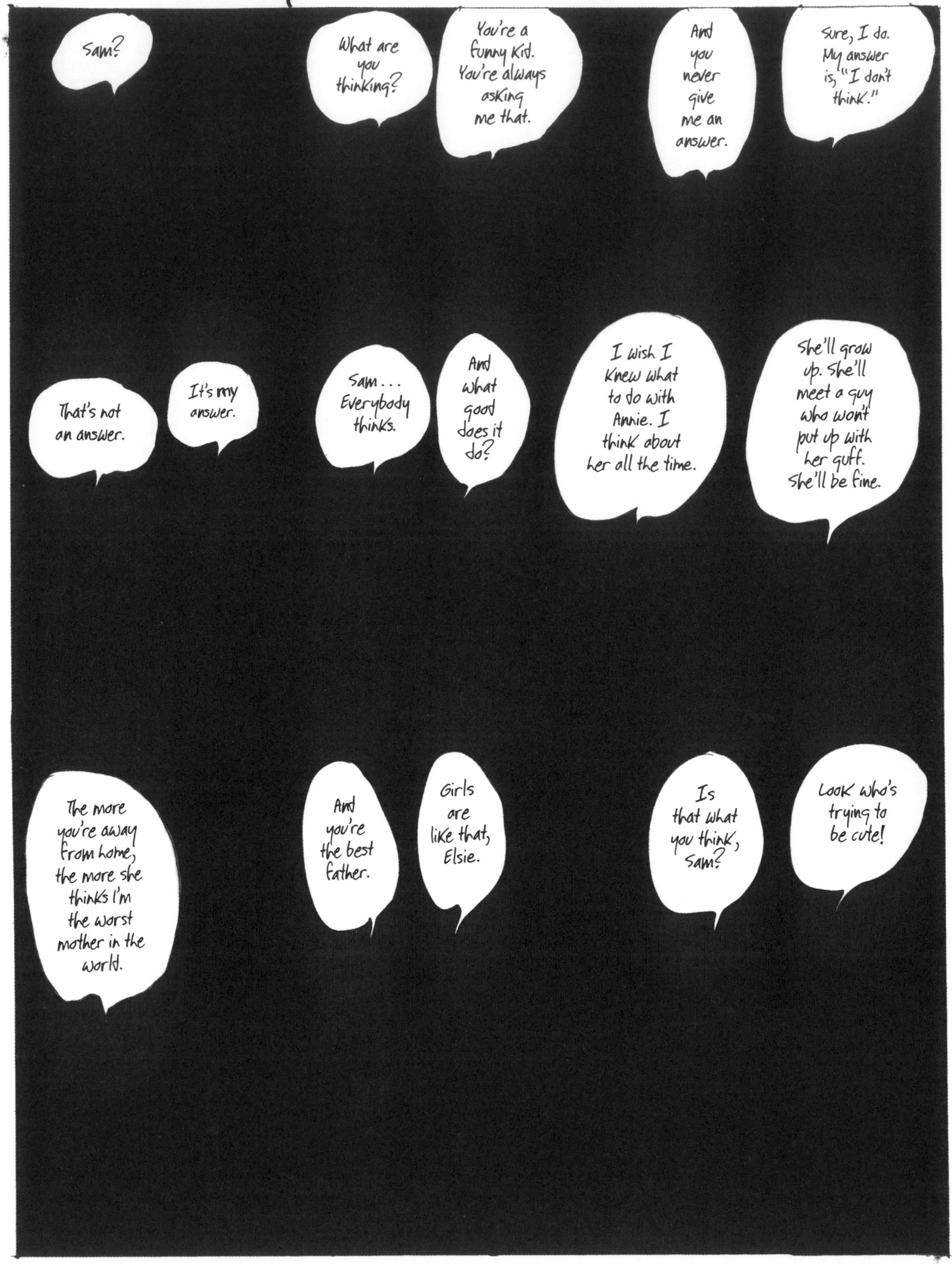
Sam?
What are you thinking?
You're a funny kid. You're always asking me that.
And you never give me an answer.
Sure, I do. My answer is, "I don't think."
That's not an answer.
It's my answer.
Sam... Everybody thinks.
And what good does it do?
I wish I knew what to do with Annie. I think about her all the time.
She'll grow up. She'll meet a guy who won't put up with her guff. She'll be fine.
The more you're away from home, the more she thinks I'm the worst mother in the world.
And you're the best father.
Girls are like that, Elsie.
Is that what you think, Sam?
Look who's trying to be cute!

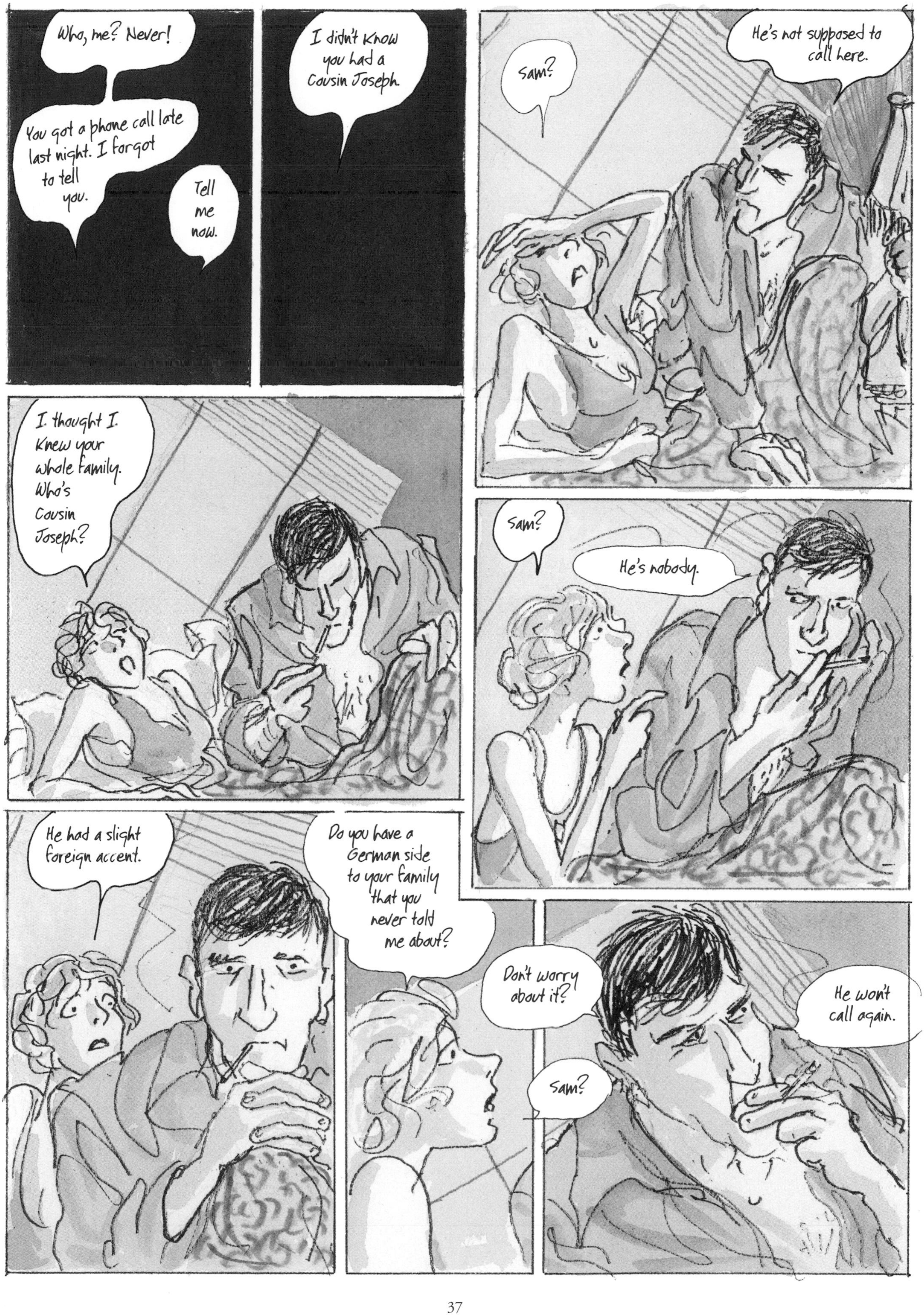
Who, me? Never!
You got a phone call late last night. I forgot to tell you.
Tell me now.
I didn't know you had a Cousin Joseph.
Sam?
He's not supposed to call here.
I thought I knew your whole family. Who's Cousin Joseph?
Sam?
He's nobody.
He had a slight foreign accent.
Do you have a German side to your family that you never told me about?
Don't worry about it?
Sam?
He won't call again.

Chapter Fourteen: Class Warfare

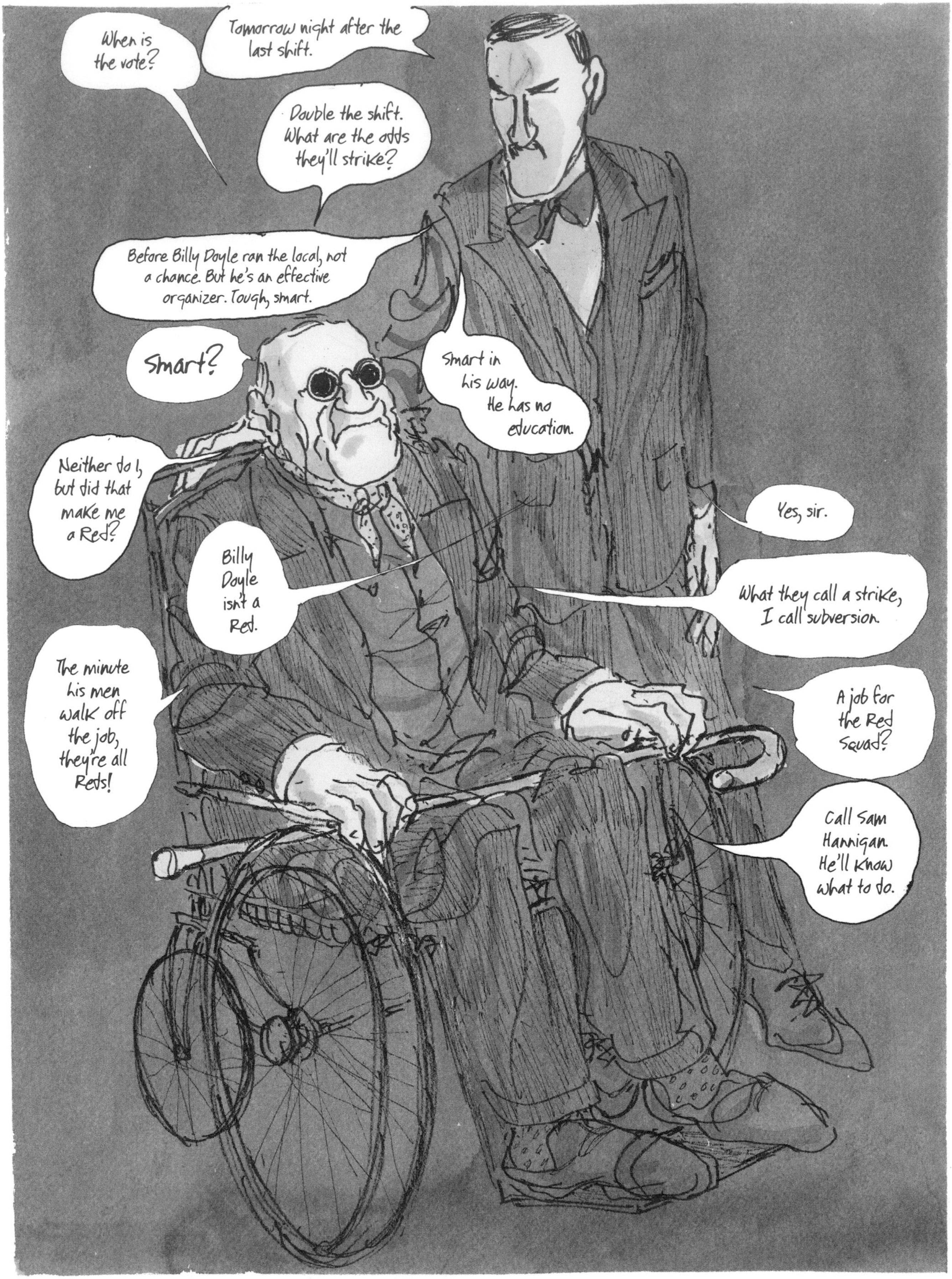
When is the vote?
Tomorrow night after the last shift.
Double the shift. What are the odds they'll strike?
Before Billy Doyle ran the local, not a chance. But he's an effective organizer. Tough, smart.
Smart?
Smart in his way. He has no education.
Neither do I, but did that make me a Red?
Billy Doyle isn't a Red.
Yes, sir.
What they call a strike, I call subversion.
The minute his men walk off the job, they're all Reds!
A job for the Red Squad?
Call Sam Hannigan. He'll know what to do.

Chapter Fifteen: High School Reunion

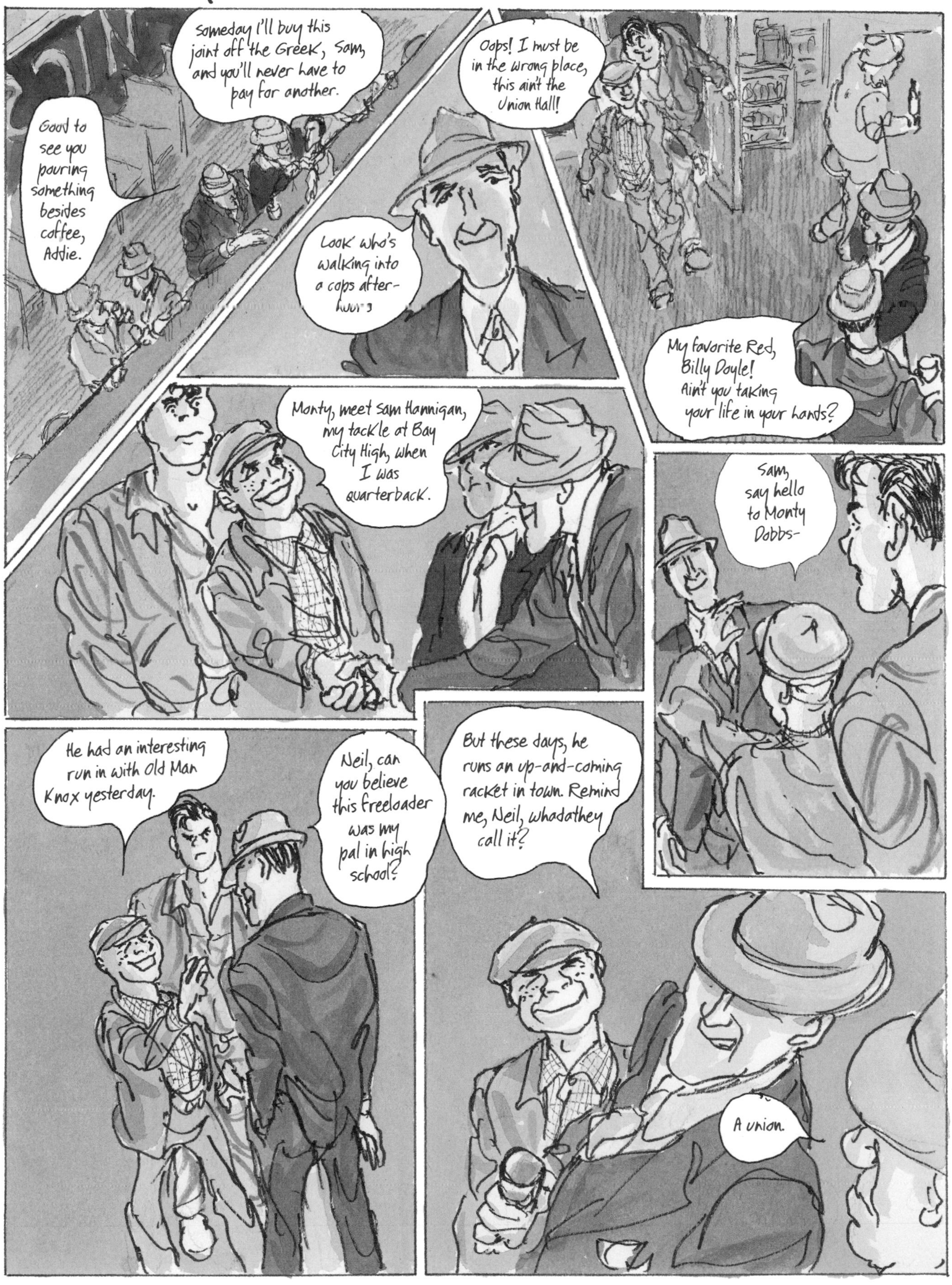
Someday I'll buy this joint off the Greek, Sam, and you'll never have to pay for another.
Good to see you pouring something besides coffee, Addie.
Look who's walking into a cops after-hours
Oops! I must be in the wrong place, this ain't the Union Hall!
My favorite Red, Billy Doyle! Ain't you taking your life in your hands?
Monty, meet Sam Hannigan, my tackle at Bay City High, when I was quarterback.
Sam, say hello to Monty Dobbs-
He had an interesting run in with Old Man Knox yesterday.
Neil, can you believe this freeloader was my pal in high school?
But these days, he runs an up-and-coming racket in town. Remind me, Neil, whadathey call it?
A union.

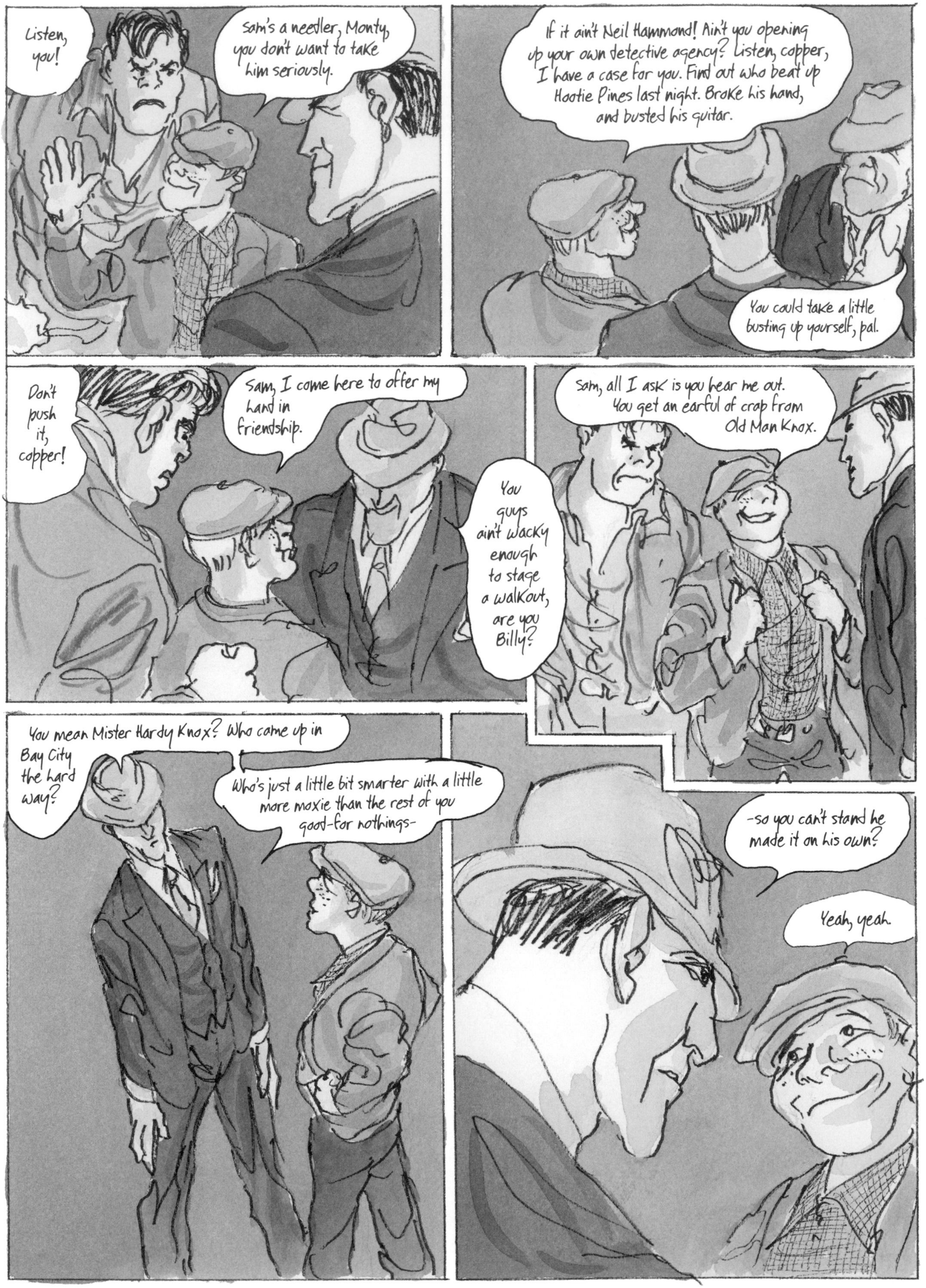

Listen, you!
Sam's a needler, Monty, you don't want to take him seriously.
If it ain't Neil Hammond! Ain't you opening up your own detective agency? Listen, copper, I have a case for you. Find out who beat up Hootie Pines last night. Broke his hand, and busted his guitar.
You could take a little busting up yourself, pal.
Don't push it, copper!
Sam, I come here to offer my hand in friendship.
You guys ain't wacky enough to stage a walkout, are you Billy?
Sam, all I ask is you hear me out. You get an earful of crap from Old Man Knox.
You mean Mister Hardy Knox? Who came up in Bay City the hard way?
Who's just a little bit smarter with a little more moxie than the rest of you good-for nothings-
-so you can't stand he made it on his own?
Yeah, yeah.

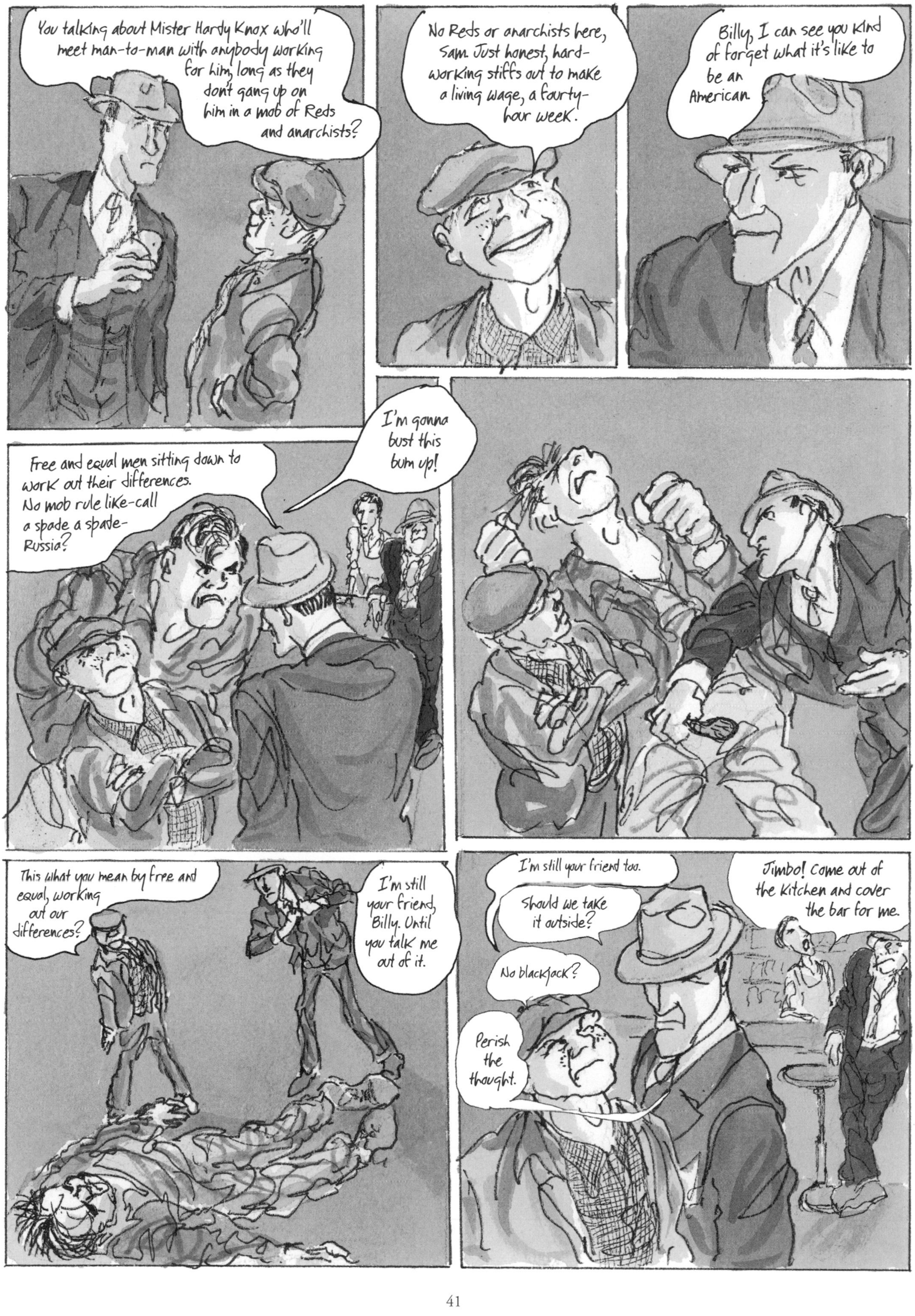
You talking about Mister Hardy Knox who'll meet man-to-man with anybody working for him, long as they don't gang up on him in a mob of Reds and anarchists?
No Reds or anarchists here, Sam. Just honest, hard-working stiffs out to make a living wage, a fourty-hour week.
Billy, I can see you kind of forget what it's like to be an American.
Free and equal men sitting down to work out their differences. No mob rule like-call a spade a spade-Russia?
I'm gonna bust this bum up!
This what you mean by free and equal, working out our differences?
I'm still your friend, Billy. Until you talk me out of it.
I'm still your friend too.
Should we take it outside?
No blackjack?
Perish the thought.
Jimbo! Come out of the kitchen and cover the bar for me.

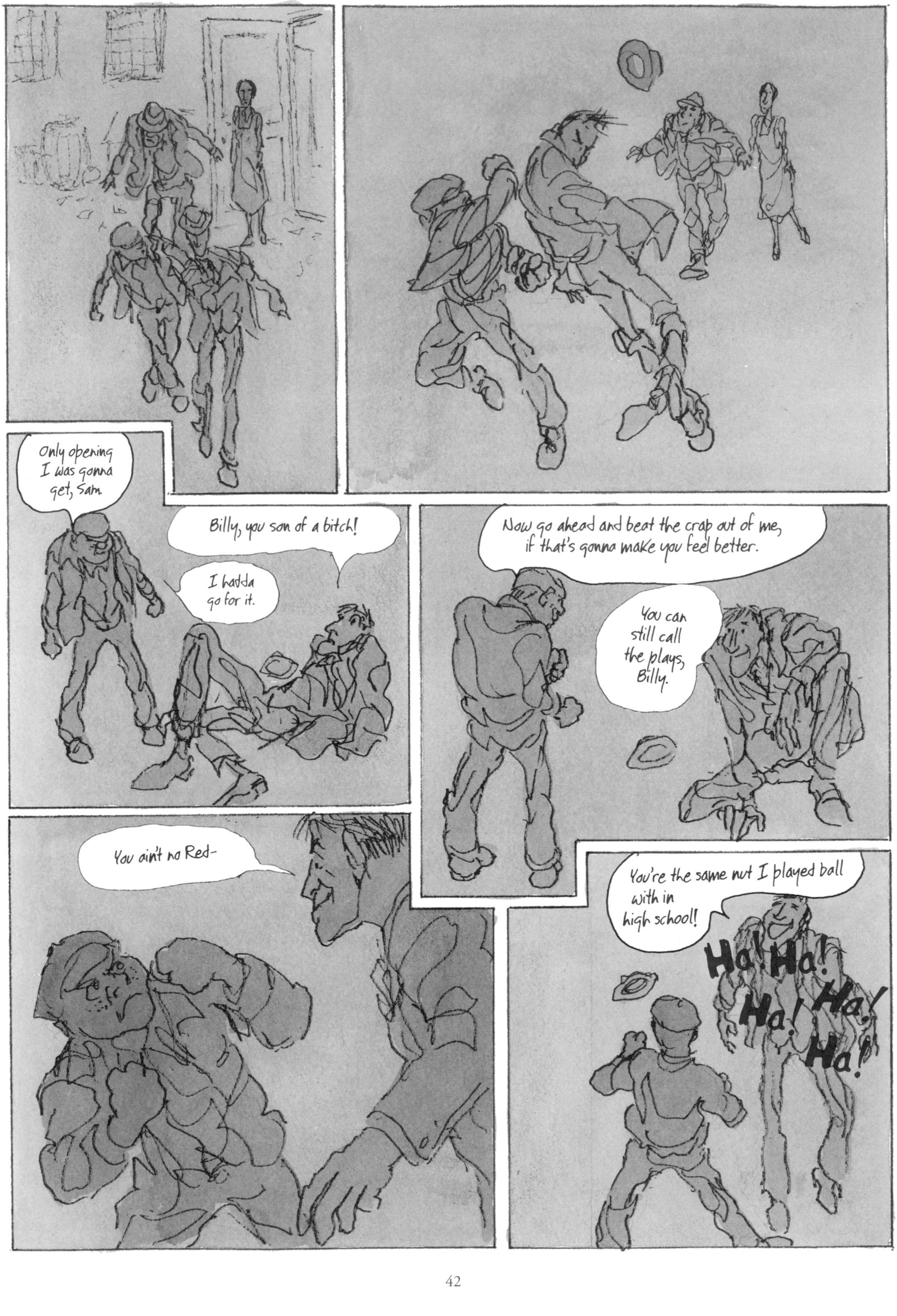
Only opening I was gonna get, Sam.
Billy, you son of a bitch!
I hadda go for it.
Now go ahead and beat the crap out of me, if that's gonna make you feel better.
You can still call the plays, Billy.
You ain't no Red-
You're the same nut I played ball with in high school!
Ha! Ha! Ha! Ha! Ha!

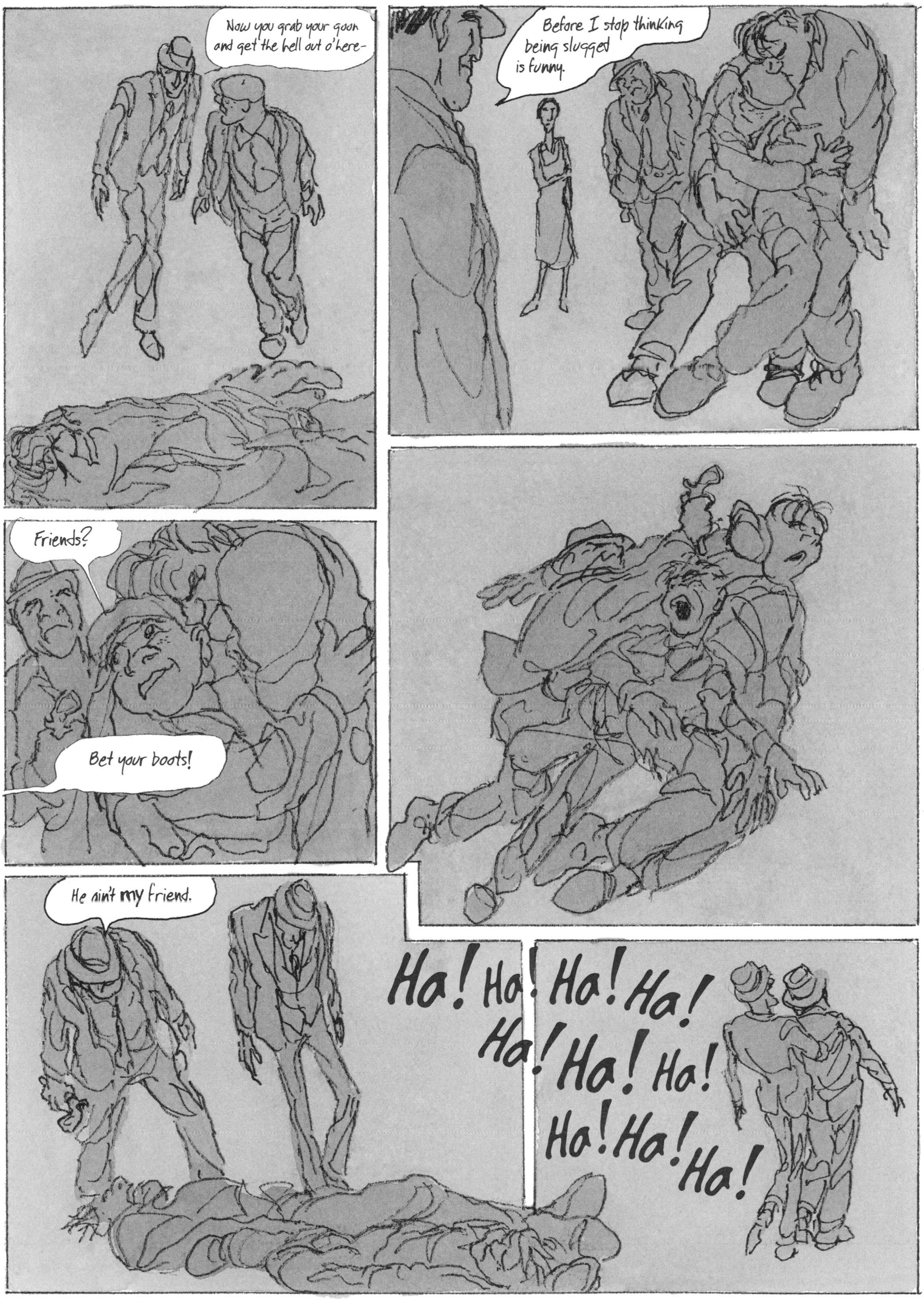
Now you grab your goon and get the hell out o'here-
Before I stop thinking being slugged is funny.
Friends?
Bet your boots!
He ain't my friend.
Ha! Ha! Ha! Ha! Ha! Ha! Ha! Ha! Ha! Ha!

Chapter Sixteen: Blackmail in the Schoolyard

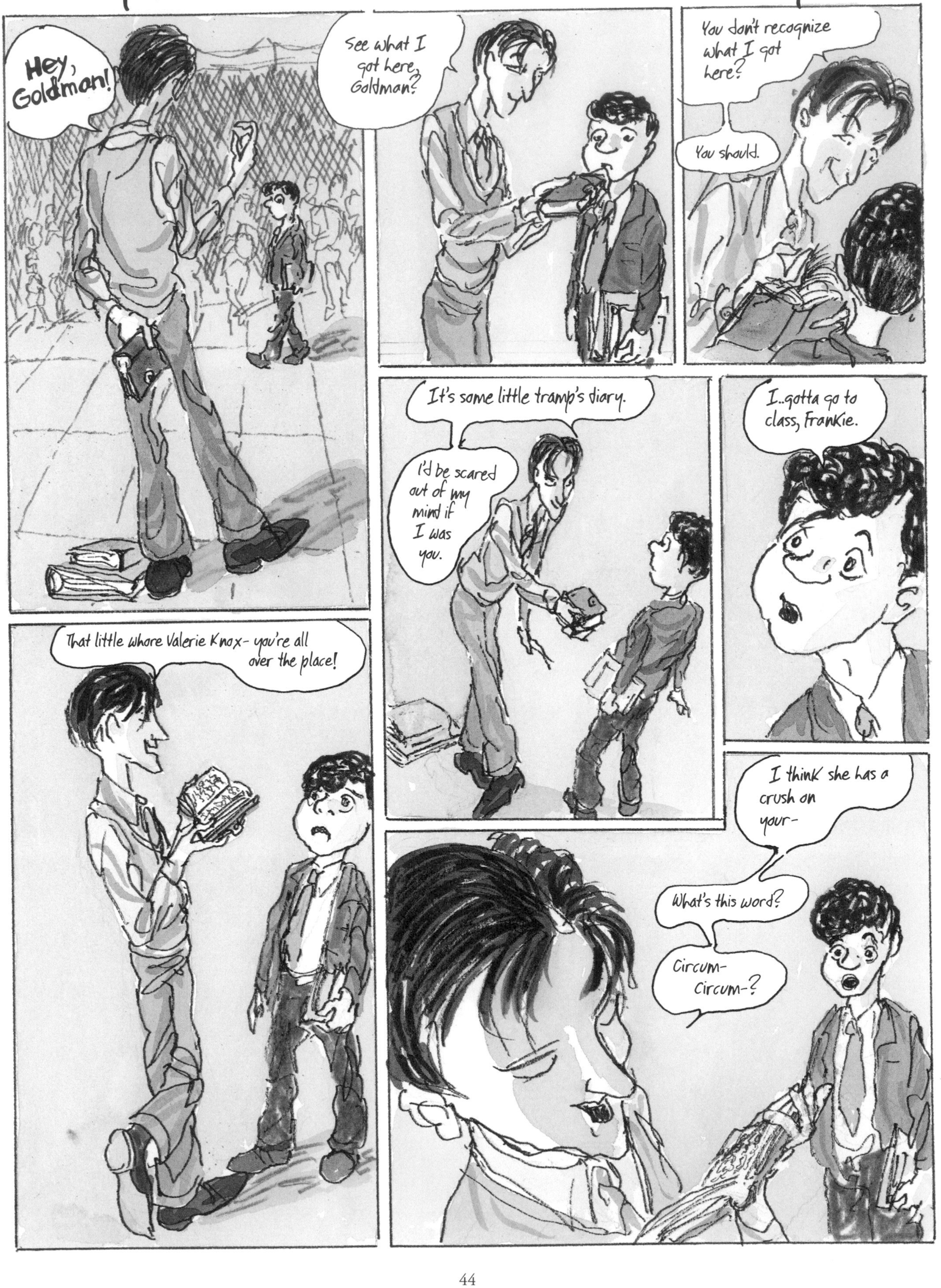

Hey, Goldman!
See what I got here, Goldman?
You don't recognize what I got here?
You should.
It's some little tramp's diary.
I'd be scared out of my mind if I was you.
I..gotta go to class, Frankie.
That little whore Valerie Knox- you're all over the place!
I think she has a crush on your-
What's this word?
Circum-Circum-?

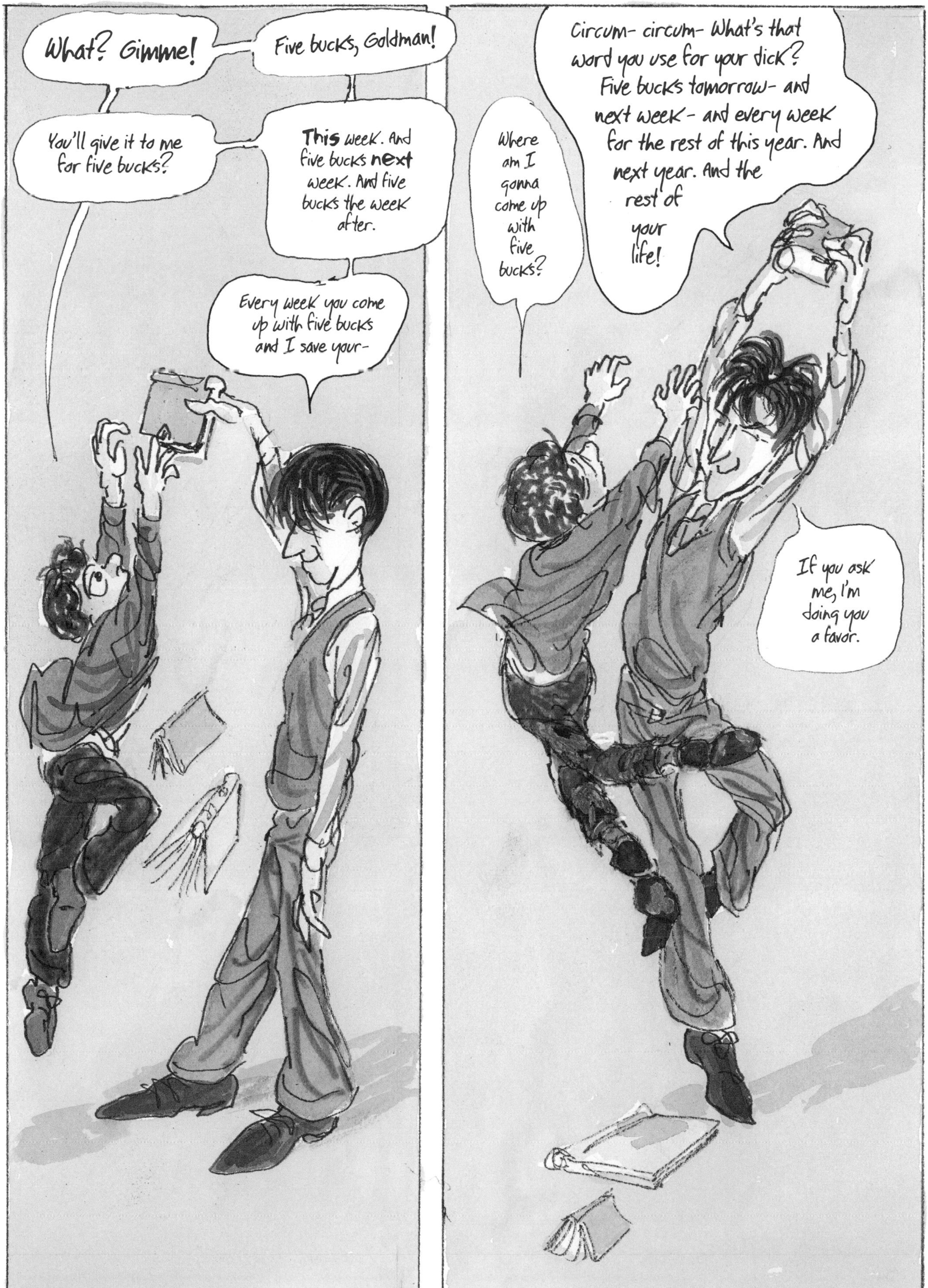
What? Gimme!
Five bucks, Goldman!
You'll give it to me for five bucks?
This week. And five bucks next week. And five bucks the week after.
Every week you come up with five bucks and I save your-
Where am I gonna come up with five bucks?
Circum- circum- What's that word you use for your dick? Five bucks tomorrow- and next week- and every week for the rest of this year. And next year. And the rest of your life!
If you ask me, I'm doing you a favor.

Chapter Seventeen: The Union Maid

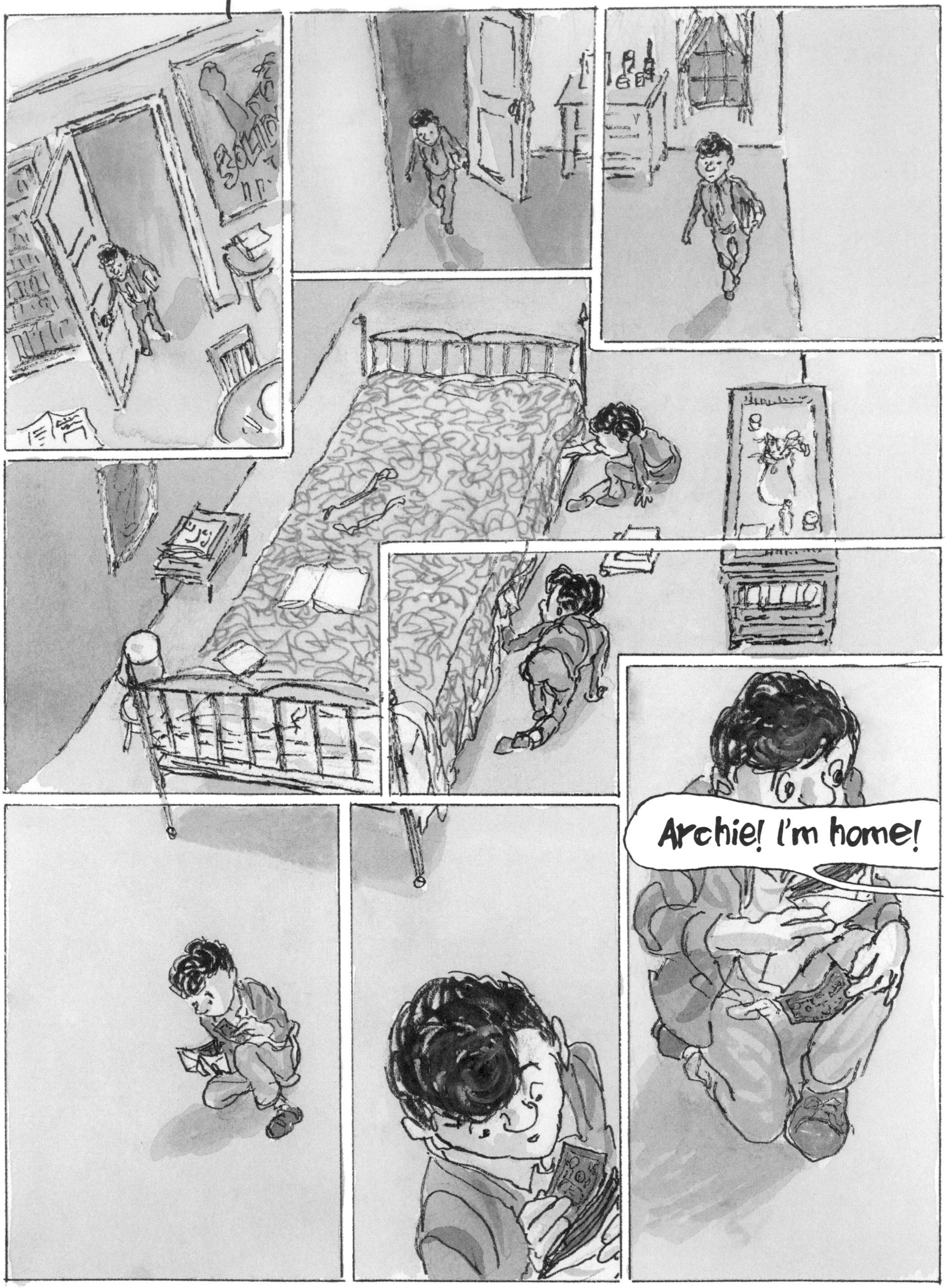
Archie! I'm home!

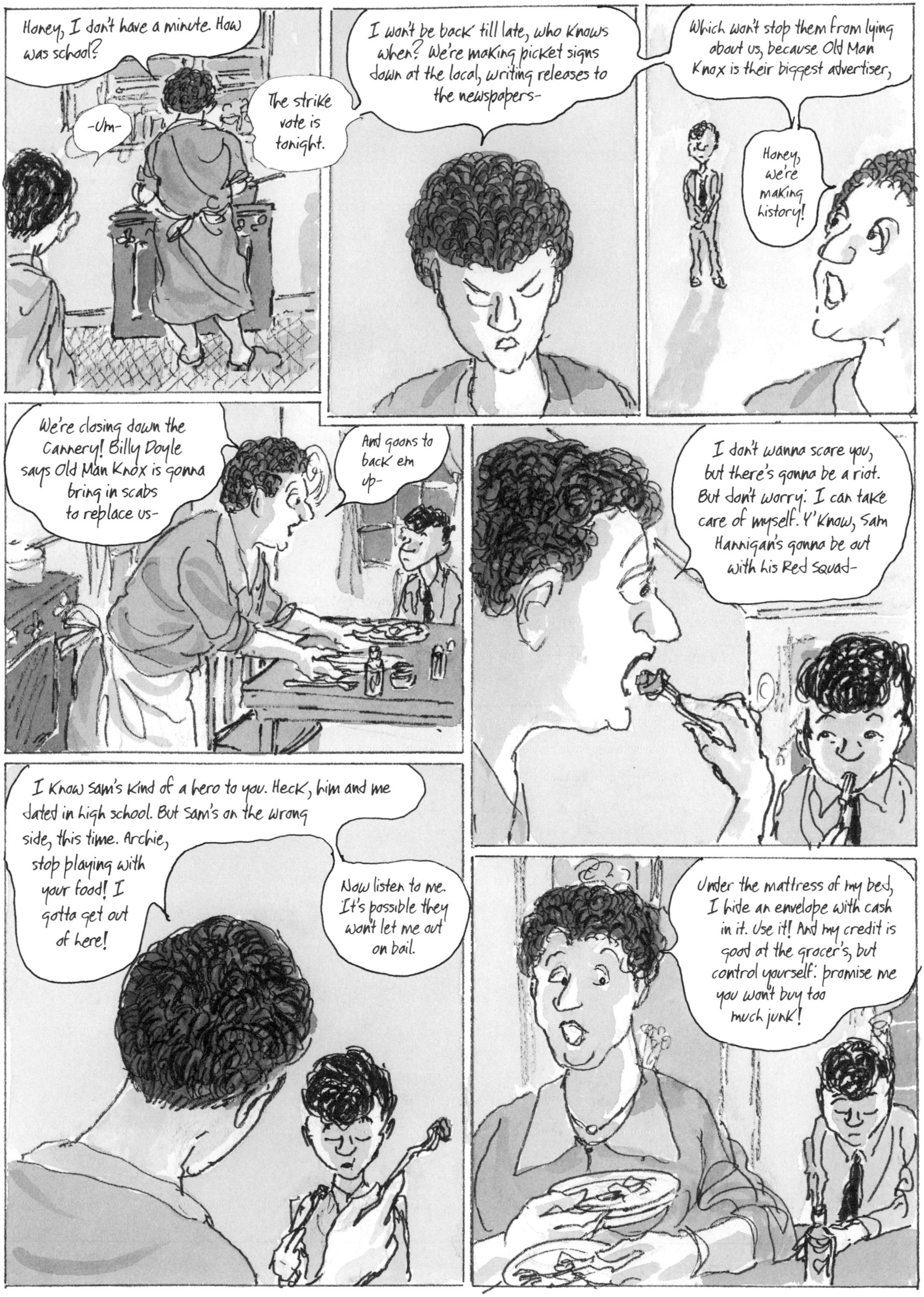
Honey, I don't have a minute. How was school?
-Um-
The strike vote is tonight.
I won't be back till late, who knows when? We're making picket signs down at the local, writing releases to the newspapers-
Which won't stop them from lying about us, because Old Man Knox is their biggest advertiser,
Honey, we're making history!
We're closing down the cannery! Billy Doyle says Old Man Knox is gonna bring in scabs to replace us-
And goons to back em up-
I don't wanna scare you, but there's gonna be a riot. But don't worry: I can take care of myself. Y'know, Sam Hannigan's gonna be out with his Red Squad-
I know Sam's kind of a hero to you. Heck, him and me dated in high school. But Sam's on the wrong side, this time. Archie, stop playing with your food! I gotta get out of here!
Now listen to me. It's possible they won't let me out on bail.
Under the mattress of my bed, I hide an envelope with cash in it. Use it! And my credit is good at the grocer's, but control yourself: promise me you won't buy too much junk!

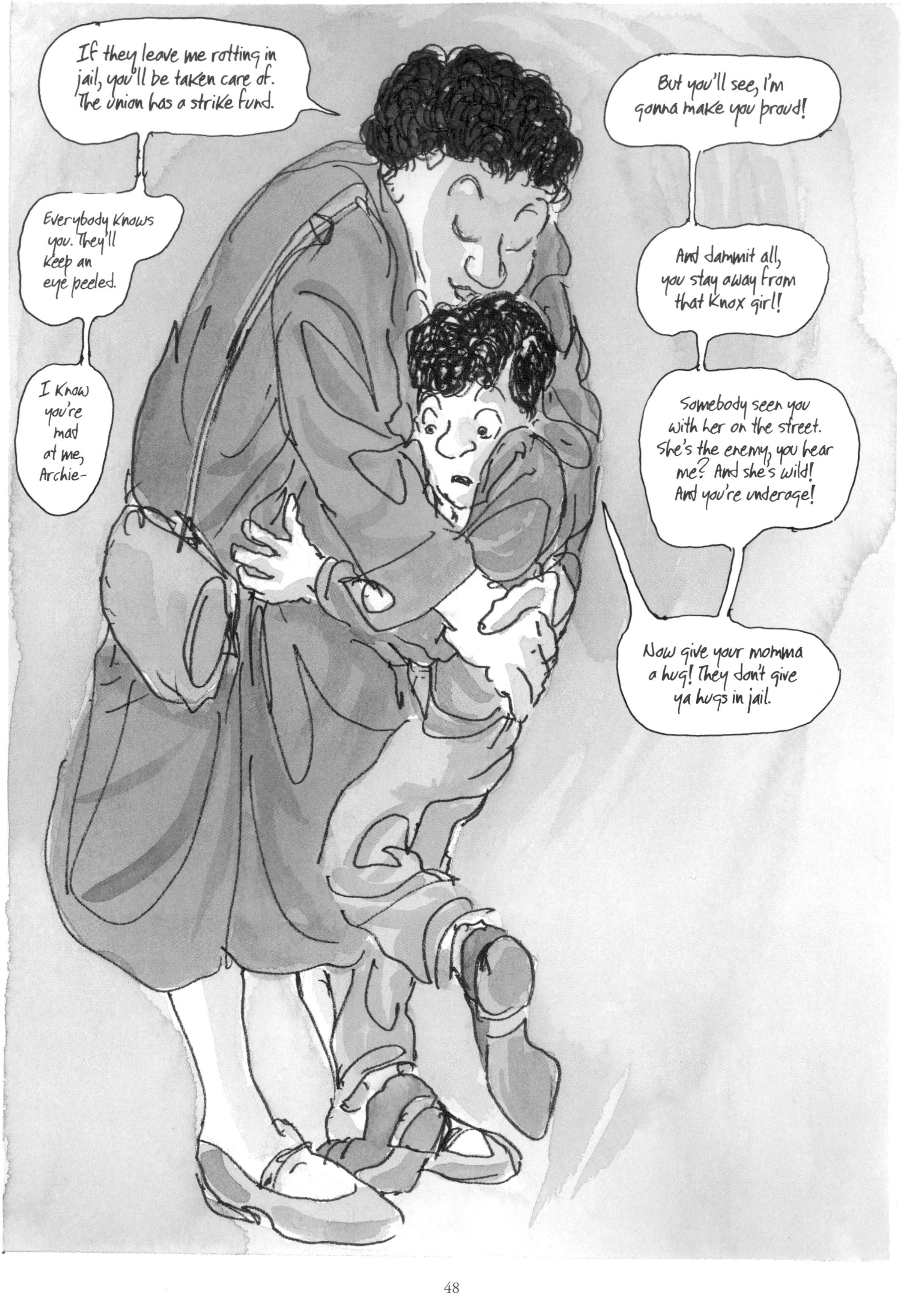
If they leave me rotting in jail, you'll be taken care of. The union has a strike fund.
Everybody knows you. They'll keep an eye peeled.
I know you're mad at me, Archie-
But you'll see, I'm gonna make you proud!
And dammit all, you stay away from that Knox girl!
Somebody seen you with her on the street. She's the enemy, you hear me? And she's wild! And you're underage!
Now give your momma a hug! They don't give ya hugs in jail.

Chapter Eighteen: Cousin Joseph and the Immigrant Parable

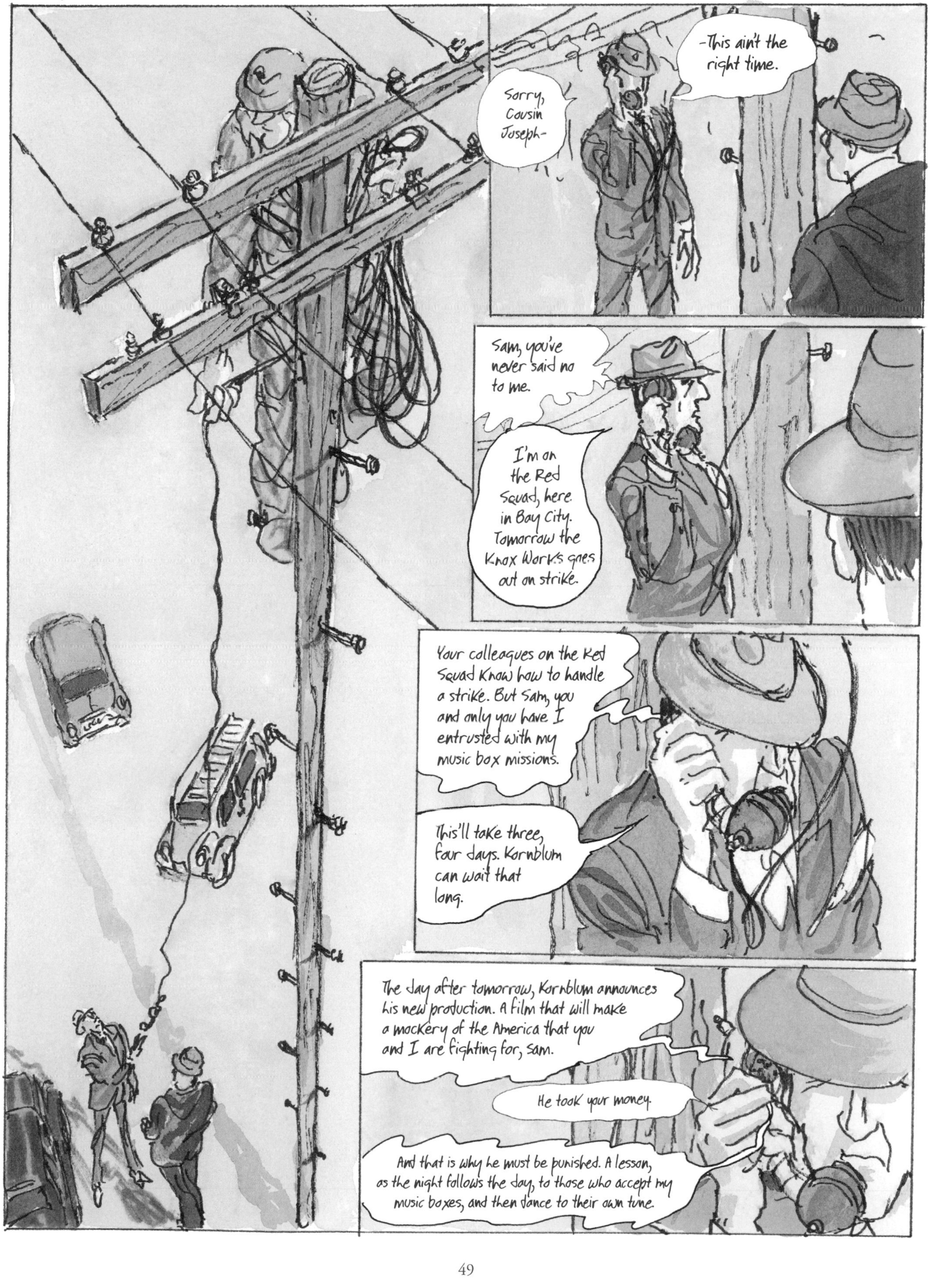

Sorry, Cousin Joseph-
-This ain't the right time.
Sam, you've never said no to me.
I'm on the Red Squad, here in Bay City. Tomorrow the Knox Works goes out on strike.
Your colleagues on the Red Squad know how to handle a strike. But Sam, you and only you have I entrusted with my music box missions.
This'll take three, four days. Kornblum can wait that long.
The day after tomorrow, Kornblum announces his new production. A film that will make a mockery of the America that you and I are fighting for, Sam.
He took your money.
And that is why he must be punished. A lesson, as the night follows the day, to those who accept my music boxes, and then dance to their own tune.

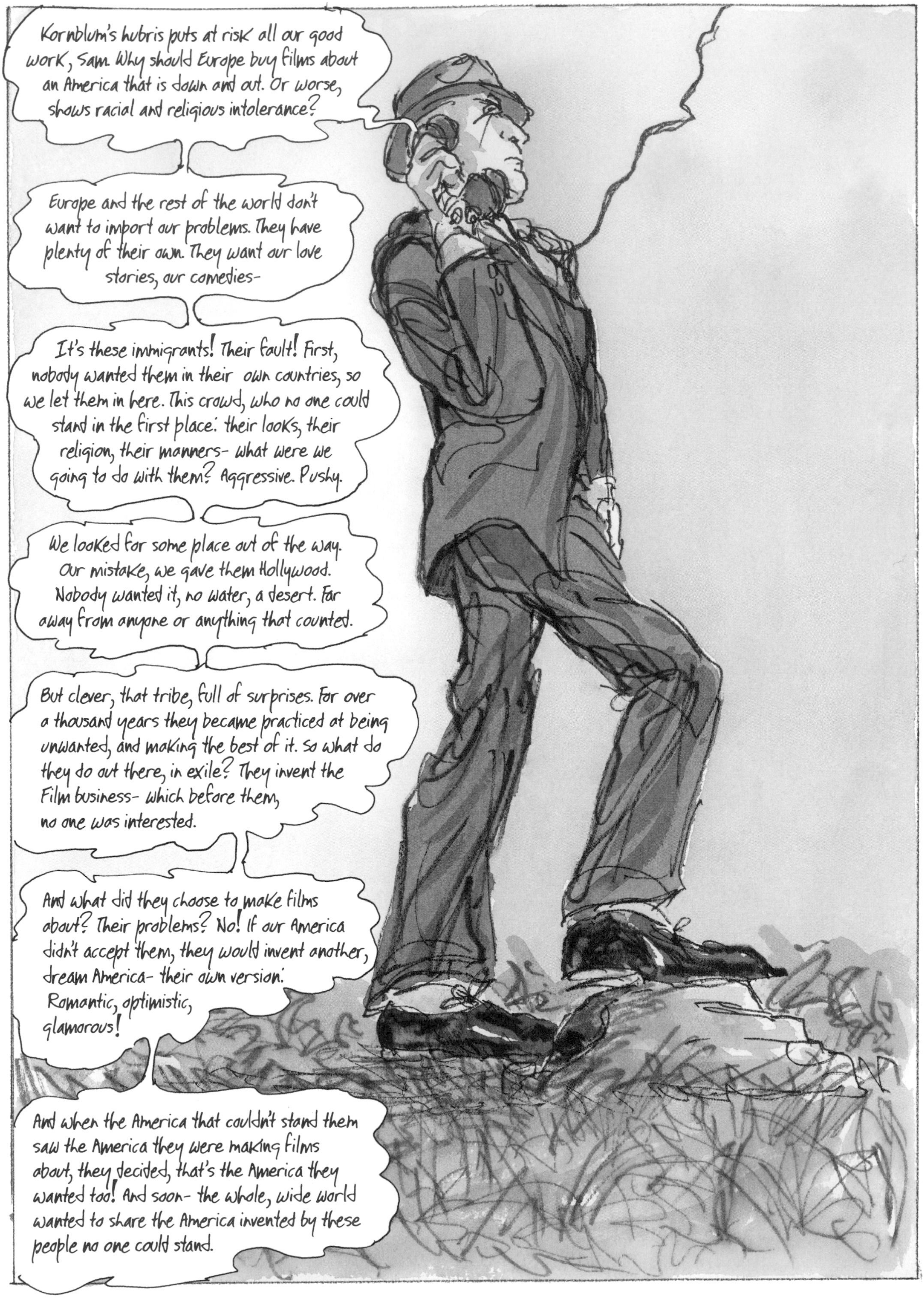
Kornblum's hubris puts at risk all our good work, Sam. Why should Europe buy films about an America that is down and out. Or worse, shows racial and religious intolerance?
Europe and the rest of the world don't want to import our problems. They have plenty of their own. They want our love stories, our comedies-
It's these immigrants! Their fault! First, nobody wanted them in their own countries, so we let them in here. This crowd, who no one could stand in the first place: their looks, their religion, their manners- what were we going to do with them? Aggressive. Pushy.
We looked for some place out of the way. Our mistake, we gave them Hollywood. Nobody wanted it, no water, a desert. Far away from anyone or anything that counted.
But clever, that tribe, full of surprises. For over a thousand years they became practiced at being unwanted, and making the best of it. So what do they do out there, in exile? They invent the Film business- which before them, no one was interested.
And what did they choose to make films about? Their problems? No! If our America didn't accept them, they would invent another, dream America- their own version: Romantic, optimistic, glamorous!
And when the America that couldn't stand them saw the America they were making films about, they decided, that's the America they wanted too! And soon- the whole, wide world wanted to share the America invented by these people no one could stand.

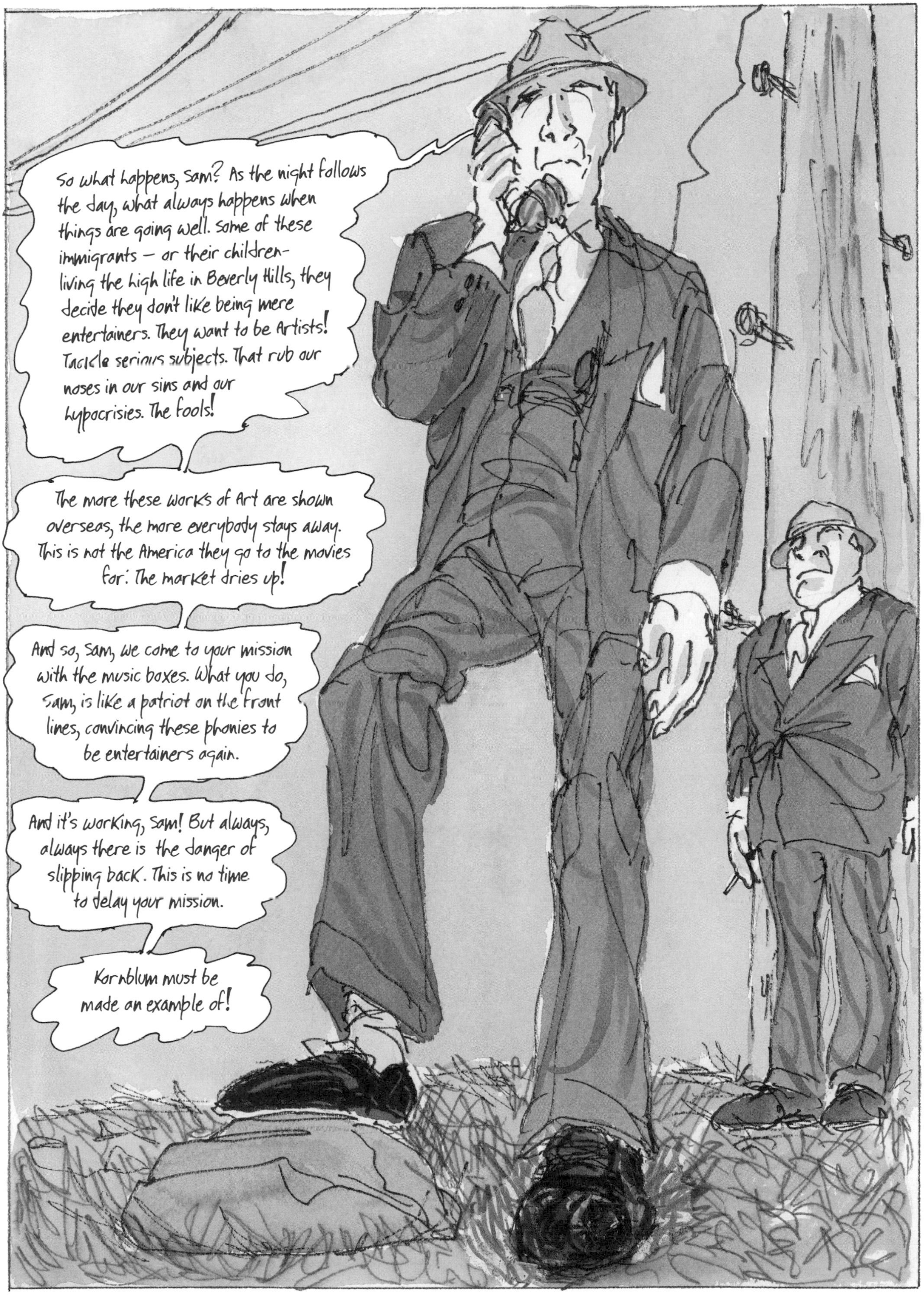
So what happens, Sam? As the night follows the day, what always happens when things are going well. Some of these immigrants – or their children- living the high life in Beverly Hills, they decide they don't like being mere entertainers. They want to be Artists! Tackle serious subjects. That rub our noses in our sins and our hypocrisies. The fools!
The more these works of Art are shown overseas, the more everybody stays away. This is not the America they go to the movies for: The market dries up!
And so, Sam, we come to your mission with the music boxes. What you do, Sam, is like a patriot on the front lines, convincing these phonies to be entertainers again.
And it's working, Sam! But always, always there is the danger of slipping back. This is no time to delay your mission.
Kornblum must be made an example of!

Chapter Nineteen: The Surprise

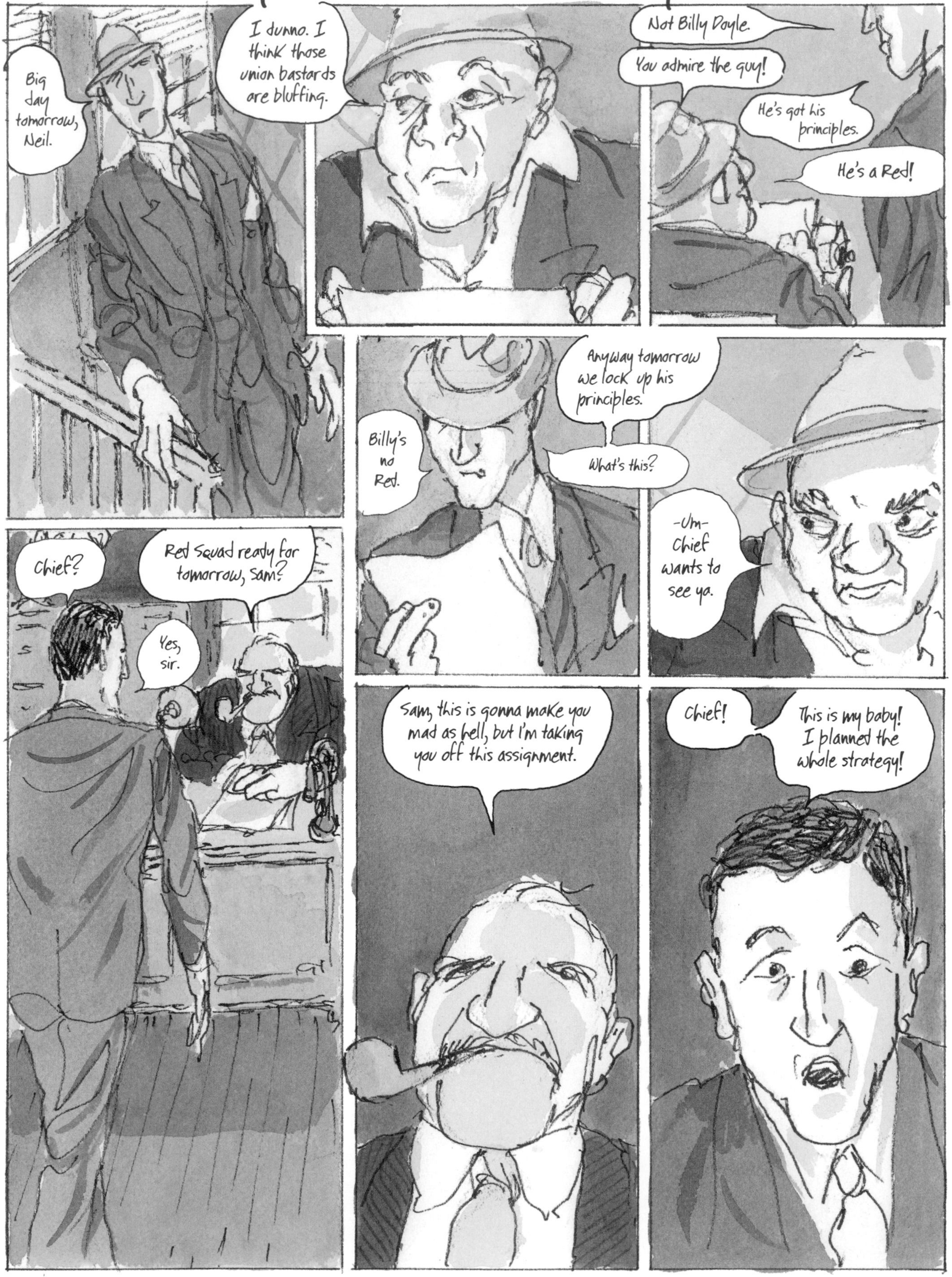

Big day tomorrow, Neil.
I dunno. I think those union bastards are bluffing.
Not Billy Doyle.
You admire the guy!
He's got his principles.
He's a Red!
Billy's no Red.
Anyway tomorrow we lock up his principles.
What's this?
-Um- Chief wants to see ya.
Chief?
Red Squad ready for tomorrow, Sam?
Yes, sir.
Sam, this is gonna make you mad as hell, but I'm taking you off this assignment.
Chief!
This is my baby! I planned the whole strategy!

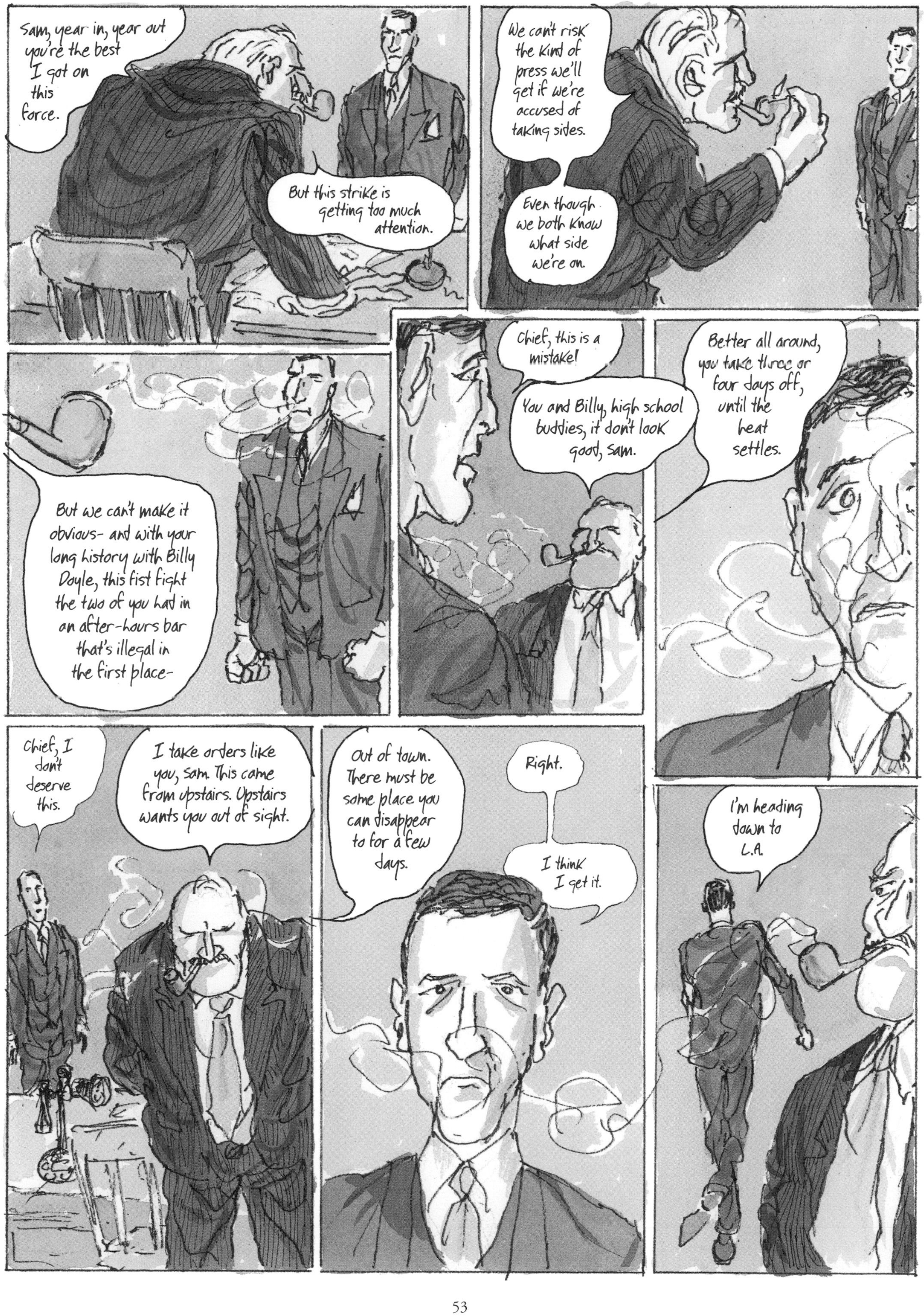
Sam, year in, year out you're the best I got on this force.
But this strike is getting too much attention.
We can't risk the kind of press we'll get if we're accused of taking sides.
Even though we both know what side we're on.
But we can't make it obvious- and with your long history with Billy Doyle, this fist fight the two of you had in an after-hours bar that's illegal in the first place-
Chief, this is a mistake!
You and Billy, high school buddies, it don't look good, Sam.
Better all around, you take three or four days off, until the heat settles.
Chief, I don't deserve this.
I take orders like you, Sam. This came from upstairs. Upstairs wants you out of sight.
Out of town. There must be some place you can disappear to for a few days.
Right.
I think I get it.
I'm heading down to L.A.

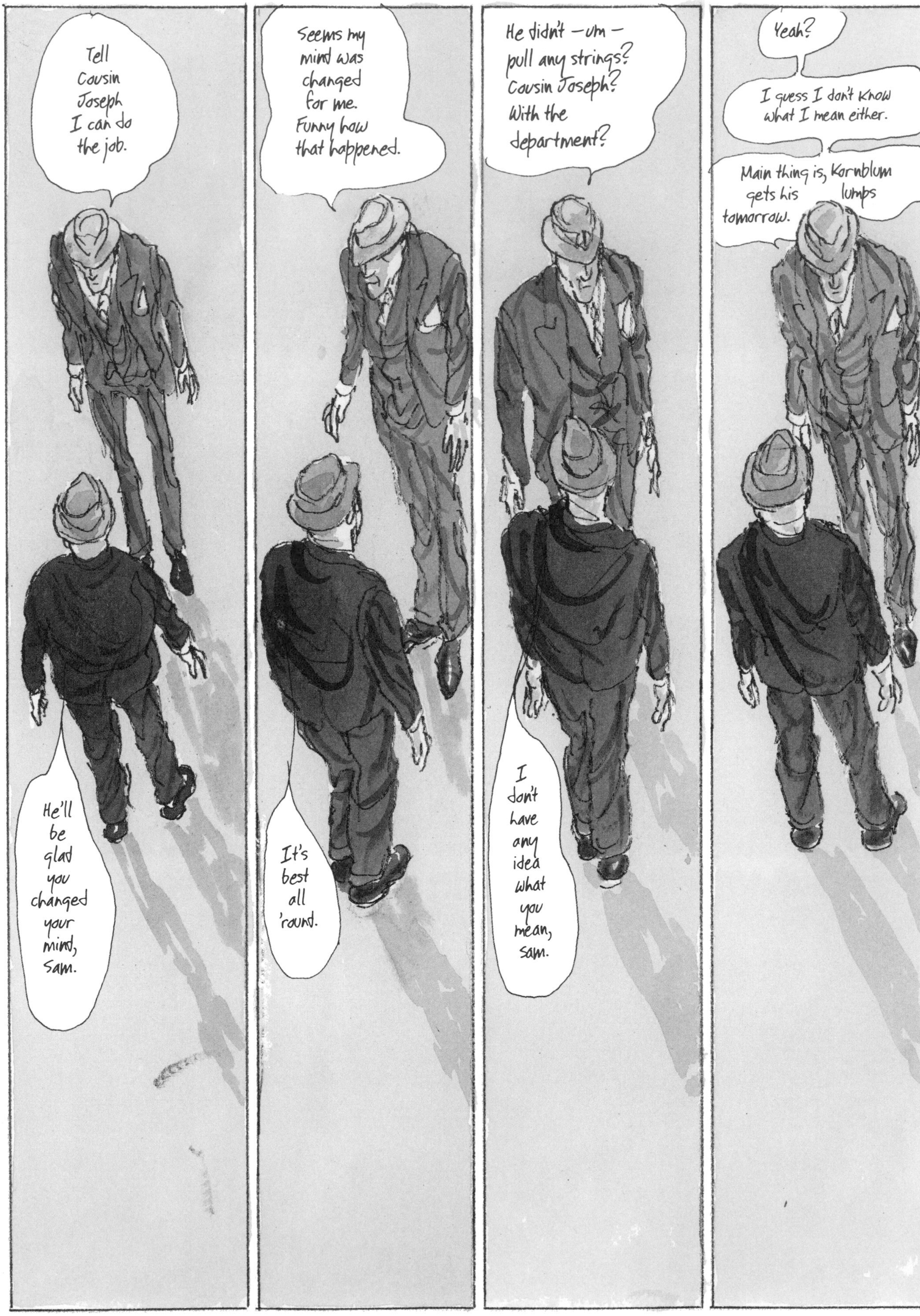
Tell Cousin Joseph I can do the job.
He'll be glad you changed your mind, Sam.
Seems my mind was changed for me. Funny how that happened.
It's best all 'round.
He didn't —um— pull any strings? Cousin Joseph? With the department?
I don't have any idea what you mean, Sam.
Yeah?
I guess I don't know what I mean either.
Main thing is, Kornblum gets his lumps tomorrow.

Chapter Twenty: Where's Frankie?

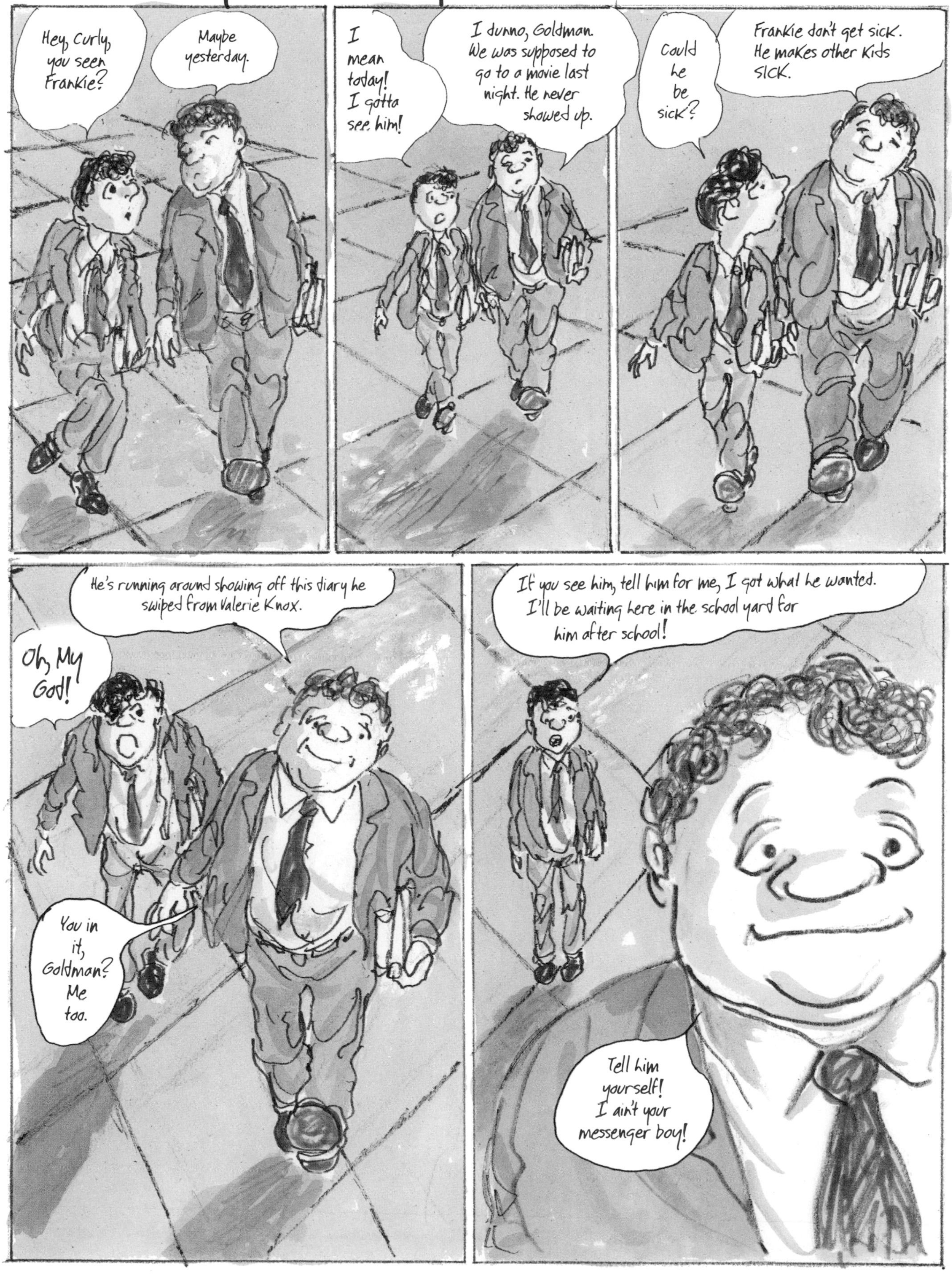
Hey, Curly, you seen Frankie?
Maybe yesterday.
I mean today! I gotta see him!
I dunno, Goldman. We was supposed to go to a movie last night. He never showed up.
Could he be sick?
Frankie don't get sick. He makes other kids SICK.
He's running around showing off this diary he swiped from Valerie Knox.
Oh, My God!
You in it, Goldman? Me too.
If you see him, tell him for me, I got what he wanted. I'll be waiting here in the school yard for him after school!
Tell him yourself! I ain't your messenger boy!

Chapter Twenty-One: Strike!

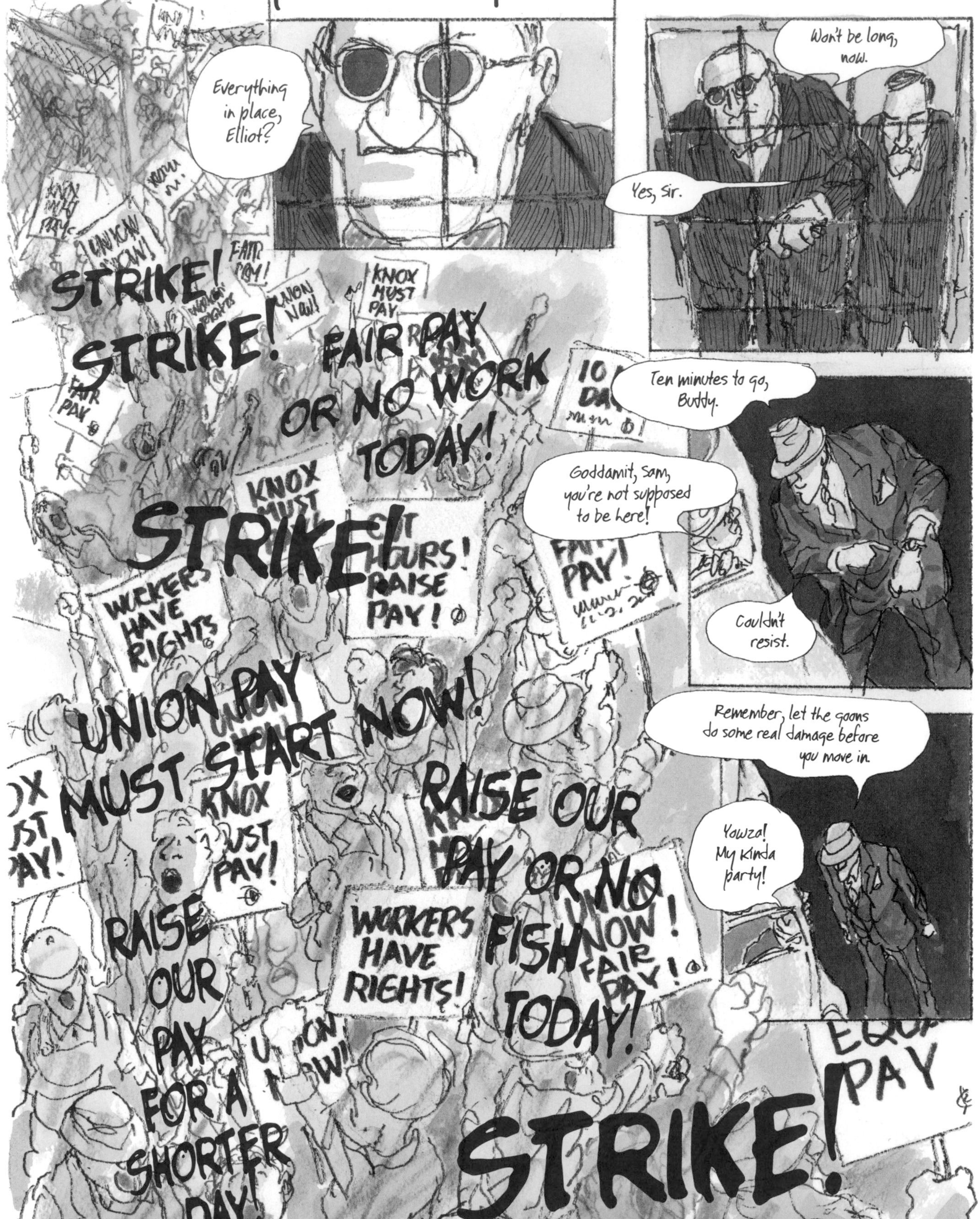
Everything in place, Elliot?
Won't be long, now.
Yes, Sir.
Ten minutes to go, Buddy.
Goddamit, Sam, you're not supposed to be here!
Couldn't resist.
Remember, let the goons do some real damage before you move in.
Yowza! My kinda party!
STRIKE!
STRIKE!
FAIR PAY OR NO WORK TODAY!
STRIKE!
KNOX MUST PAY
UNION NOW!
FAIR PAY
WORKERS HAVE RIGHTS
CUT HOURS! RAISE PAY!
UNION PAY MUST START NOW!
RAISE OUR PAY OR NO FISH TODAY!
KNOX MUST PAY!
RAISE OUR PAY FOR A SHORTER DAY!
WORKERS HAVE RIGHTS!
UNION NOW! FAIR PAY!
STRIKE!

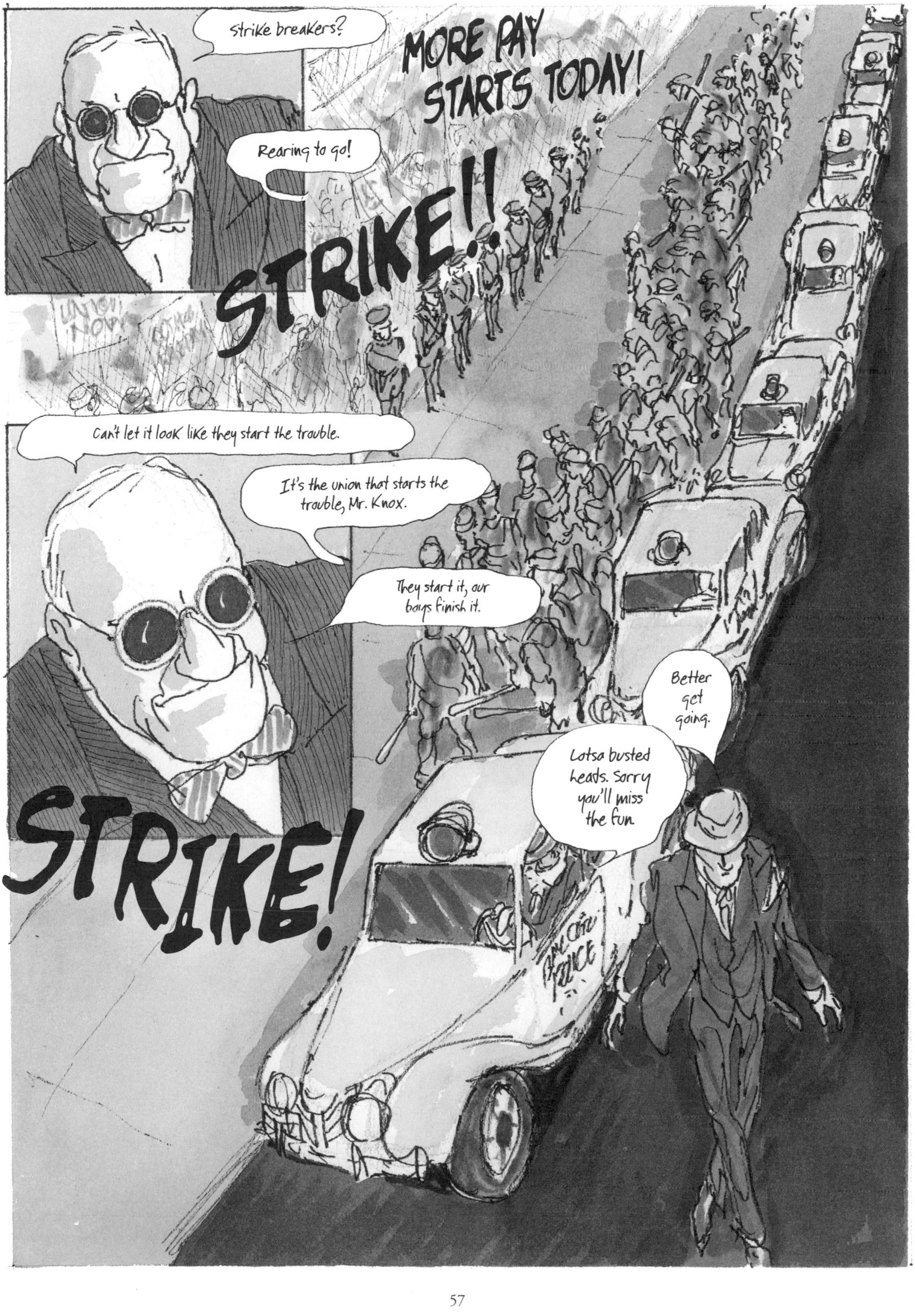
strike breakers?
MORE PAY STARTS TODAY!
Rearing to go!
STRIKE!!
Can't let it look like they start the trouble.
It's the union that starts the trouble, Mr. Knox.
They start it, our boys finish it.
Better get going.
Lotsa busted heads. Sorry you'll miss the fun.
STRIKE!

Chapter Twenty-Two: America!

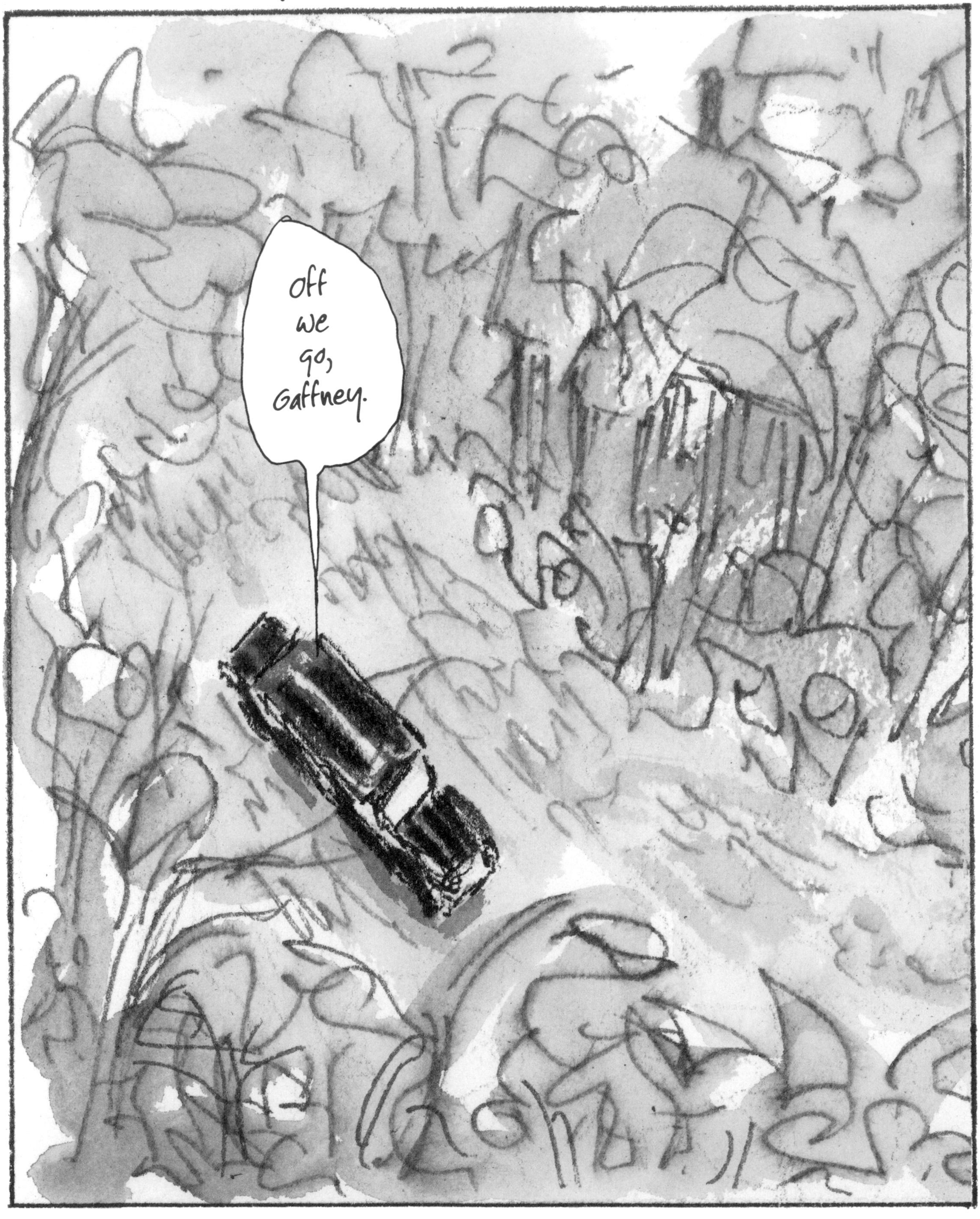
Off we go, Gaffney.

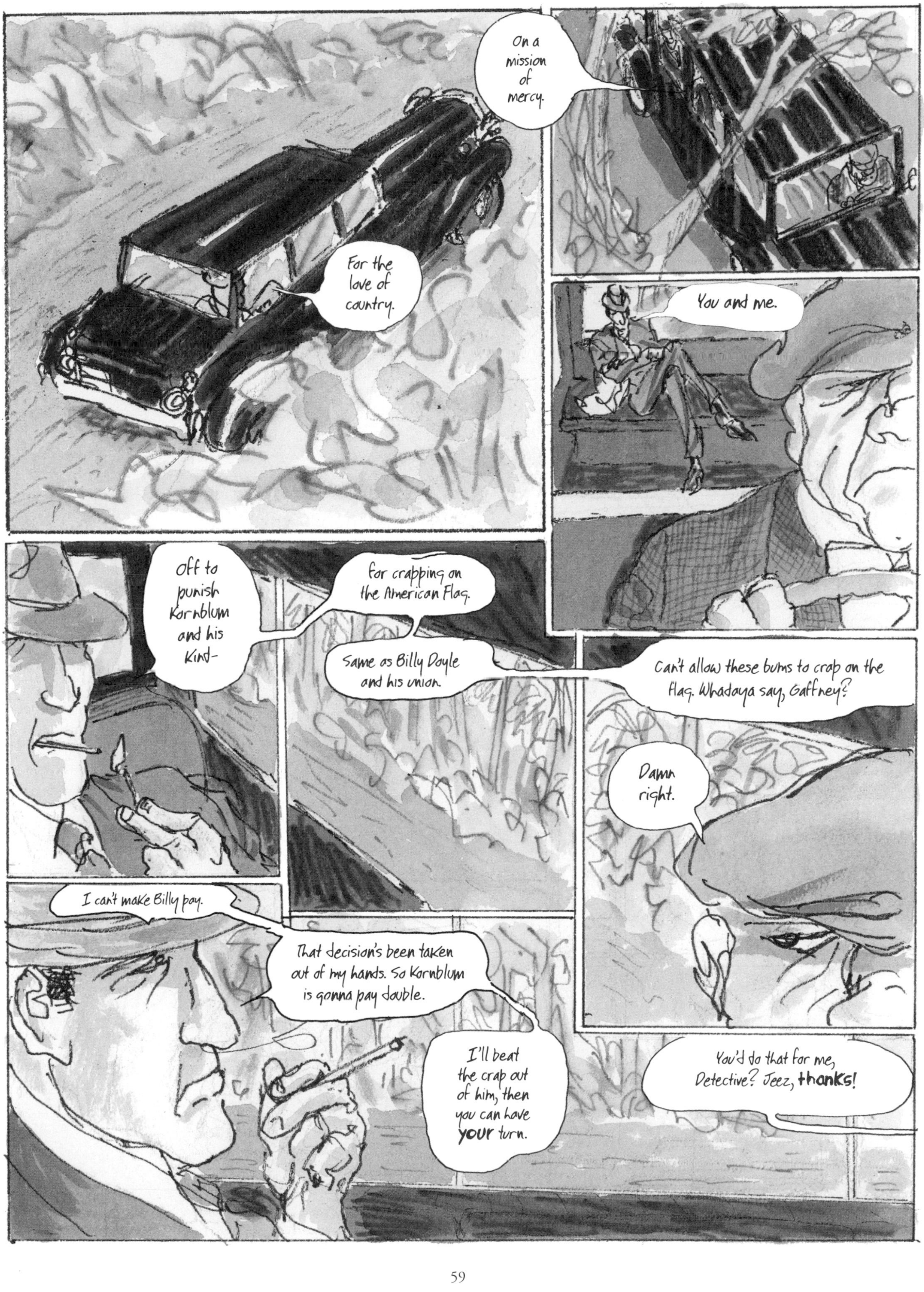
On a mission of mercy.
For the love of country.
You and me.
Off to punish Kornblum and his kind-
for crapping on the American Flag.
Same as Billy Doyle and his union.
Can't allow these bums to crap on the Flag. Whadaya say, Gaffney?
Damn right.
I can't make Billy pay.
That decision's been taken out of my hands. So Kornblum is gonna pay double.
I'll beat the crap out of him, then you can have **your** turn.
You'd do that for me, Detective? Jeez, **thanks!**

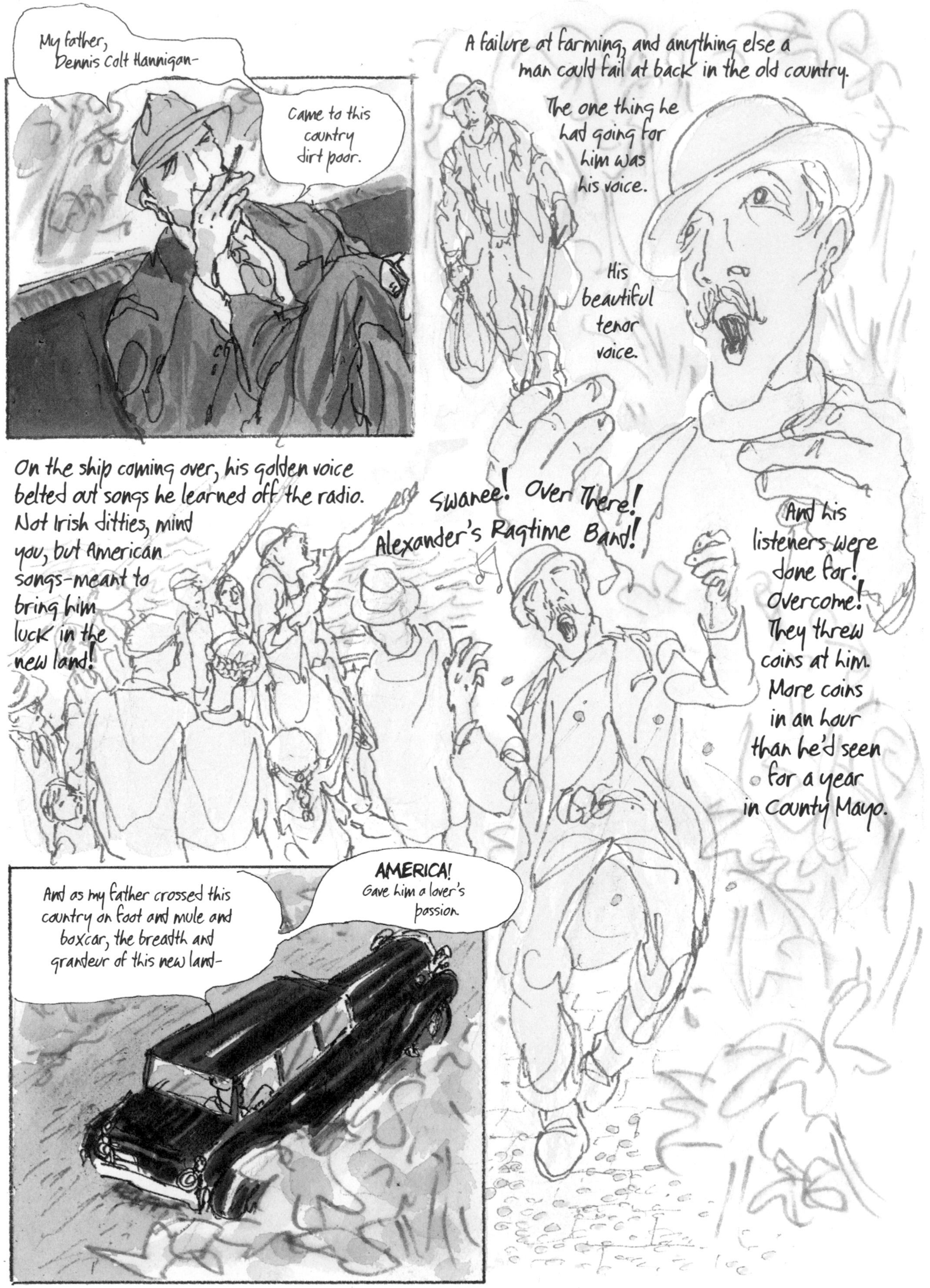

My father, Dennis Colt Hannigan-
Came to this country dirt poor.
A failure at farming, and anything else a man could fail at back in the old country.
The one thing he had going for him was his voice.
His beautiful tenor voice.
On the ship coming over, his golden voice belted out songs he learned off the radio. Not Irish ditties, mind you, but American songs-meant to bring him luck in the new land!
Swanee! Over There! Alexander's Ragtime Band!
And his listeners were done for! Overcome! They threw coins at him. More coins in an hour than he'd seen for a year in County Mayo.
And as my father crossed this country on foot and mule and boxcar, the breadth and grandeur of this new land-
AMERICA! Gave him a lover's passion.

And the shower of coins went on. He taught himself more up-to-date songs. Toot-Toot-Tootsie Goodbye.... Luck and more luck! And then one day, it was over. Stopped cold. And then a month or so later, began again. And then, stop again. And that's how it went with my dad.

A married man, by now, five mouths to feed. Stops and starts, rich or on the skid, no complaints. Never joining a union. Always good for a laugh.

—the good lord gave me, fighting in my father's name to beat back the weak sisters, and the un-Americans who'd sell us down the river for a plugged nickel.

Till the day he died, on his fortieth birthday, my old man taught us we were the best family in the world living in the best country in the world. And here I am today, carrying on his legacy. Can't sing a note, but with the wit and muscle—

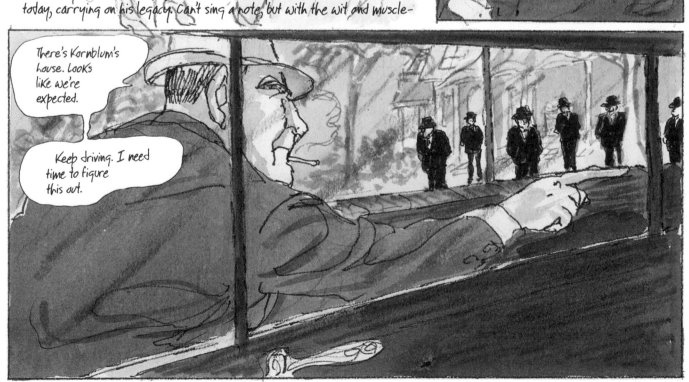

There's Kornblum's house. Looks like we're expected.

Keep driving. I need time to figure this out.

Chapter Twenty-Three: Riot!

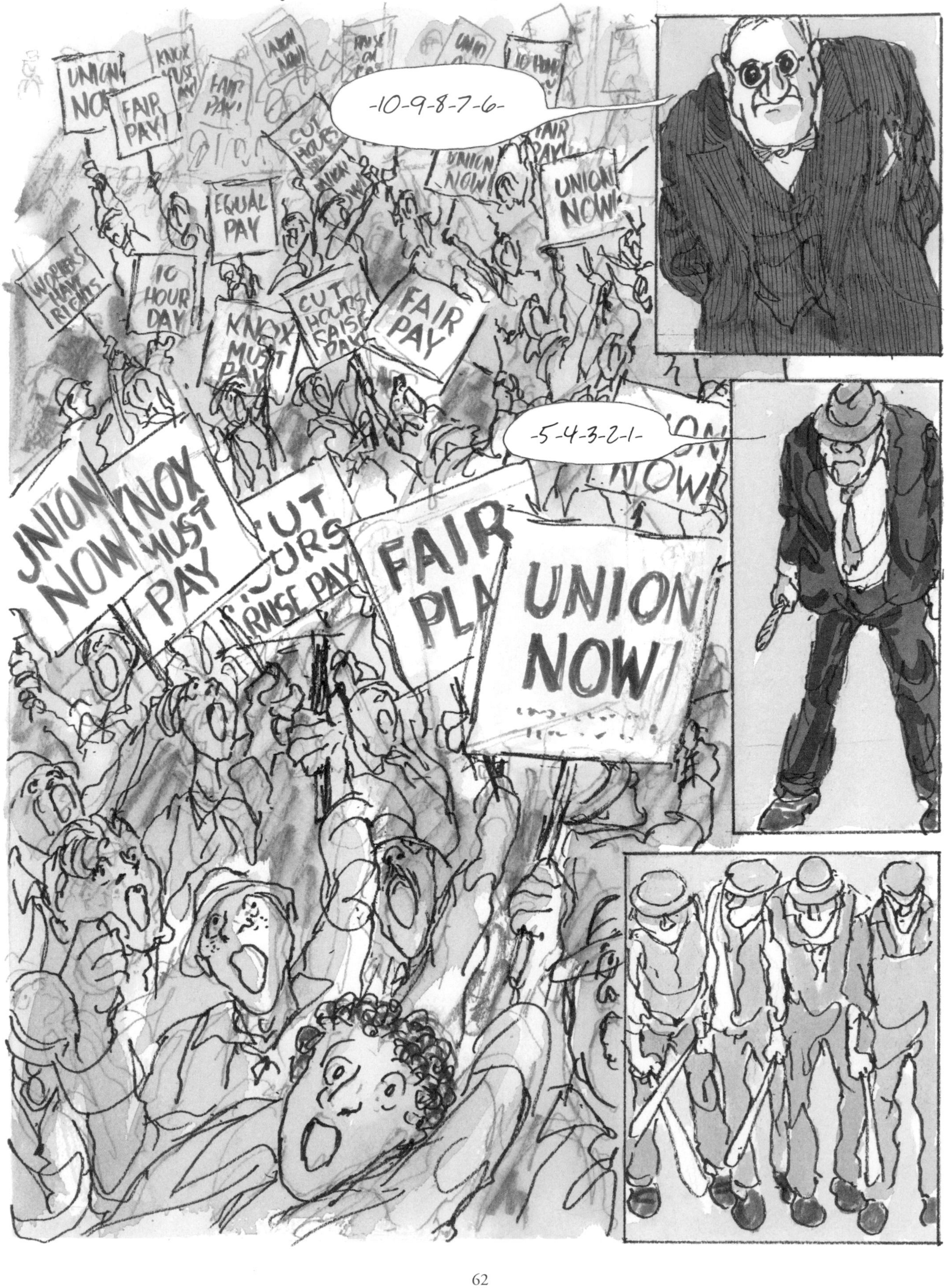
-10-9-8-7-6-
-5-4-3-2-1-
UNION NOW
FAIR PAY!
EQUAL PAY
WORKERS HAVE RIGHTS
10 HOUR DAY
KNOX MUST PAY
CUT HOURS RAISE PAY
FAIR PLA
UNION NOW!

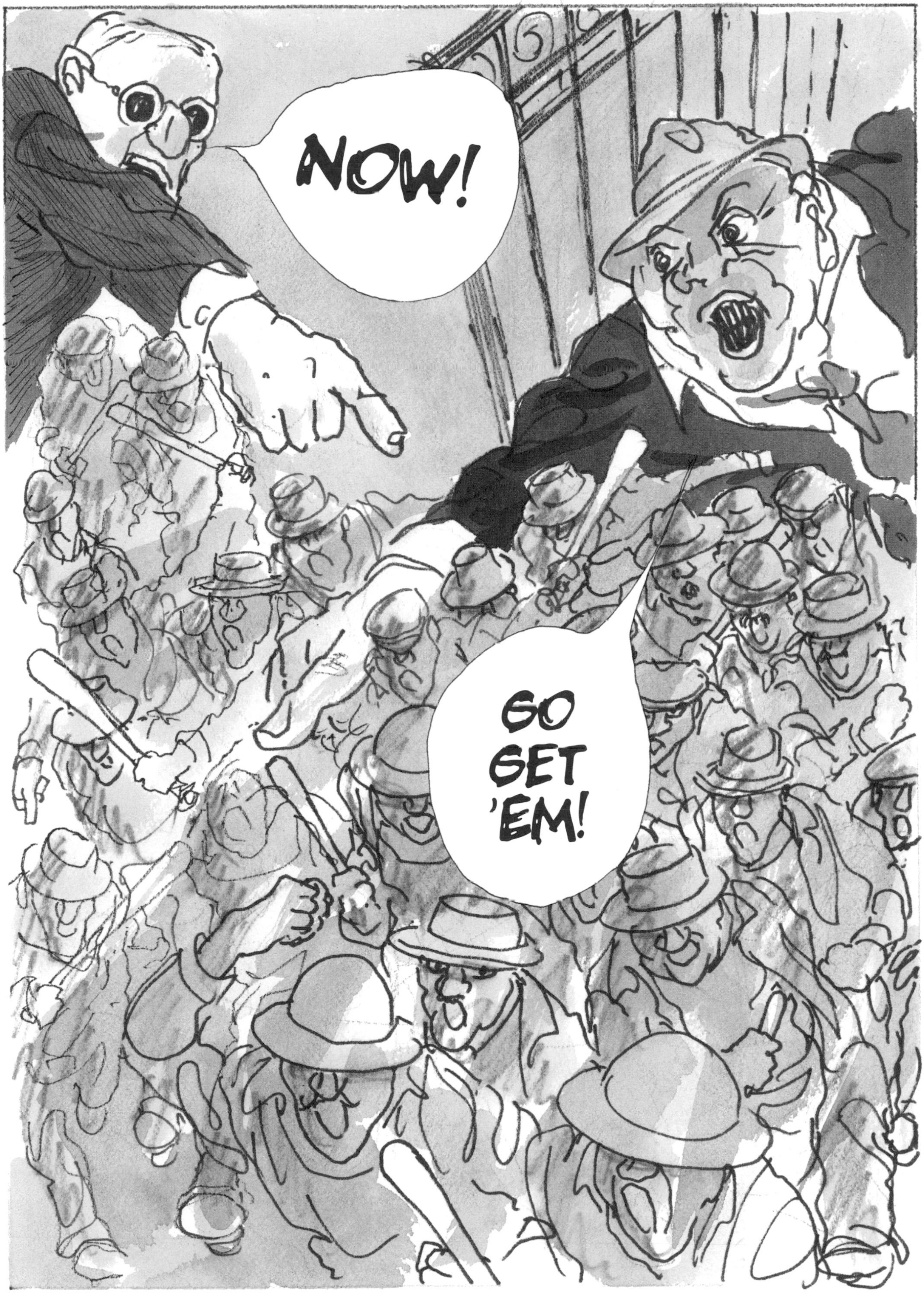
NOW!
GO GET 'EM!

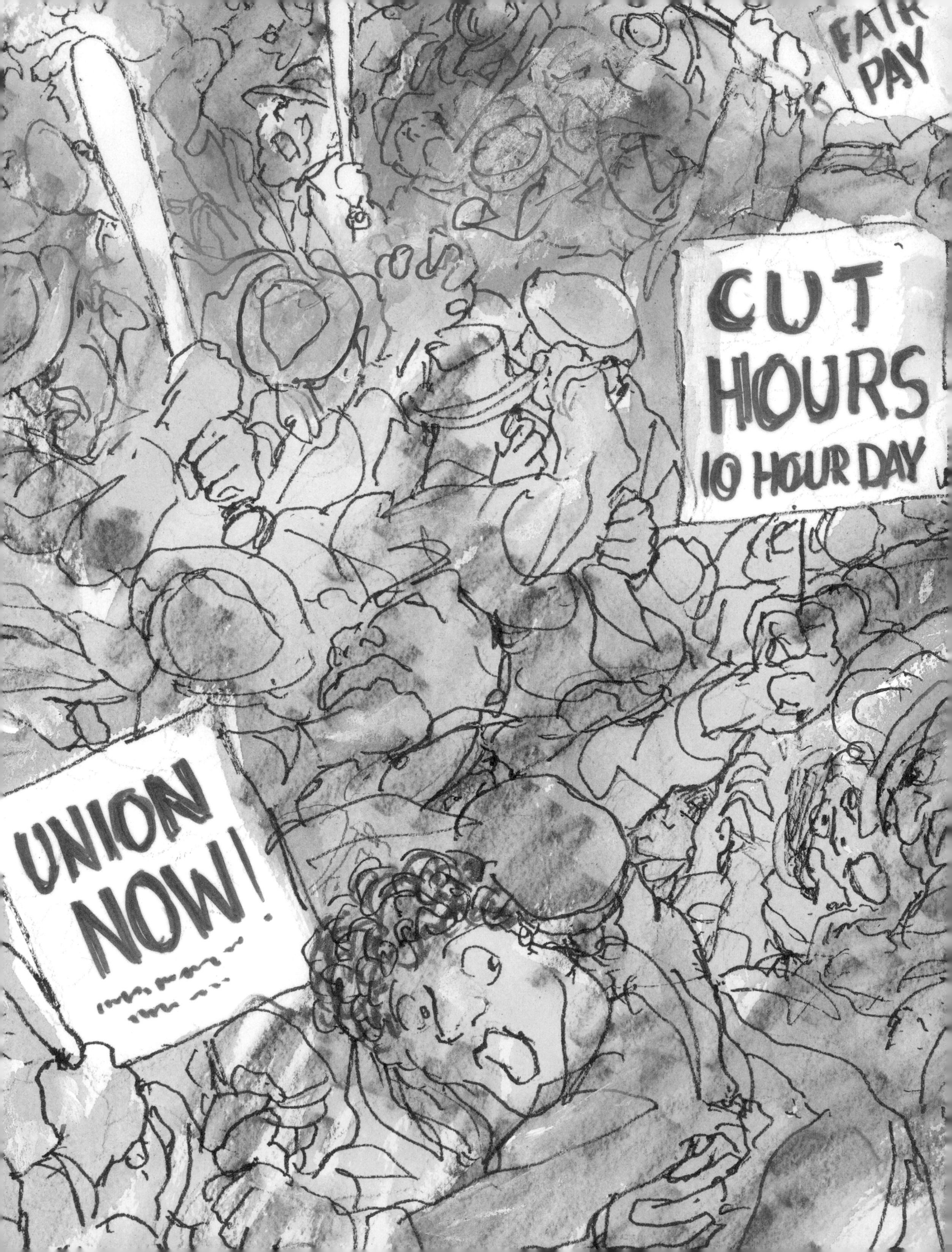
FAIR PAY
CUT HOURS
10 HOUR DAY
UNION NOW!

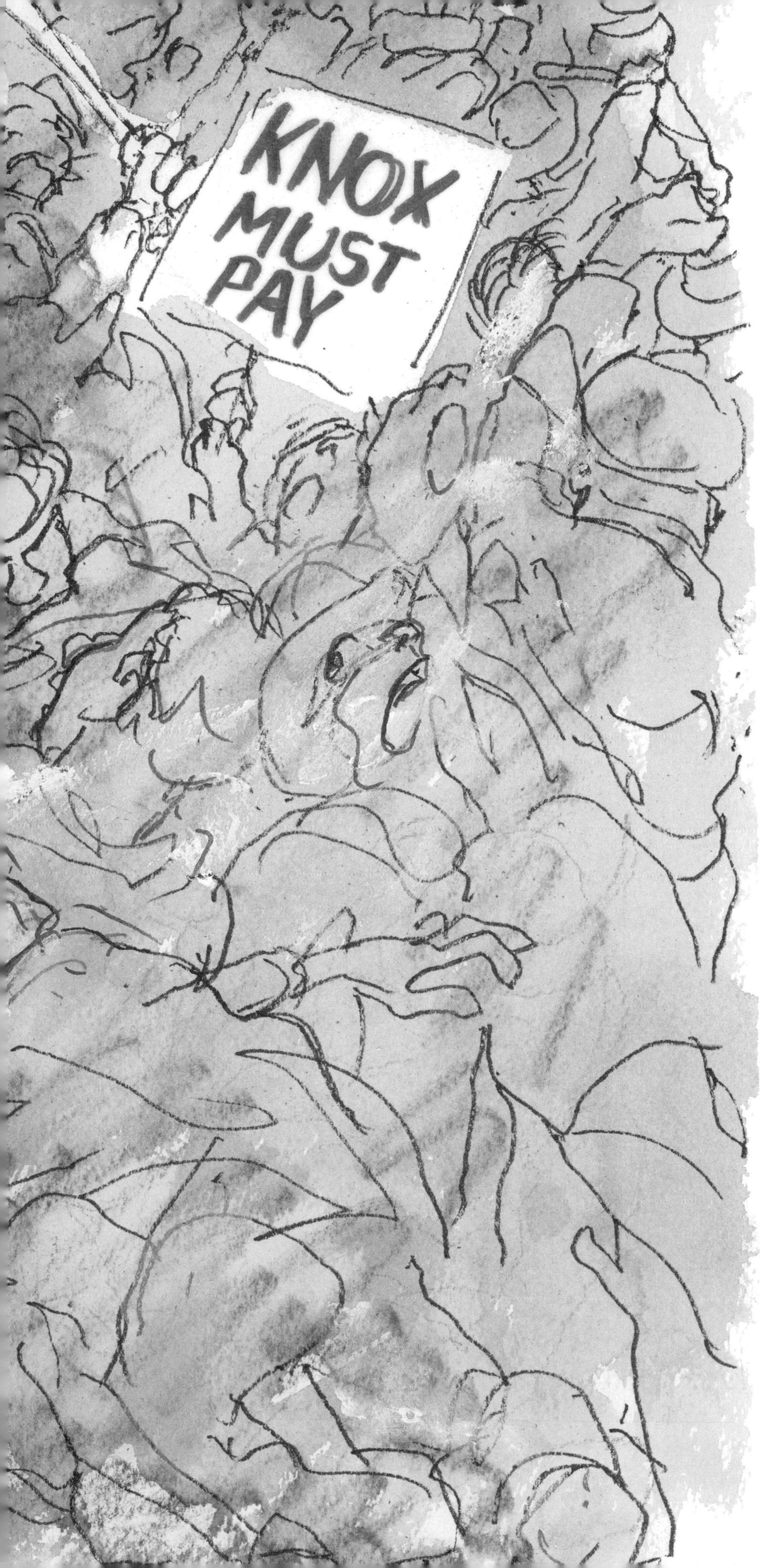
KNOX
MUST
PAY

Chapter Twenty-Four: Diversion

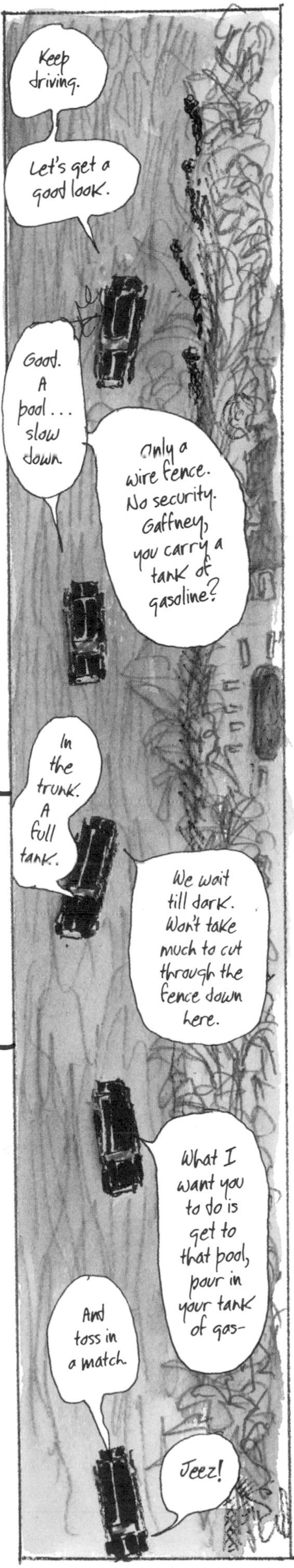
Keep driving.
Let's get a good look.
Good. A pool . . . slow down.
Only a wire fence. No security. Gaffney, you carry a tank of gasoline?
In the trunk. A full tank.
We wait till dark. Won't take much to cut through the fence down here.
What I want you to do is get to that pool, pour in your tank of gas-
And toss in a match.
Jeez!

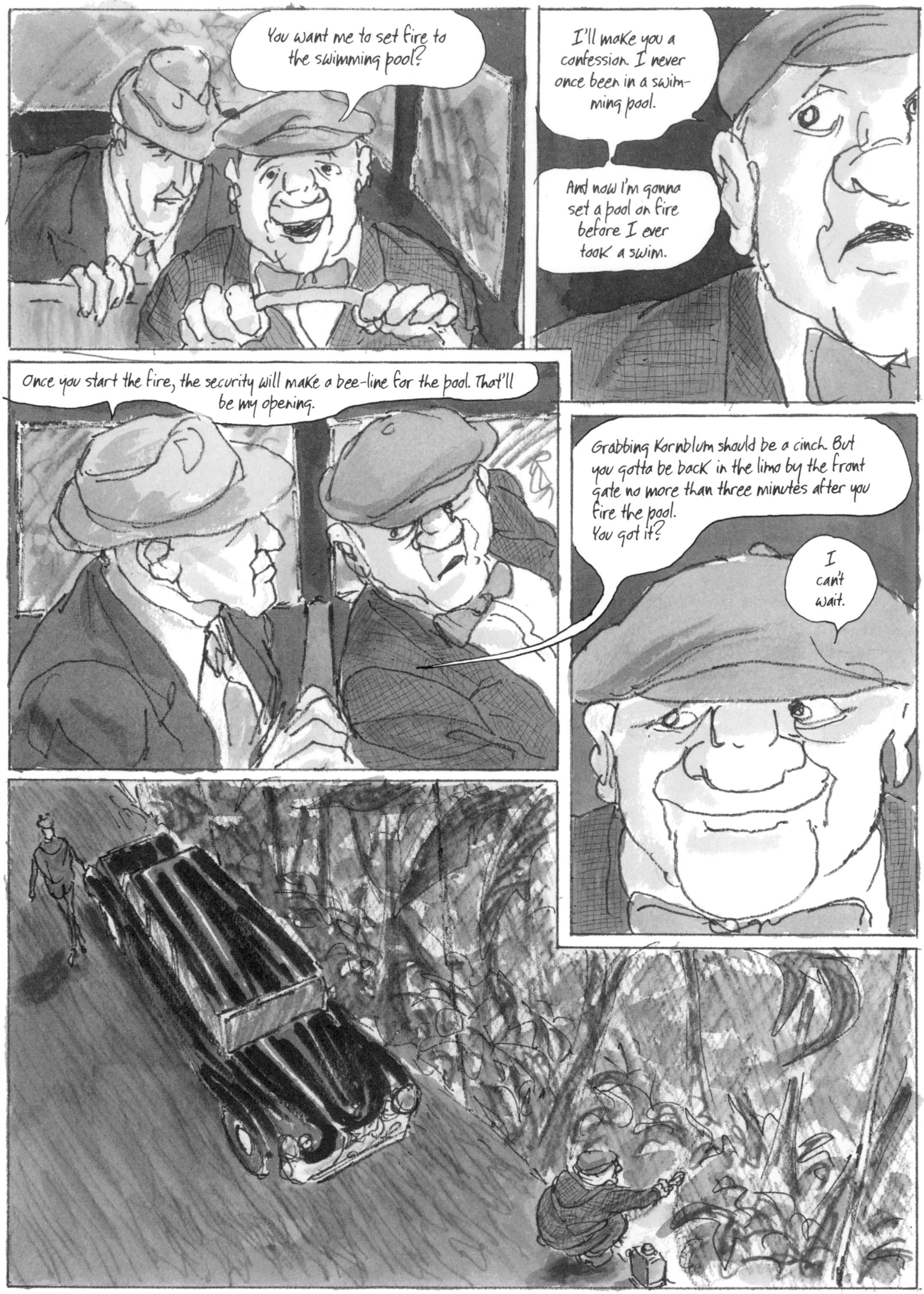
You want me to set fire to the swimming pool?
I'll make you a confession. I never once been in a swimming pool.
And now I'm gonna set a pool on fire before I ever took a swim.
Once you start the fire, the security will make a bee-line for the pool. That'll be my opening.
Grabbing Kornblum should be a cinch. But you gotta be back in the limo by the front gate no more than three minutes after you fire the pool. You got it?
I can't wait.

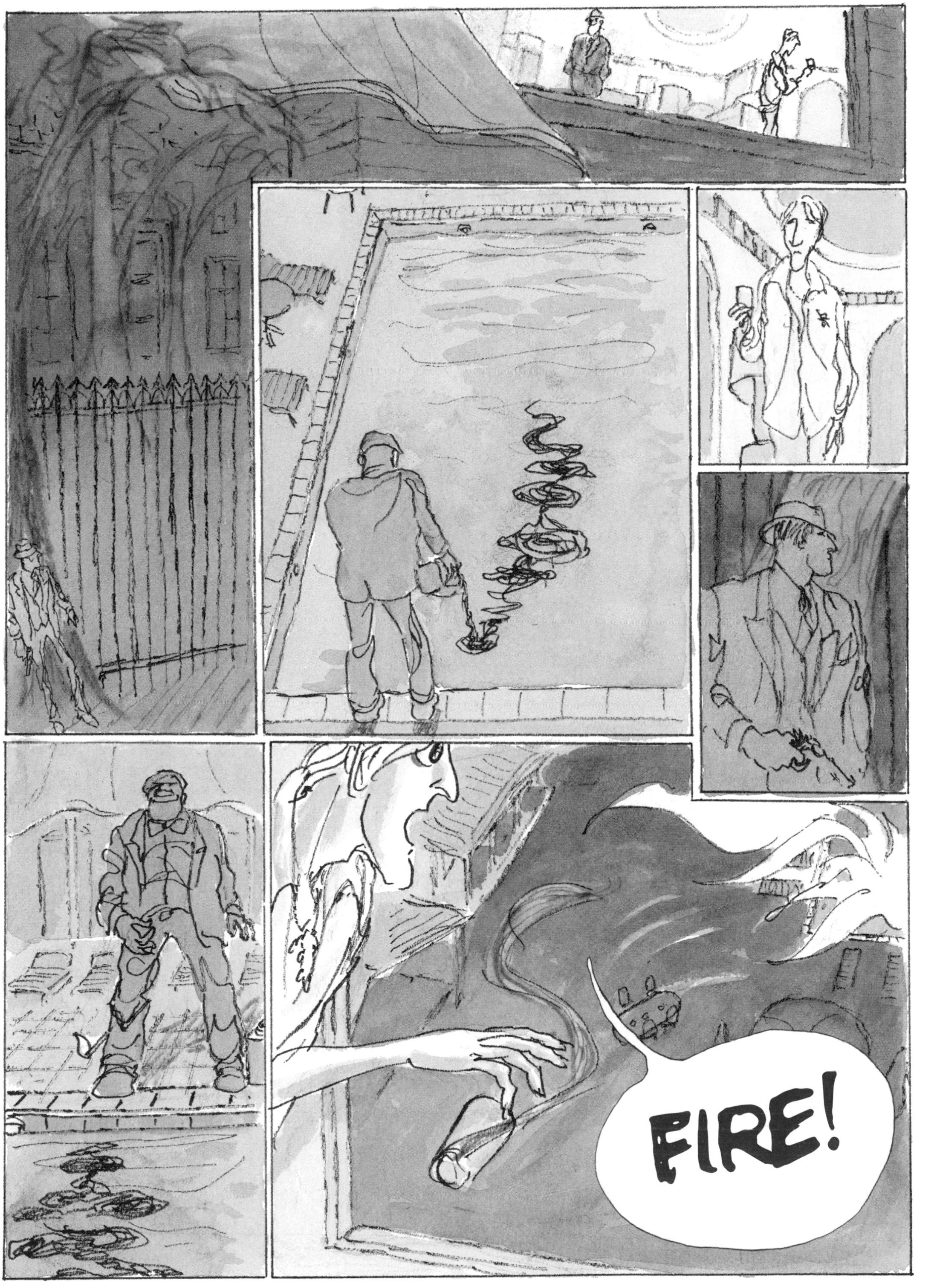
FIRE!

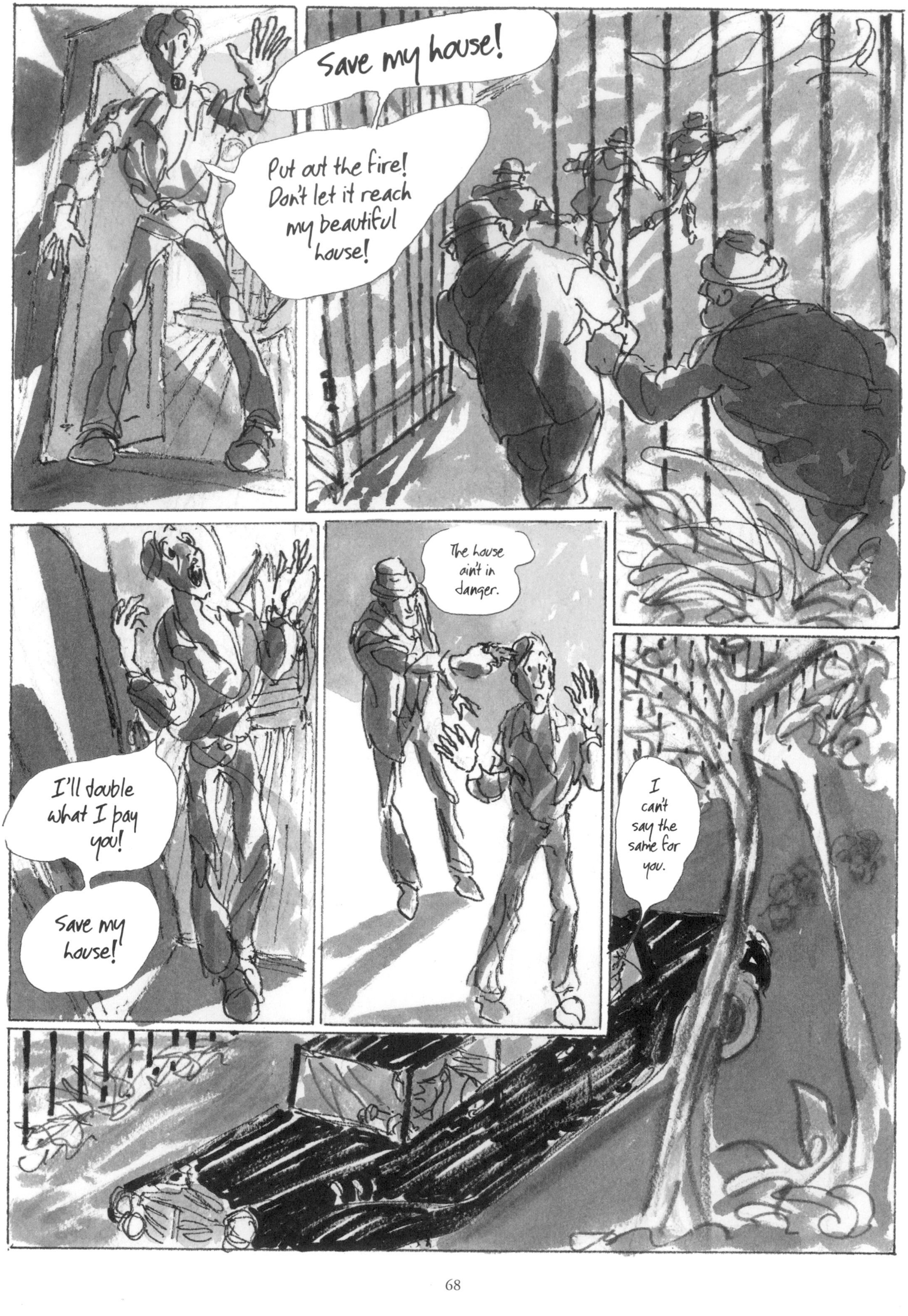
Save my house!
Put out the fire! Don't let it reach my beautiful house!
The house ain't in danger.
I'll double what I pay you!
Save my house!
I can't say the same for you.

Chapter Twenty-Five: The Body

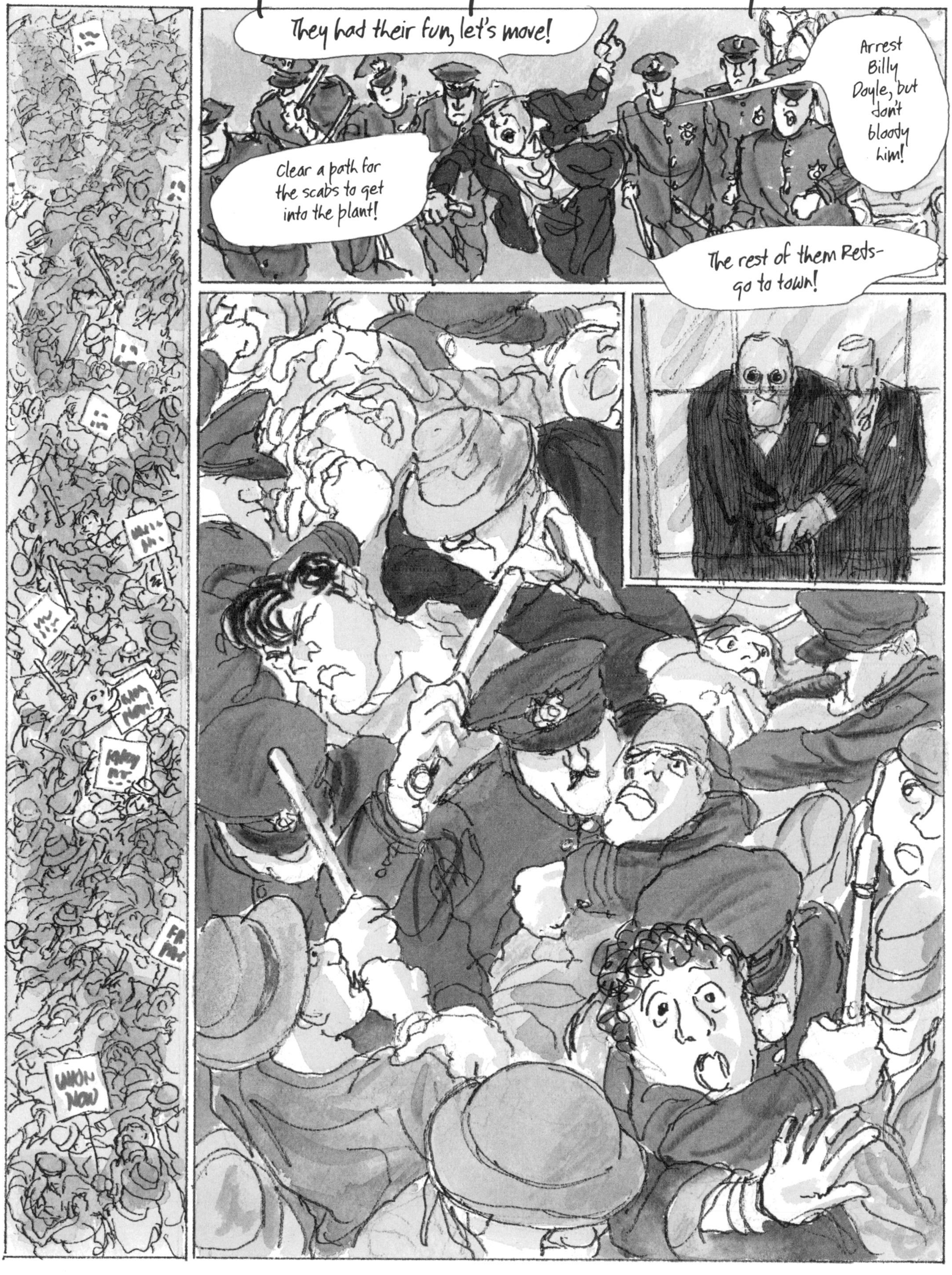

They had their fun, let's move!
Clear a path for the scabs to get into the plant!
Arrest Billy Doyle, but don't bloody him!
The rest of them Reds-go to town!
UNION NOW

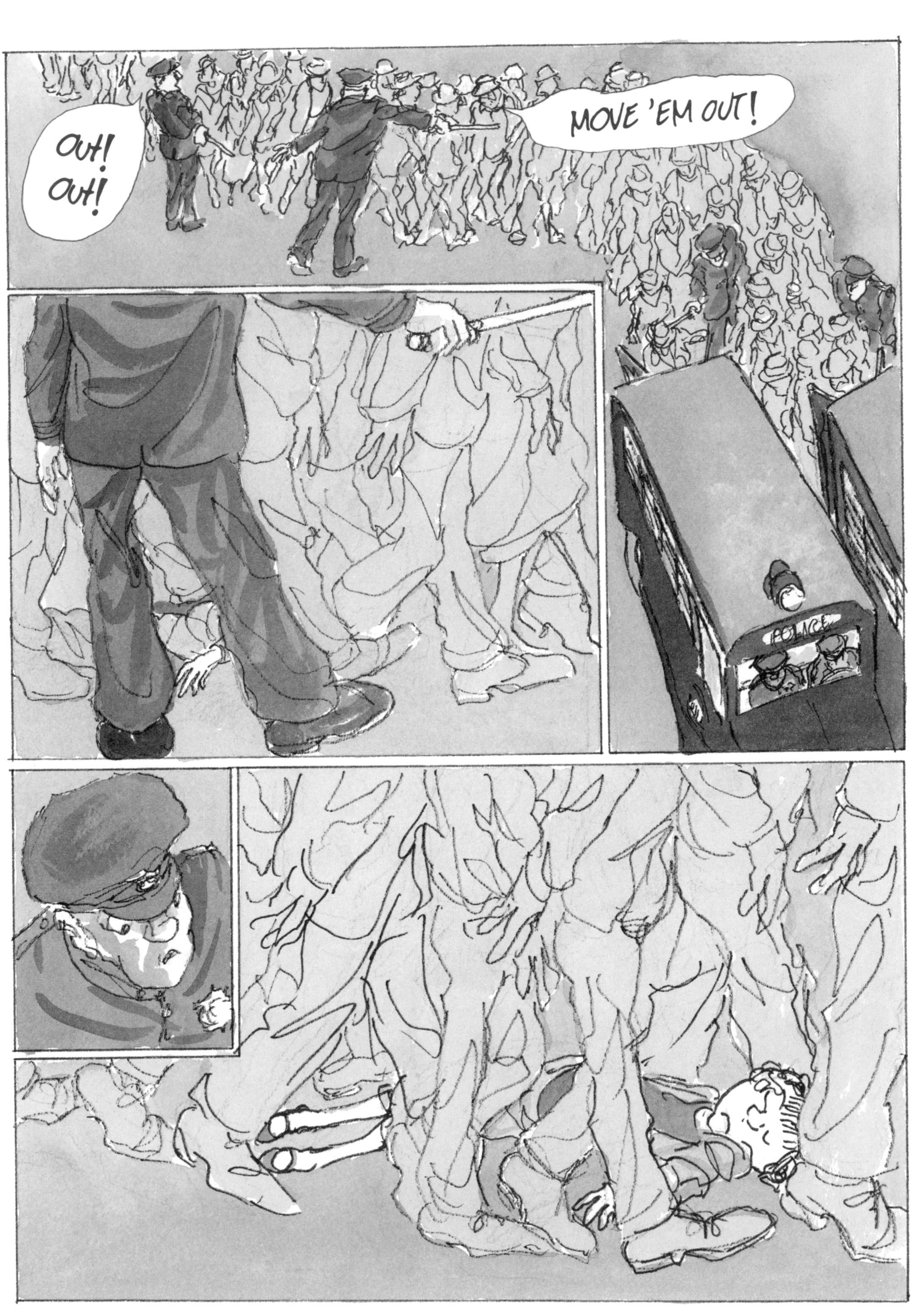
OUT! OUT!
MOVE 'EM OUT!
POLICE

Chapter Twenty-Six: The Pitch

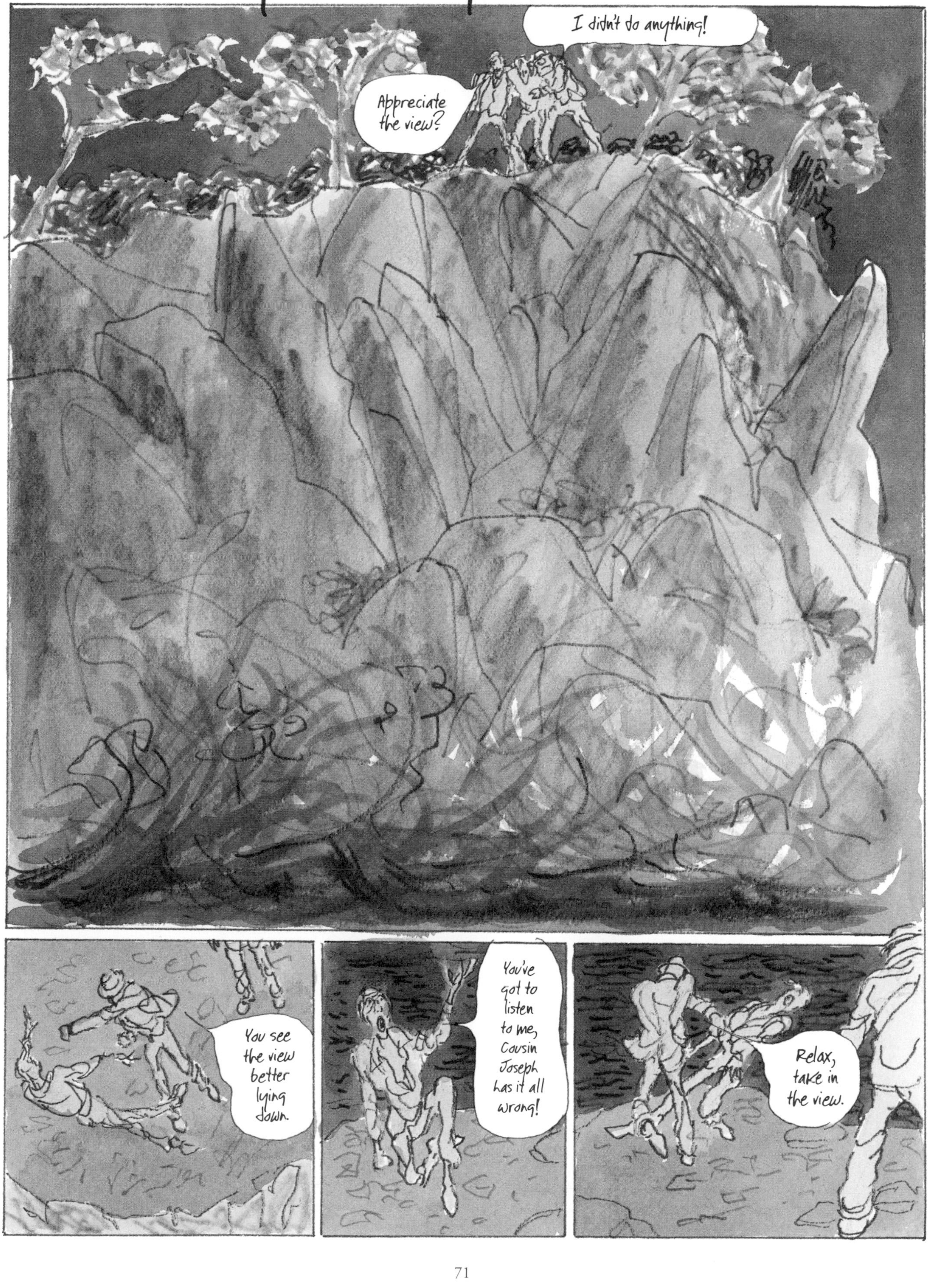
I didn't do anything!
Appreciate the view?
You see the view better lying down.
You've got to listen to me, Cousin Joseph has it all wrong!
Relax, take in the view.

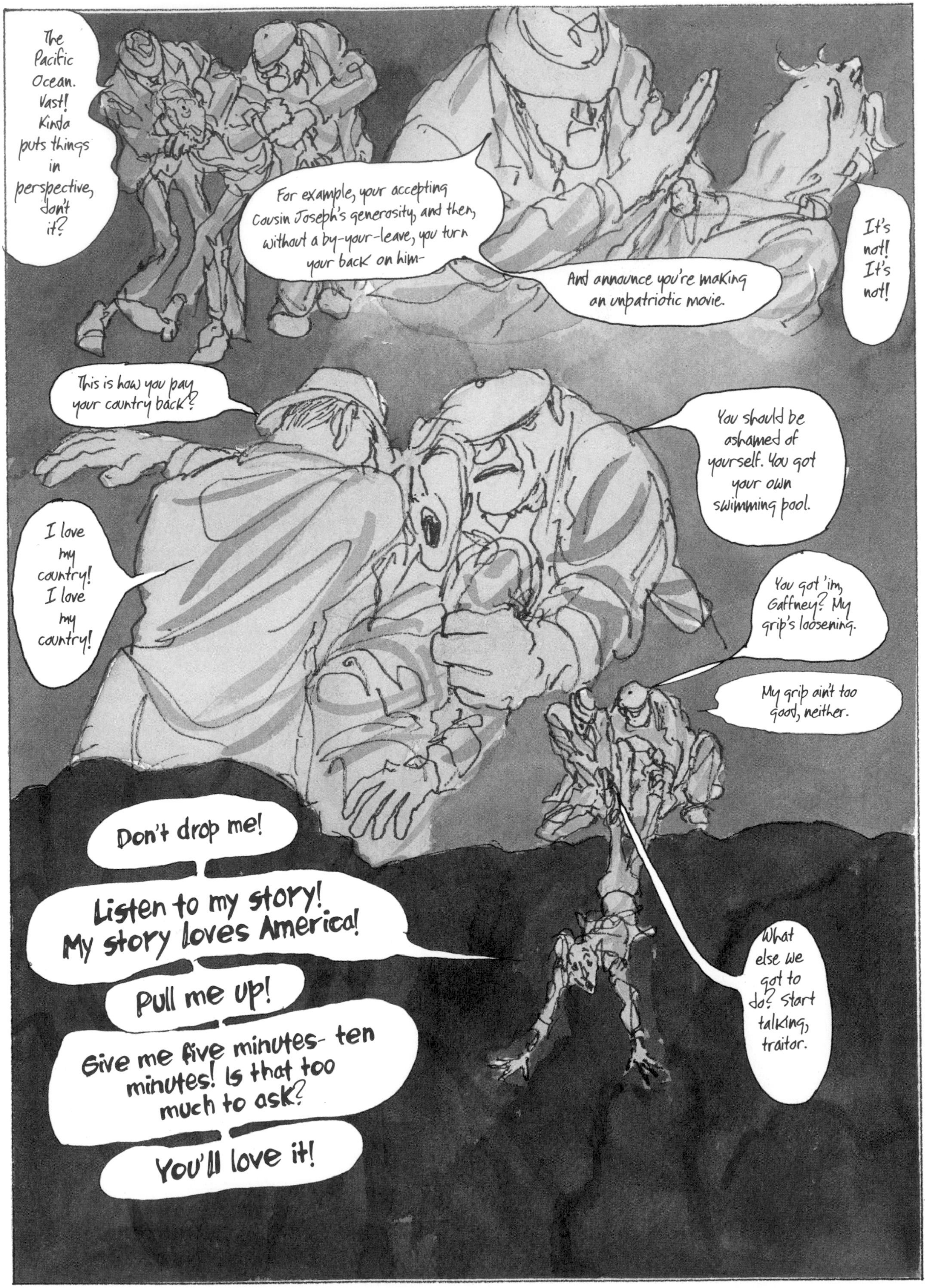
The Pacific Ocean. Vast! Kinda puts things in perspective, don't it?
For example, your accepting Cousin Joseph's generosity, and then, without a by-your-leave, you turn your back on him-
And announce you're making an unpatriotic movie.
It's not! It's not!
This is how you pay your country back?
You should be ashamed of yourself. You got your own swimming pool.
I love my country! I love my country!
You got 'im, Gaffney? My grip's loosening.
My grip ain't too good, neither.
Don't drop me!
Listen to my story! My story loves America!
Pull me up!
Give me five minutes- ten minutes! Is that too much to ask?
You'll love it!
What else we got to do? Start talking, traitor.

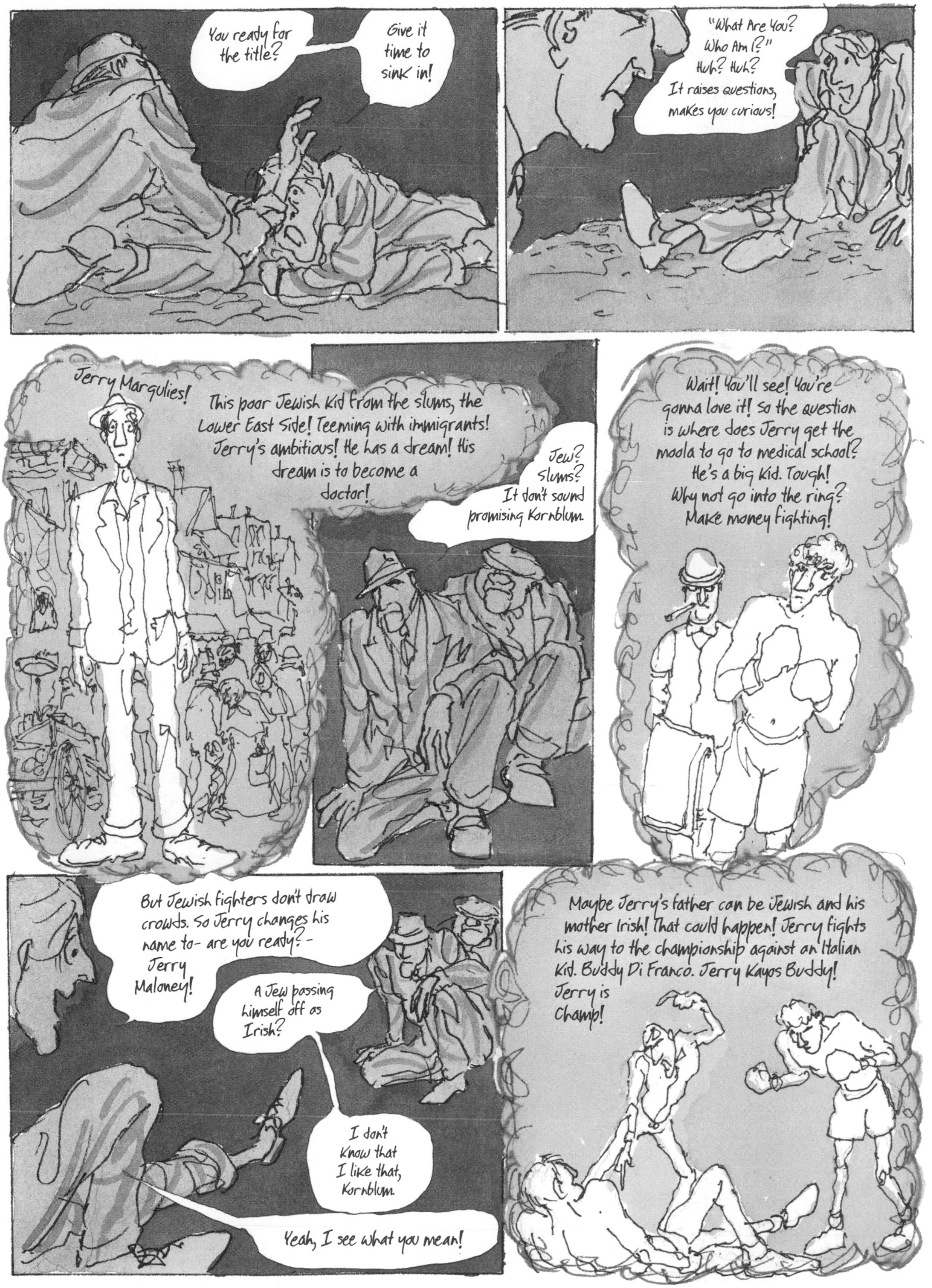
You ready for the title?
Give it time to sink in!
"What Are You? Who Am I?" Huh? Huh? It raises questions, makes you curious!
Jerry Margulies!
This poor Jewish kid from the slums, the Lower East Side! Teeming with immigrants! Jerry's ambitious! He has a dream! His dream is to become a doctor!
Jew? Slums? It don't sound promising Kornblum.
Wait! You'll see! You're gonna love it! So the question is where does Jerry get the moola to go to medical school? He's a big kid. Tough! Why not go into the ring? Make money fighting!
But Jewish fighters don't draw crowds. So Jerry changes his name to- are you ready?- Jerry Maloney!
A Jew passing himself off as Irish?
I don't know that I like that, Kornblum.
Yeah, I see what you mean!
Maybe Jerry's father can be Jewish and his mother Irish! That could happen! Jerry fights his way to the championship against an Italian kid. Buddy Di Franco. Jerry Kayos Buddy! Jerry is Champ!

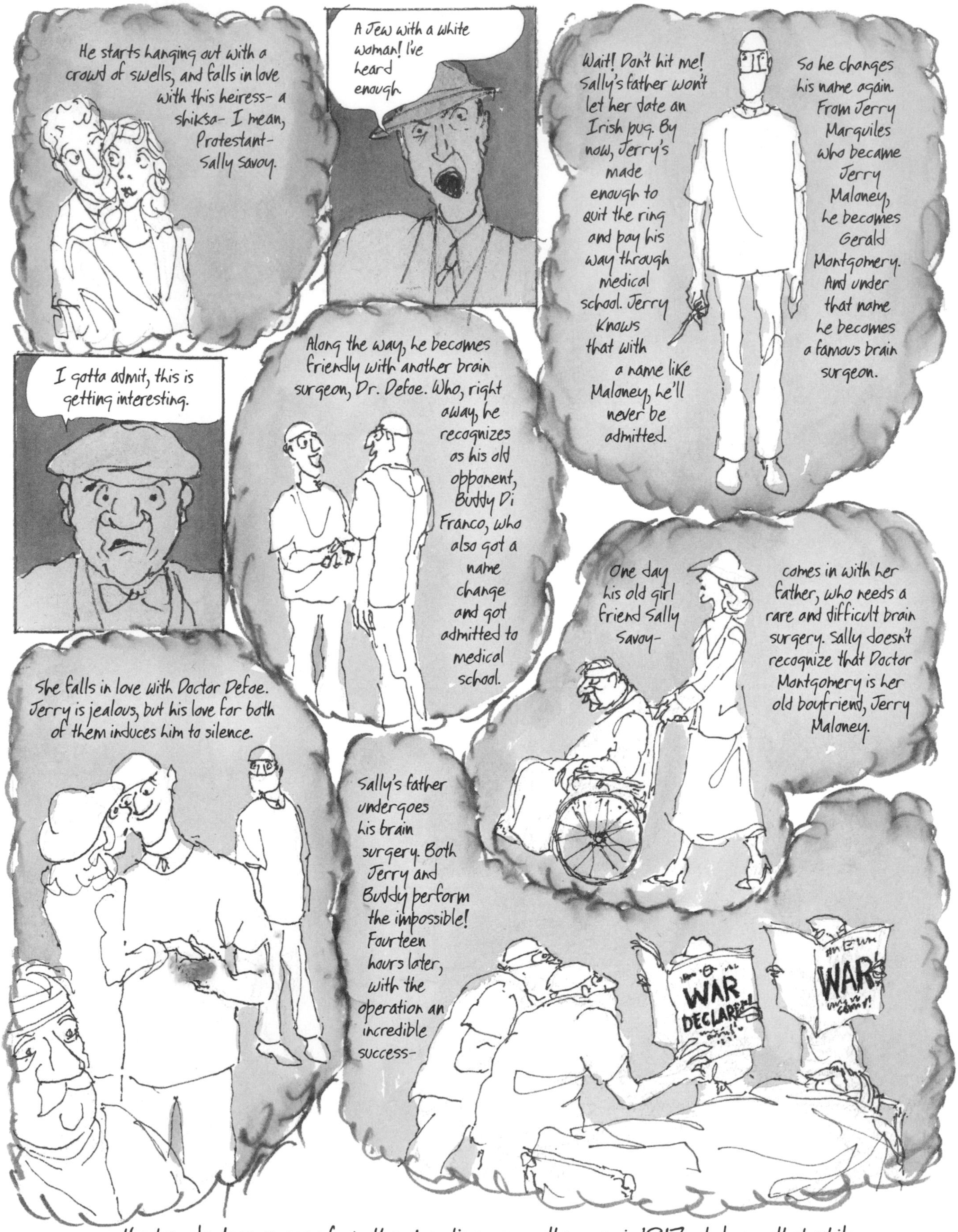
He starts hanging out with a crowd of swells, and falls in love with this heiress- a shiksa- I mean, Protestant- Sally Savoy.
A Jew with a white woman! I've heard enough.
Wait! Don't hit me! Sally's father won't let her date an Irish pug. By now, Jerry's made enough to quit the ring and pay his way through medical school. Jerry knows that with a name like Maloney, he'll never be admitted.
So he changes his name again. From Jerry Marguiles who became Jerry Maloney, he becomes Gerald Montgomery. And under that name he becomes a famous brain surgeon.
I gotta admit, this is getting interesting.
Along the way, he becomes friendly with another brain surgeon, Dr. Defoe. Who, right away, he recognizes as his old opponent, Buddy Di Franco, who also got a name change and got admitted to medical school.
One day his old girl friend Sally Savoy-
comes in with her father, who needs a rare and difficult brain surgery. Sally doesn't recognize that Doctor Montgomery is her old boyfriend, Jerry Maloney.
She falls in love with Doctor Defoe. Jerry is jealous, but his love for both of them induces him to silence.
Sally's father undergoes his brain surgery. Both Jerry and Buddy perform the impossible! Fourteen hours later, with the operation an incredible success-
WAR DECLARED!
WAR!

the two doctors emerge from the operating room- the year is 1917- to learn that while they were saving the life of the father of the girl they both love, America has gone to war with Germany! Immediately, the two surgeons enlist!

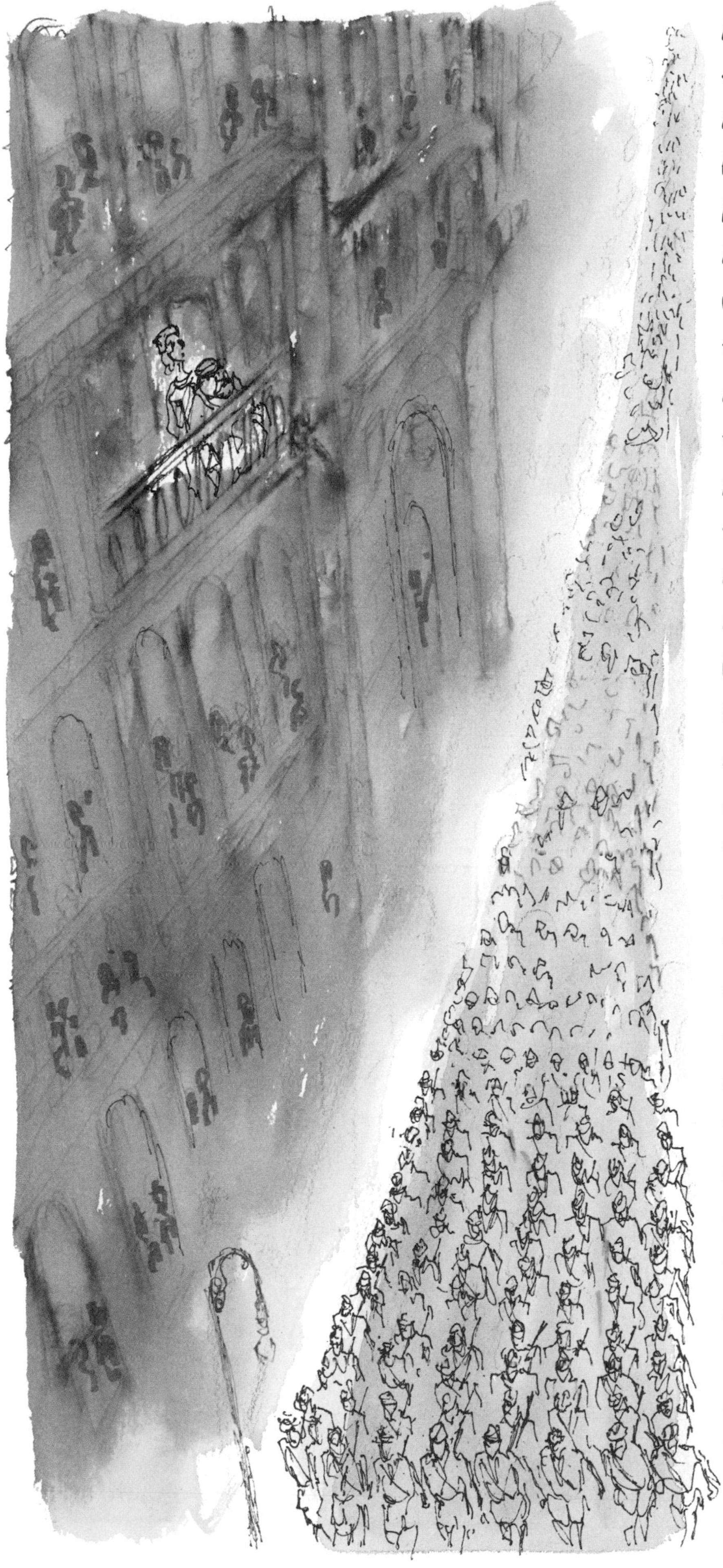

Dr. Montgomery and Dr. Defoe march down Fifth Avenue in a parade of soldiers headed for the troop ships. They pass by the mansion where the recovering Mr. Savoy sits on a balcony, tended by his daughter, Sally. She is in an army nurse's uniform. She, too, is headed off to war. Sally looks down and spots Doctors Montgomery and Defoe amid the marching troops. And at that moment, Jerry looks up at her and smiles! And she knows who he is! He is her long-lost love who her father made her give up: Jerry Maloney! A burst of love envelops Sally. But how can that be? She loves Doctor Defoe! She looks at her reflection in the window behind her. "What are you?" she asks herself. She looks down on Jerry and Buddy and she asks, "Who am I?" She surveys the thousands of men marching, and she understands. Americans! "Every last one of us! Protestant, Italian, Jew! All of us are Americans!" And she knows that the problem of one girl forced to decide between two men she loves doesn't amount to a hill of beans compared to the marching men below: on a mission, men of every race and religion, to make the world a better place. A place like America! "America!" Sally shouts. And the multitudes below shout back as one: "**AMERICA!**" Fade out. The end. What do you think?

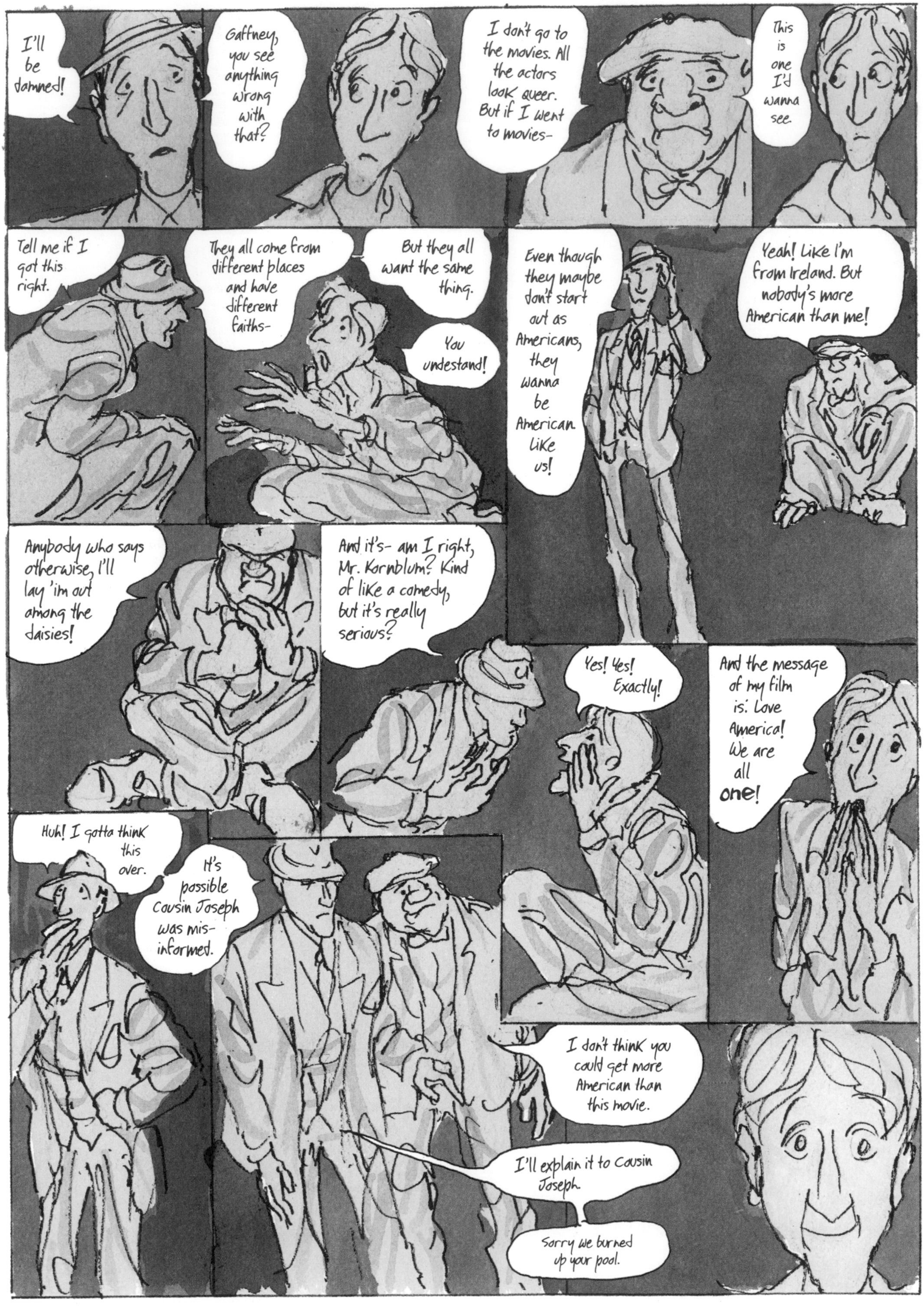
I'll be damned!
Gaffney, you see anything wrong with that?
I don't go to the movies. All the actors look queer. But if I went to movies-
This is one I'd wanna see.
Tell me if I got this right.
They all come from different places and have different faiths-
But they all want the same thing.
You undestand!
Even though they maybe don't start out as Americans, they wanna be American like us!
Yeah! Like I'm from Ireland. But nobody's more American than me!
Anybody who says otherwise, I'll lay 'im out among the daisies!
And it's- am I right, Mr. Kornblum? Kind of like a comedy, but it's really serious?
Yes! Yes! Exactly!
And the message of my film is: Love America! We are all one!
Huh! I gotta think this over.
It's possible Cousin Joseph was misinformed.
I don't think you could get more American than this movie.
I'll explain it to Cousin Joseph.
Sorry we burned up your pool.

Chapter Twenty-Seven: Mr. Elliot

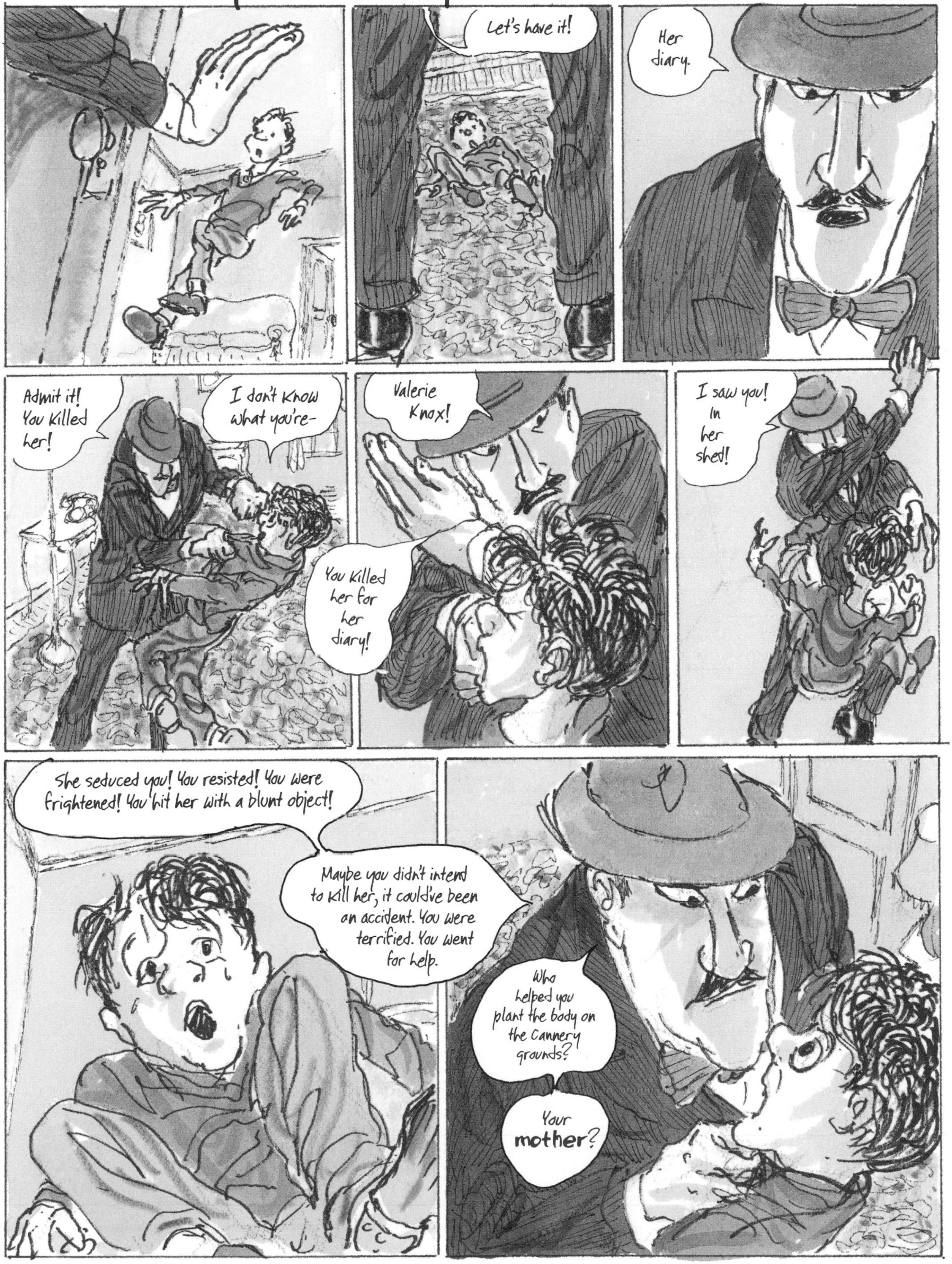

Let's have it!
Her diary.
Admit it! You killed her!
I don't know what you're-
Valerie Knox!
You killed her for her diary!
I saw you! In her shed!
She seduced you! You resisted! You were frightened! You hit her with a blunt object!
Maybe you didn't intend to kill her, it could've been an accident. You were terrified. You went for help.
Who helped you plant the body on the cannery grounds?
Your **mother**?

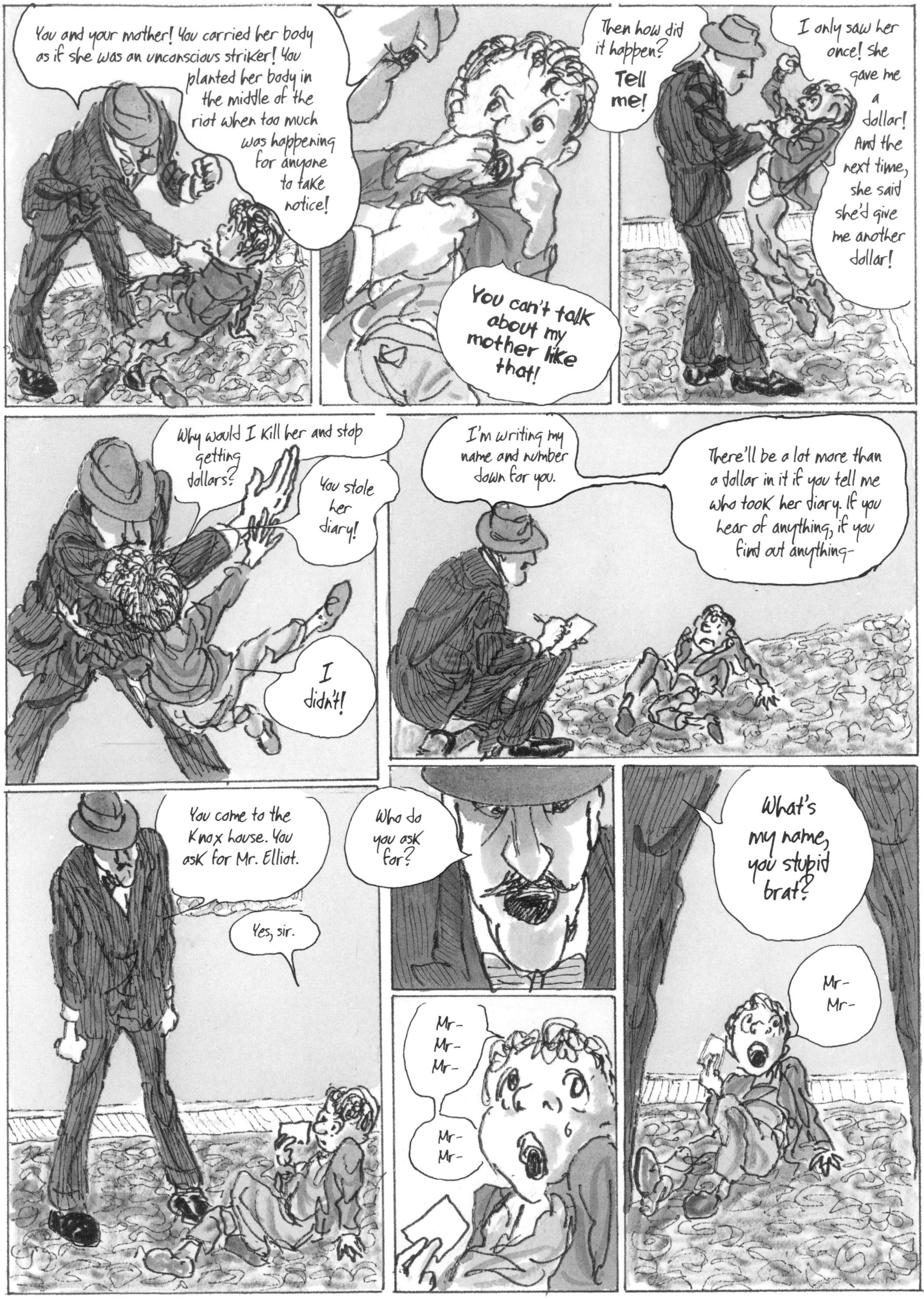

You and your mother! You carried her body as if she was an unconscious striker! You planted her body in the middle of the riot when too much was happening for anyone to take notice!
You can't talk about my mother like that!
Then how did it happen? Tell me!
I only saw her once! She gave me a dollar! And the next time, she said she'd give me another dollar!
Why would I kill her and stop getting dollars?
You stole her diary!
I didn't!
I'm writing my name and number down for you.
There'll be a lot more than a dollar in it if you tell me who took her diary. If you hear of anything, if you find out anything-
You come to the Knox house. You ask for Mr. Elliot.
Yes, sir.
Who do you ask for?
What's my name, you stupid brat?
Mr- Mr- Mr-
Mr- Mr-
Mr- Mr-

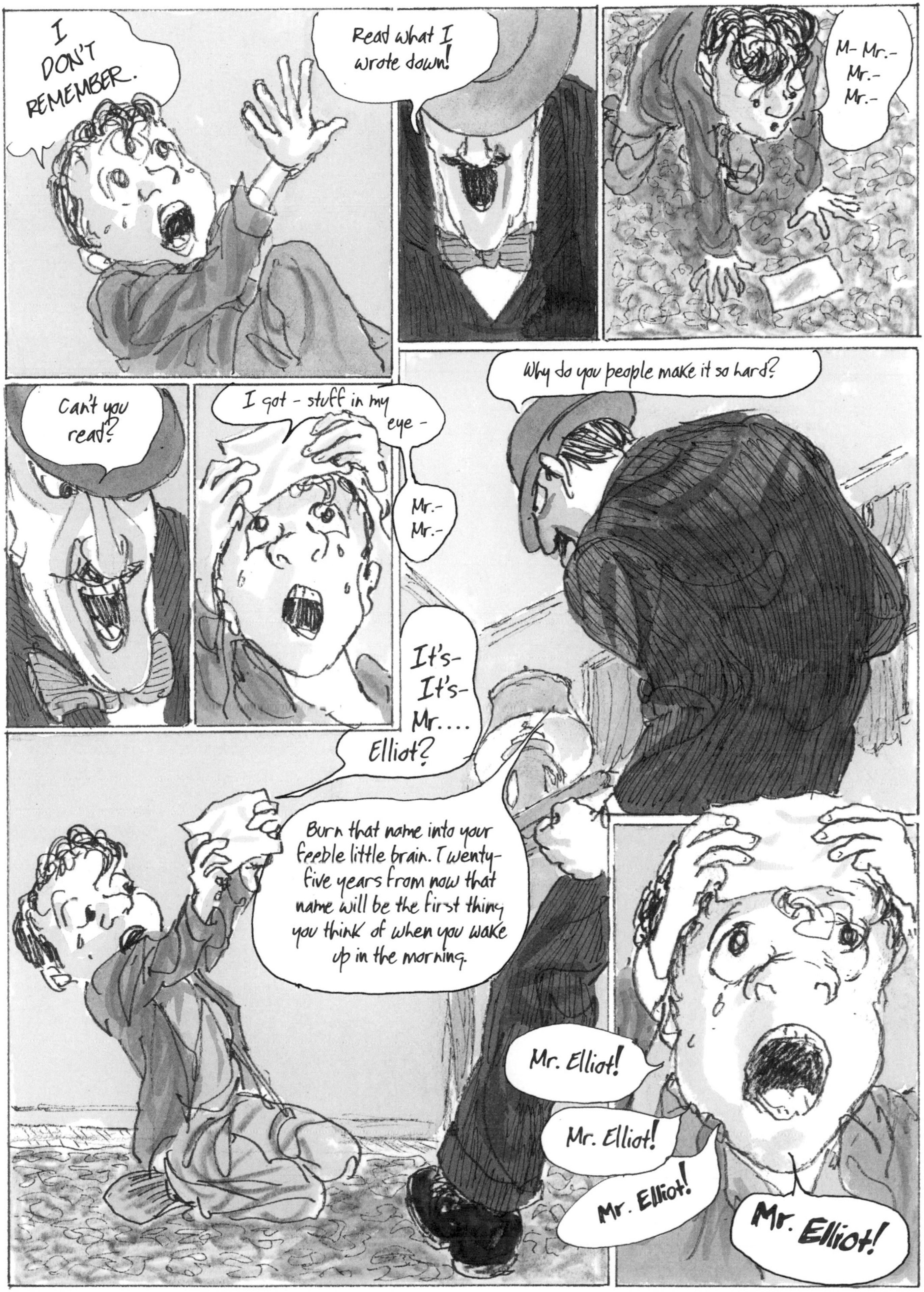
I DON'T REMEMBER.
Read what I wrote down!
M- Mr.- Mr.- Mr.-
Can't you read?
I got - stuff in my eye -
Mr.- Mr.-
Why do you people make it so hard?
It's- It's- Mr.... Elliot?
Burn that name into your feeble little brain. Twenty-five years from now that name will be the first thing you think of when you wake up in the morning.
Mr. Elliot!
Mr. Elliot!
Mr. Elliot!
Mr. Elliot!

Chapter Twenty-Eight: Post-Mortem

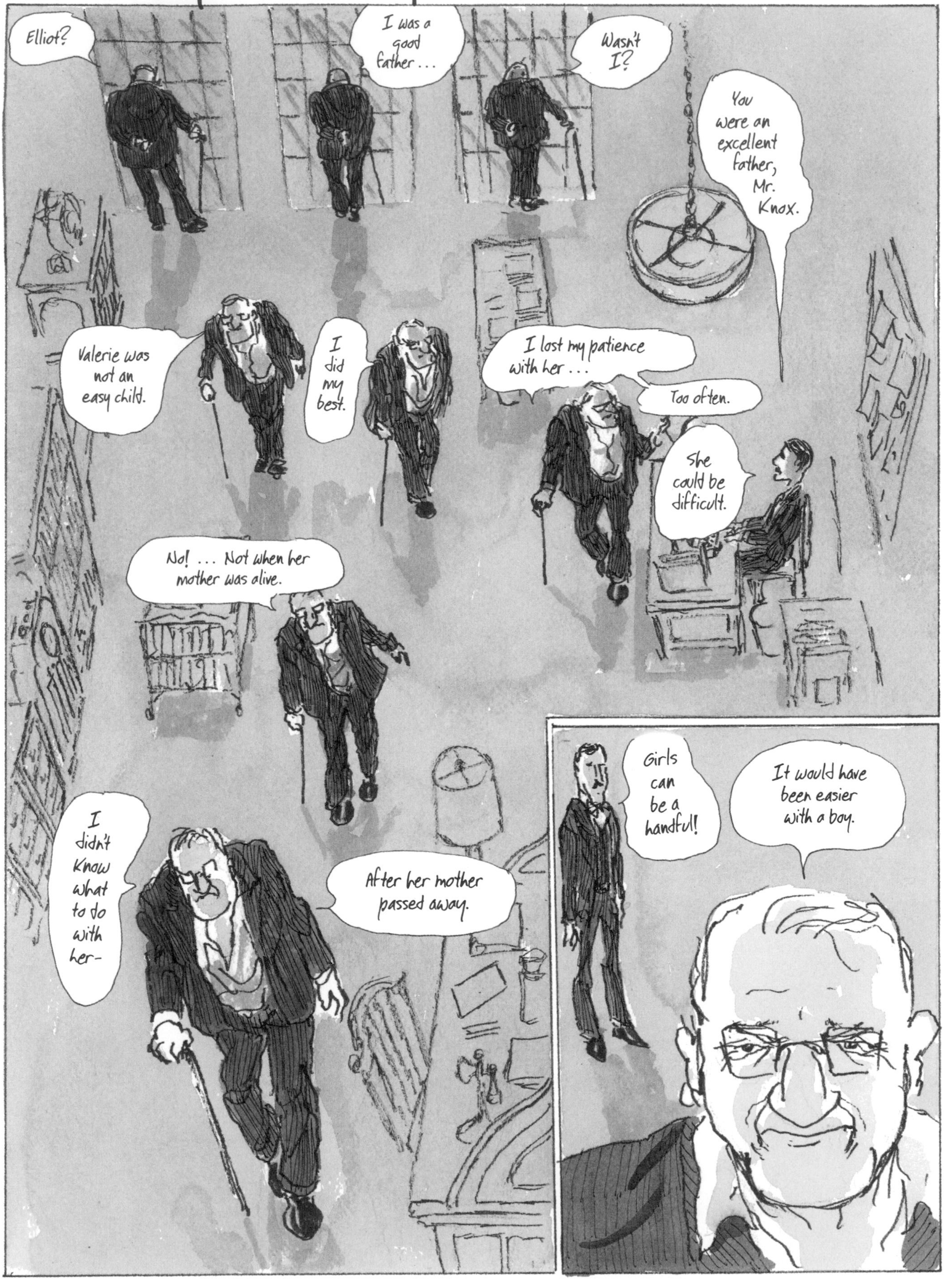
Elliot?
I was a good father...
Wasn't I?
You were an excellent father, Mr. Knox.
Valerie was not an easy child.
I did my best.
I lost my patience with her...
Too often.
She could be difficult.
No! ... Not when her mother was alive.
I didn't know what to do with her-
After her mother passed away.
Girls can be a handful!
It would have been easier with a boy.

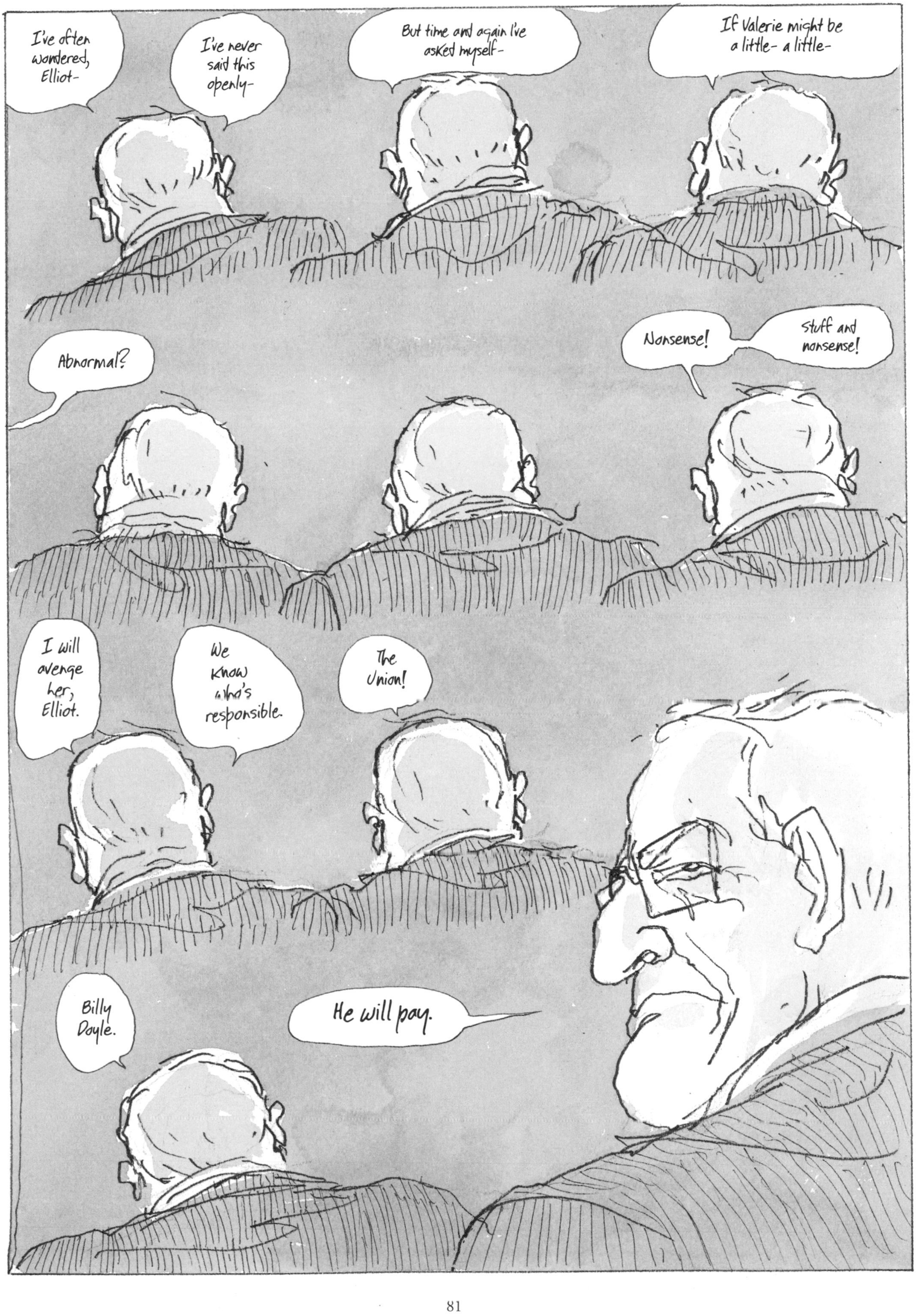
I've often wondered, Elliot-
I've never said this openly-
But time and again I've asked myself-
If Valerie might be a little- a little-
Abnormal?
Nonsense!
Stuff and nonsense!
I will avenge her, Elliot.
We know who's responsible.
The Union!
Billy Doyle.
He will pay.

Chapter Twenty-Nine: The Diary

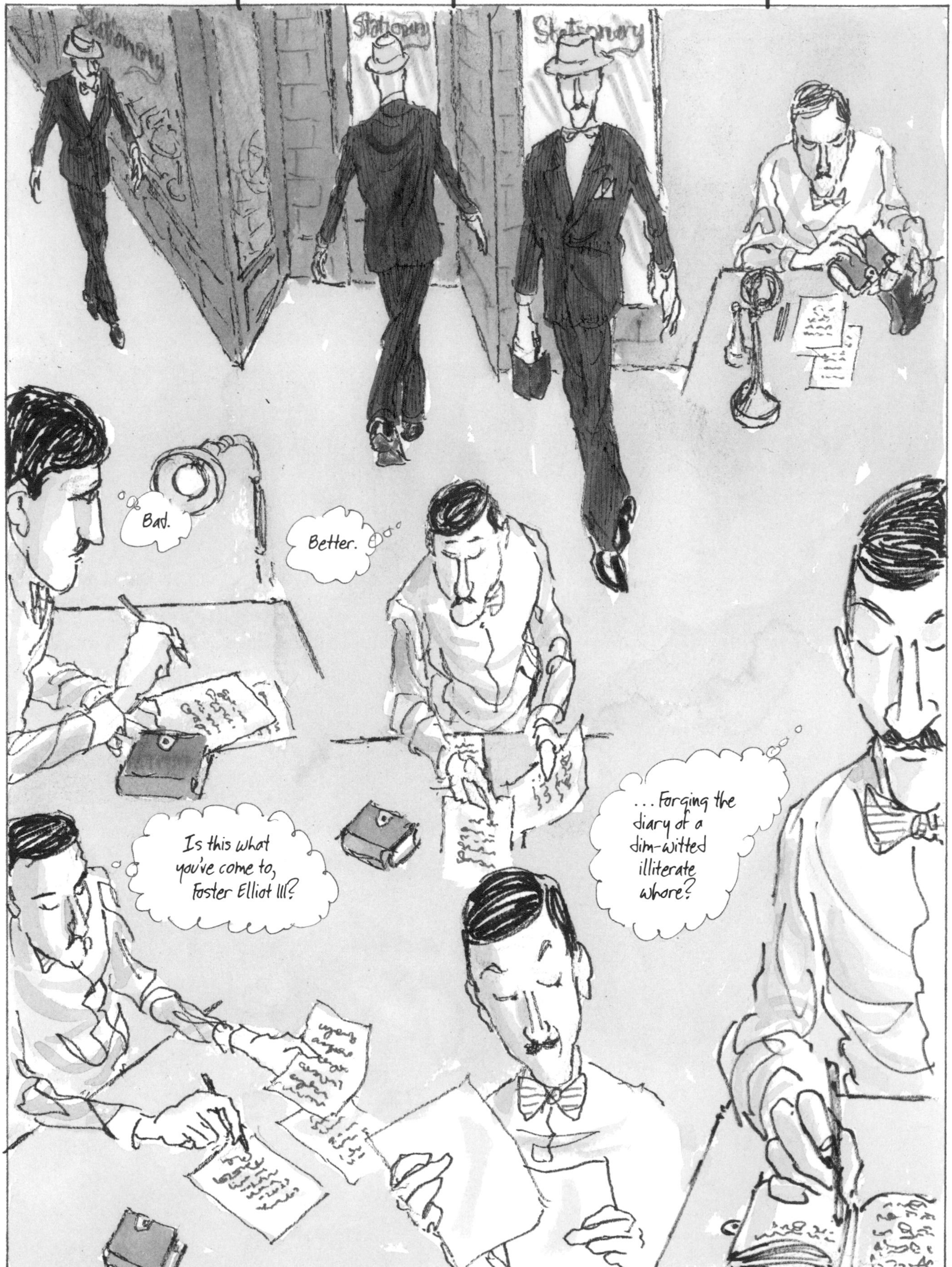

Stationery
Stationery
Stationery
Bad.
Better.
Is this what you've come to, Foster Elliot III?
. . . Forging the diary of a dim-witted illiterate whore?

Chapter Thirty: The History Lesson

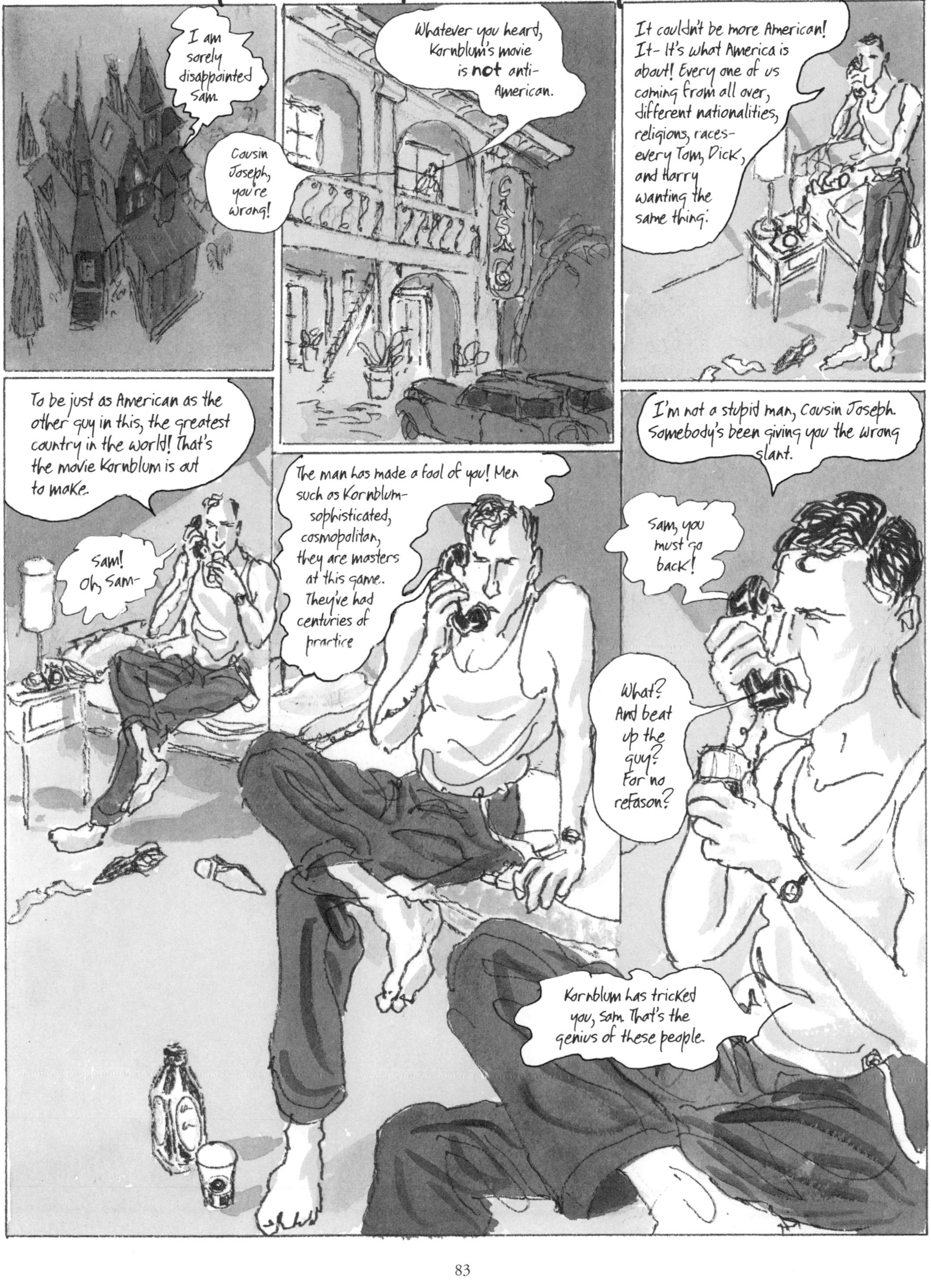
I am sorely disappointed Sam.
Cousin Joseph, you're wrong!
Whatever you heard, Kornblum's movie is **not** anti-American.
It couldn't be more American! It- It's what America is about! Every one of us coming from all over, different nationalities, religions, races- every Tom, Dick, and Harry wanting the same thing.
To be just as American as the other guy in this, the greatest country in the world! That's the movie Kornblum is out to make.
Sam! Oh, Sam-
The man has made a fool of you! Men such as Kornblum- sophisticated, cosmopolitan, they are masters at this game. They've had centuries of practice
I'm not a stupid man, Cousin Joseph. Somebody's been giving you the wrong slant.
Sam, you must go back!
What? And beat up the guy? For no refason?
Kornblum has tricked you, Sam. That's the genius of these people.

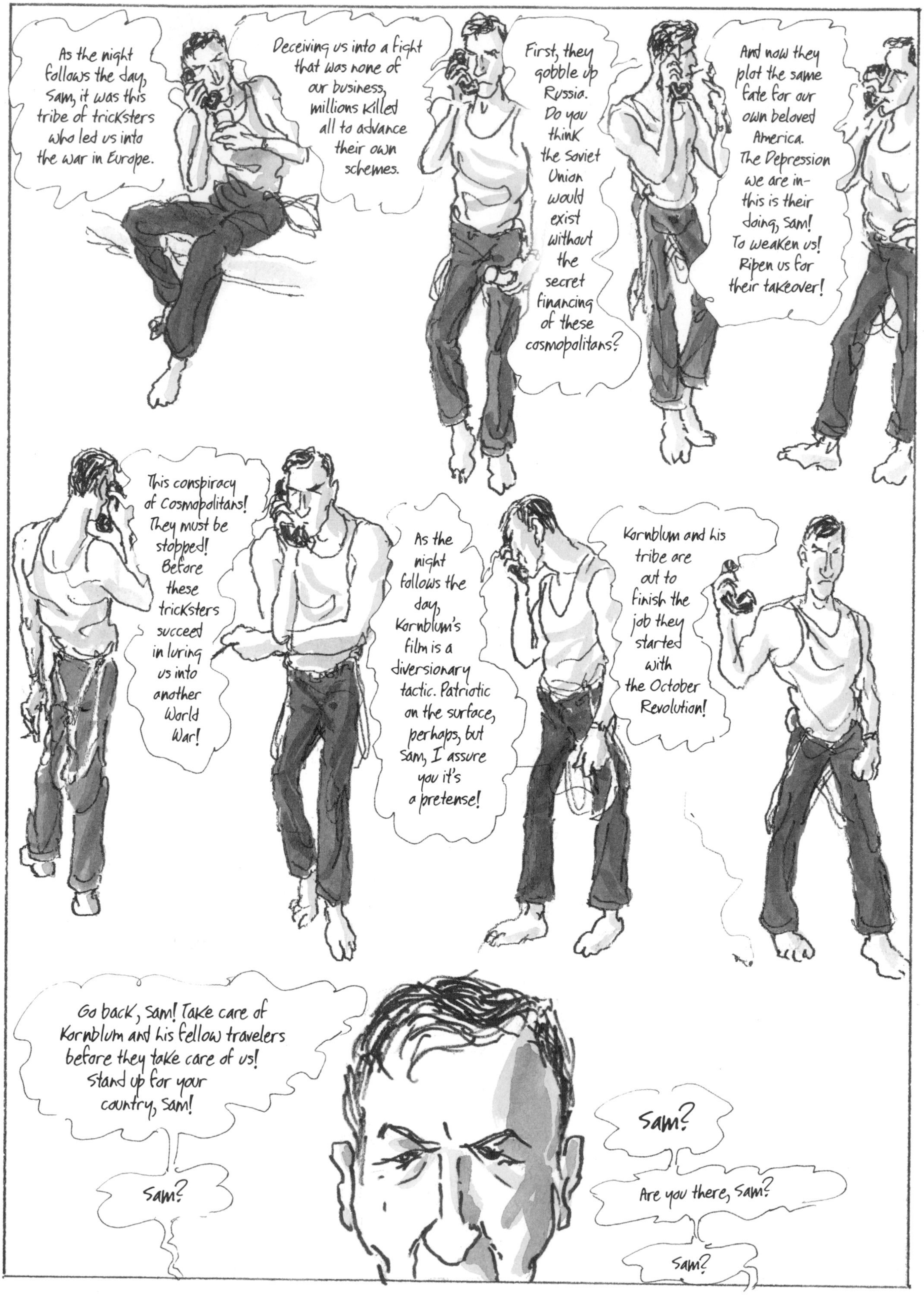

As the night follows the day, Sam, it was this tribe of tricksters who led us into the war in Europe.
Deceiving us into a fight that was none of our business, millions killed all to advance their own schemes.
First, they gobble up Russia. Do you think the Soviet Union would exist without the secret financing of these cosmopolitans?
And now they plot the same fate for our own beloved America. The Depression we are in-this is their doing, Sam! To weaken us! Ripen us for their takeover!
This conspiracy of cosmopolitans! They must be stopped! Before these tricksters succeed in luring us into another World War!
As the night follows the day, Kornblum's film is a diversionary tactic. Patriotic on the surface, perhaps, but Sam, I assure you it's a pretense!
Kornblum and his tribe are out to finish the job they started with the October Revolution!
Go back, Sam! Take care of Kornblum and his fellow travelers before they take care of us! Stand up for your country, Sam!
Sam?
Sam?
Are you there, Sam?
Sam?

Chapter Thirty-One: The Breaking Point

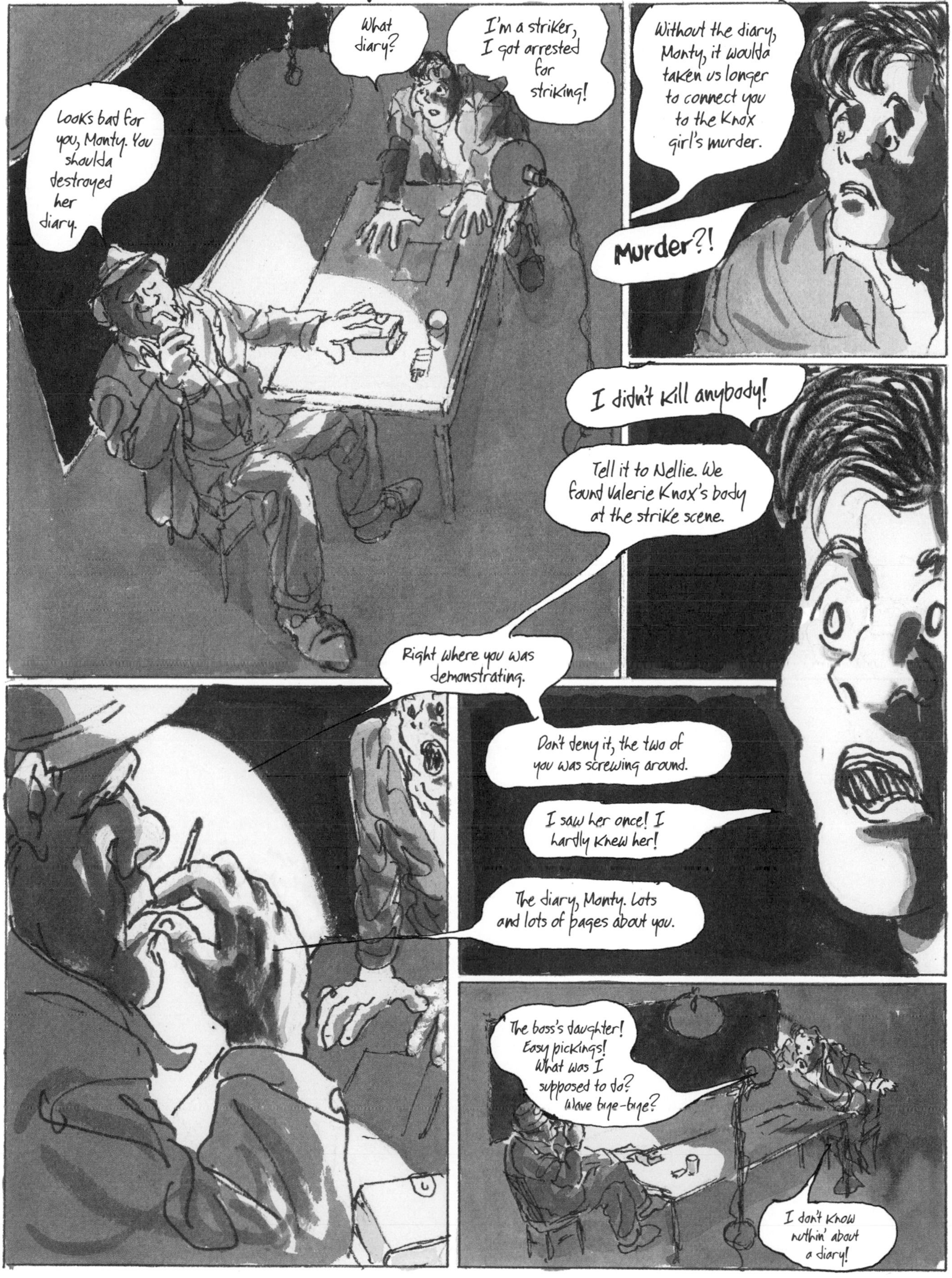

Looks bad for you, Monty. You shoulda destroyed her diary.
What diary?
I'm a striker, I got arrested for striking!
Without the diary, Monty, it woulda taken us longer to connect you to the Knox girl's murder.
Murder?!
I didn't kill anybody!
Tell it to Nellie. We found Valerie Knox's body at the strike scene.
Right where you was demonstrating.
Don't deny it, the two of you was screwing around.
I saw her once! I hardly knew her!
The diary, Monty. Lots and lots of pages about you.
The boss's daughter! Easy pickings! What was I supposed to do? Wave bye-bye?
I don't know nuthin' about a diary!

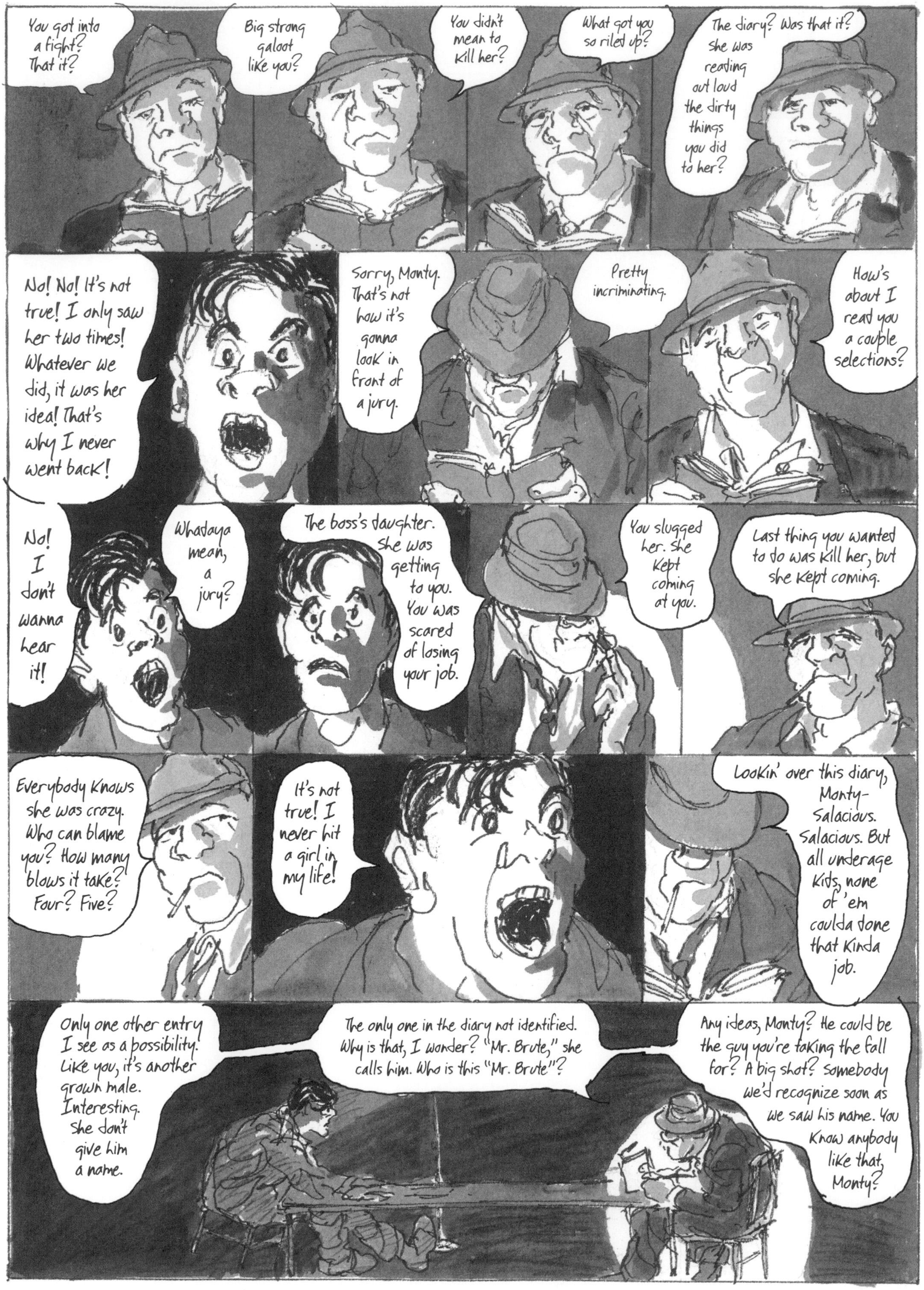

You got into a fight? That it?
Big strong galoot like you?
You didn't mean to kill her?
What got you so riled up?
The diary? Was that it? She was reading out loud the dirty things you did to her?
No! No! It's not true! I only saw her two times! Whatever we did, it was her idea! That's why I never went back!
Sorry, Monty. That's not how it's gonna look in front of a jury.
Pretty incriminating.
How's about I read you a couple selections?
No! I don't wanna hear it!
Whadaya mean, a jury?
The boss's daughter. She was getting to you. You was scared of losing your job.
You slugged her. She kept coming at you.
Last thing you wanted to do was kill her, but she kept coming.
Everybody knows she was crazy. Who can blame you? How many blows it take? Four? Five?
It's not true! I never hit a girl in my life!
Lookin' over this diary, Monty- Salacious. Salacious. But all underage kids, none of 'em coulda done that kinda job.
Only one other entry I see as a possibility. Like you, it's another grown male. Interesting. She don't give him a name.
The only one in the diary not identified. Why is that, I wonder? "Mr. Brute," she calls him. Who is this "Mr. Brute"?
Any ideas, Monty? He could be the guy you're taking the fall for? A big shot? Somebody we'd recognize soon as we saw his name. You know anybody like that, Monty?

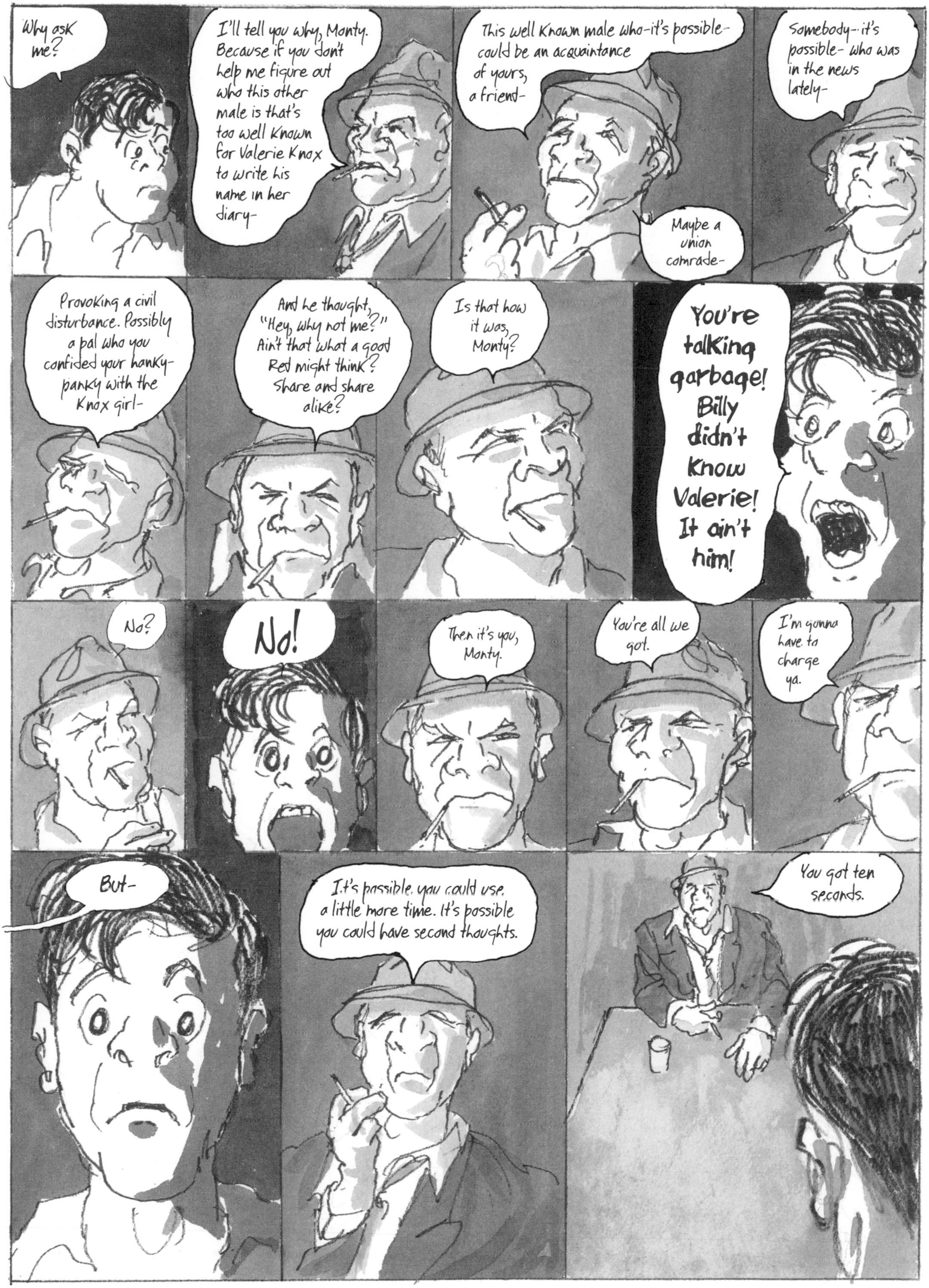
Why ask me?
I'll tell you why, Monty. Because if you don't help me figure out who this other male is that's too well Known for Valerie Knox to write his name in her diary-
This well Known male who-it's possible-could be an acquaintance of yours, a friend-
Maybe a union comrade-
Somebody-it's possible-who was in the news lately-
Provoking a civil disturbance. Possibly a pal who you confided your hanky-panky with the Knox girl-
And he thought, "Hey, why not me?" Ain't that what a good Red might think? Share and share alike?
Is that how it was, Monty?
You're talking garbage! Billy didn't Know Valerie! It ain't him!
No?
No!
Then it's you, Monty.
You're all we got.
I'm gonna have to charge ya.
But-
It's possible you could use a little more time. It's possible you could have second thoughts.
You got ten seconds.

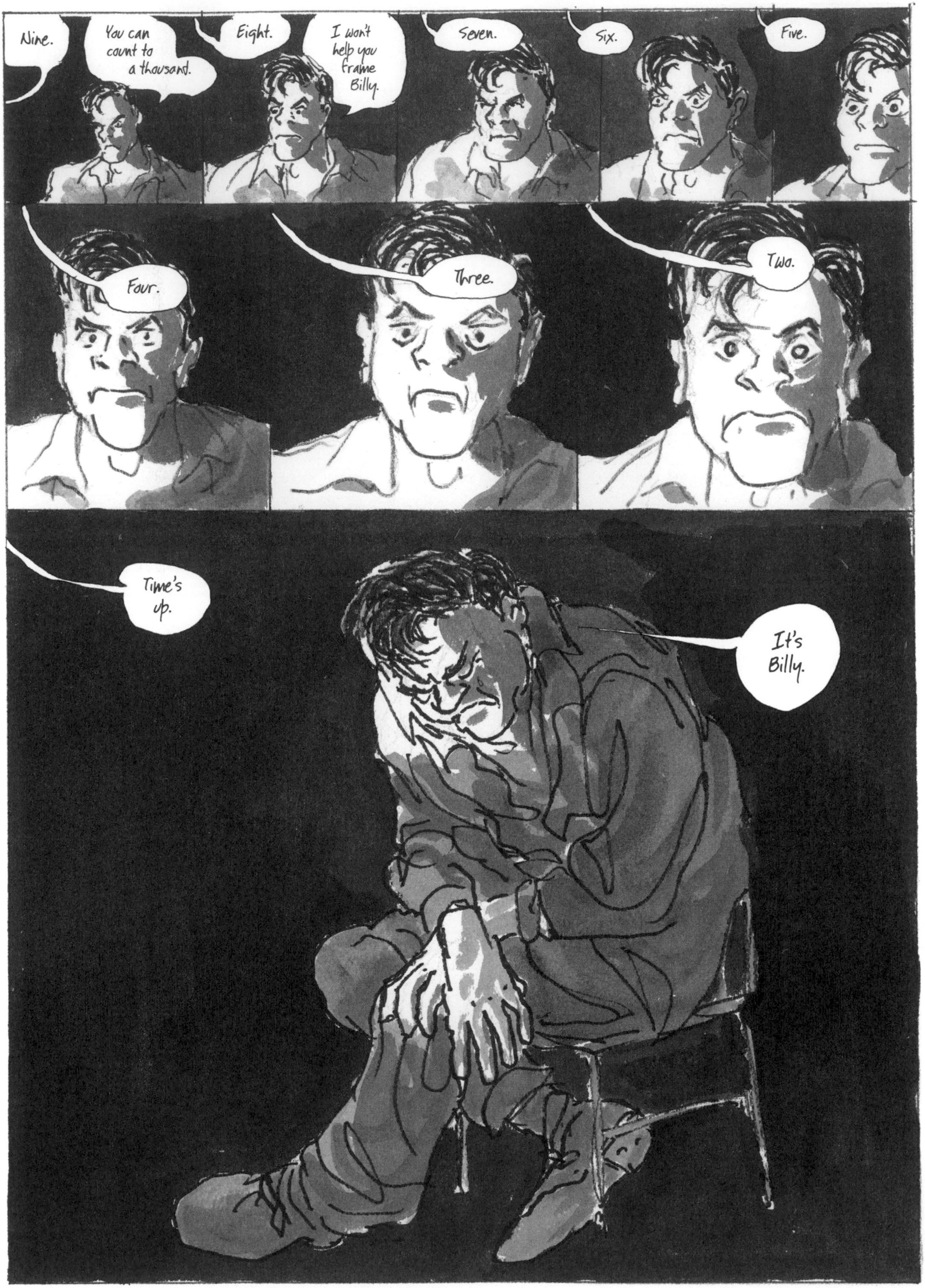
Nine.
You can count to a thousand.
Eight.
I won't help you frame Billy.
Seven.
Six.
Five.
Four.
Three.
Two.
Time's up.
It's Billy.

Chapter Thirty-Two: Epiphany

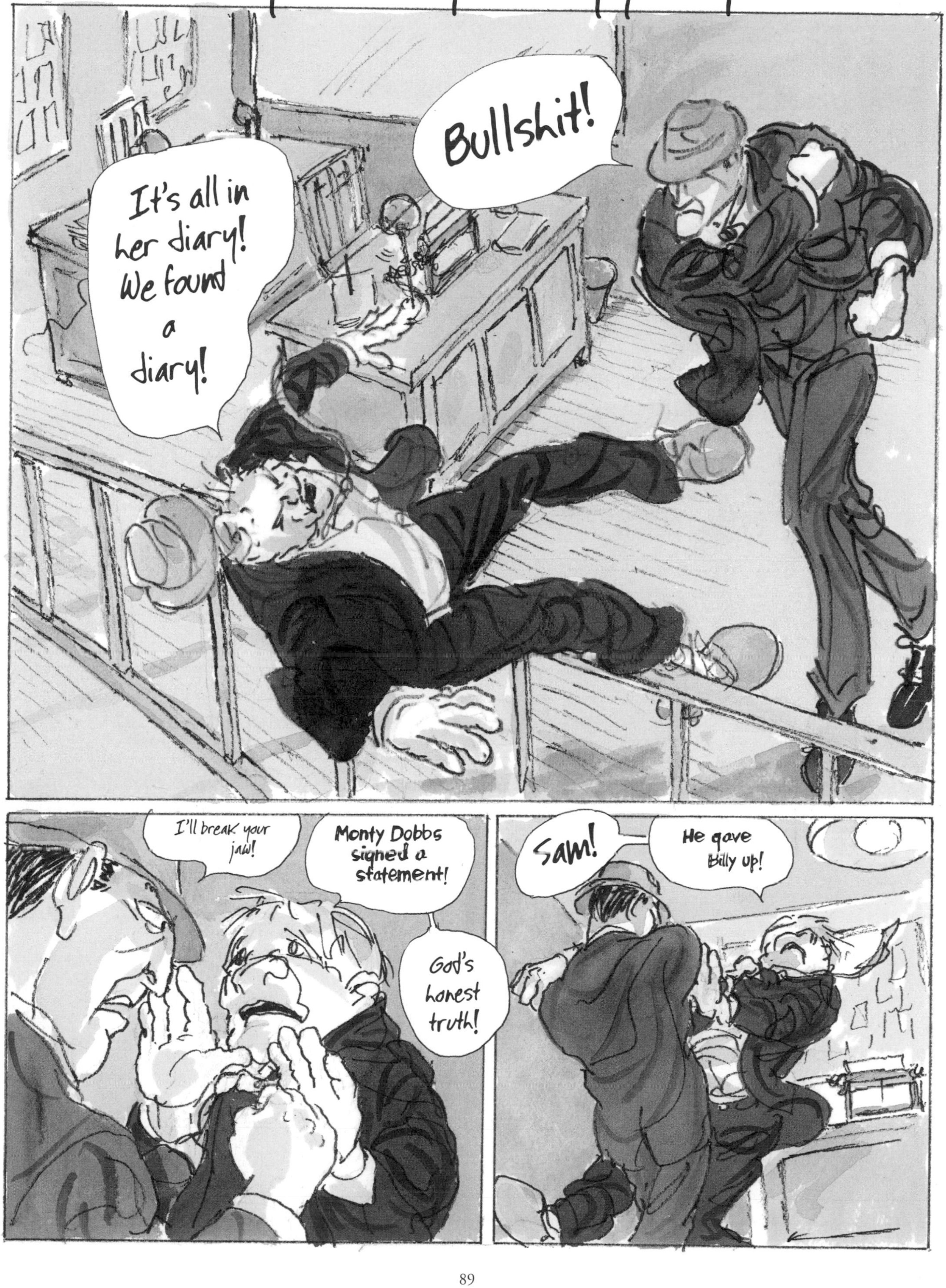
It's all in her diary! We found a diary!
Bullshit!
I'll break your jaw!
Monty Dobbs signed a statement!
God's honest truth!
Sam!
He gave Billy up!

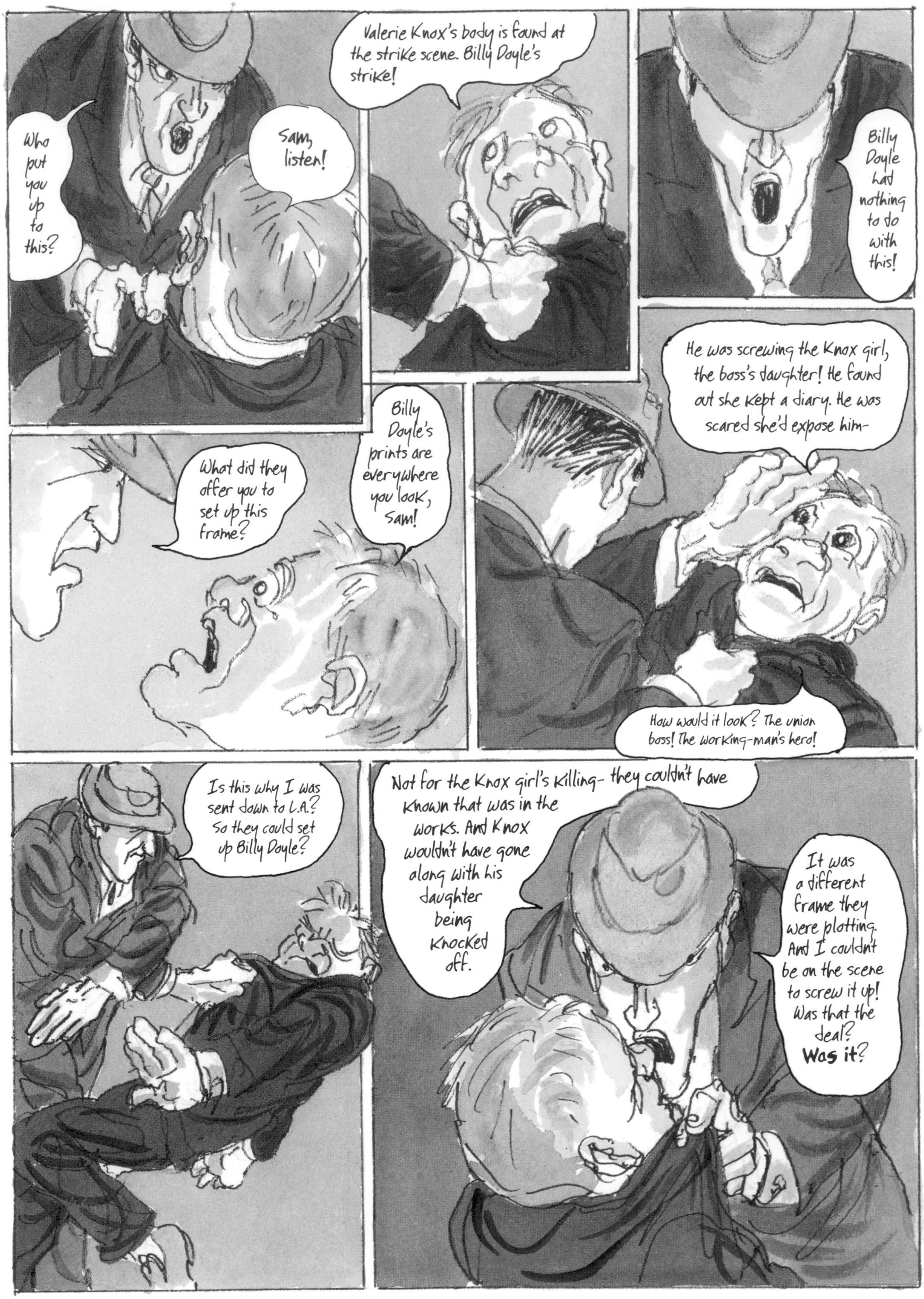
Who put you up to this?
Sam, listen!
Valerie Knox's body is found at the strike scene. Billy Doyle's strike!
Billy Doyle had nothing to do with this!
He was screwing the Knox girl, the boss's daughter! He found out she kept a diary. He was scared she'd expose him-
What did they offer you to set up this frame?
Billy Doyle's prints are everywhere you look, Sam!
How would it look? The union boss! The working-man's hero!
Is this why I was sent down to L.A.? So they could set up Billy Doyle?
Not for the Knox girl's killing- they couldn't have known that was in the works. And Knox wouldn't have gone along with his daughter being knocked off.
It was a different frame they were plotting. And I couldn't be on the scene to screw it up! Was that the deal? **Was it?**

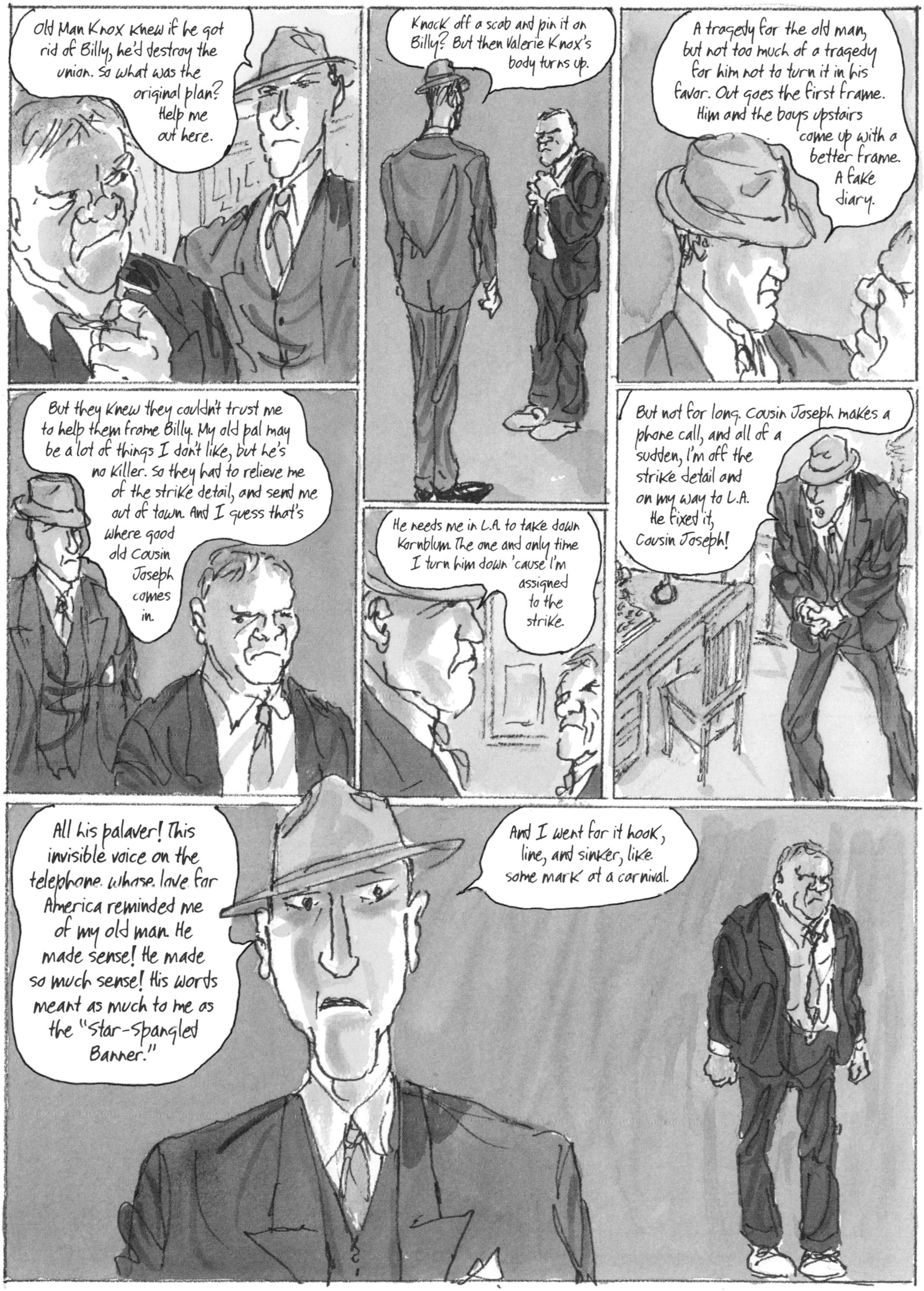

Old Man Knox knew if he got rid of Billy, he'd destroy the union. So what was the original plan? Help me out here.
Knock off a scab and pin it on Billy? But then Valerie Knox's body turns up.
A tragedy for the old man, but not too much of a tragedy for him not to turn it in his favor. Out goes the first frame. Him and the boys upstairs come up with a better frame. A fake diary.
But they knew they couldn't trust me to help them frame Billy. My old pal may be a lot of things I don't like, but he's no killer. So they had to relieve me of the strike detail, and send me out of town. And I guess that's where good old Cousin Joseph comes in.
He needs me in L.A. to take down Kornblum. The one and only time I turn him down 'cause I'm assigned to the strike.
But not for long. Cousin Joseph makes a phone call, and all of a sudden, I'm off the strike detail and on my way to L.A. He fixed it, Cousin Joseph!
All his palaver! This invisible voice on the telephone, whose love for America reminded me of my old man. He made sense! He made so much sense! His words meant as much to me as the "Star-Spangled Banner."
And I went for it hook, line, and sinker, like some mark at a carnival.

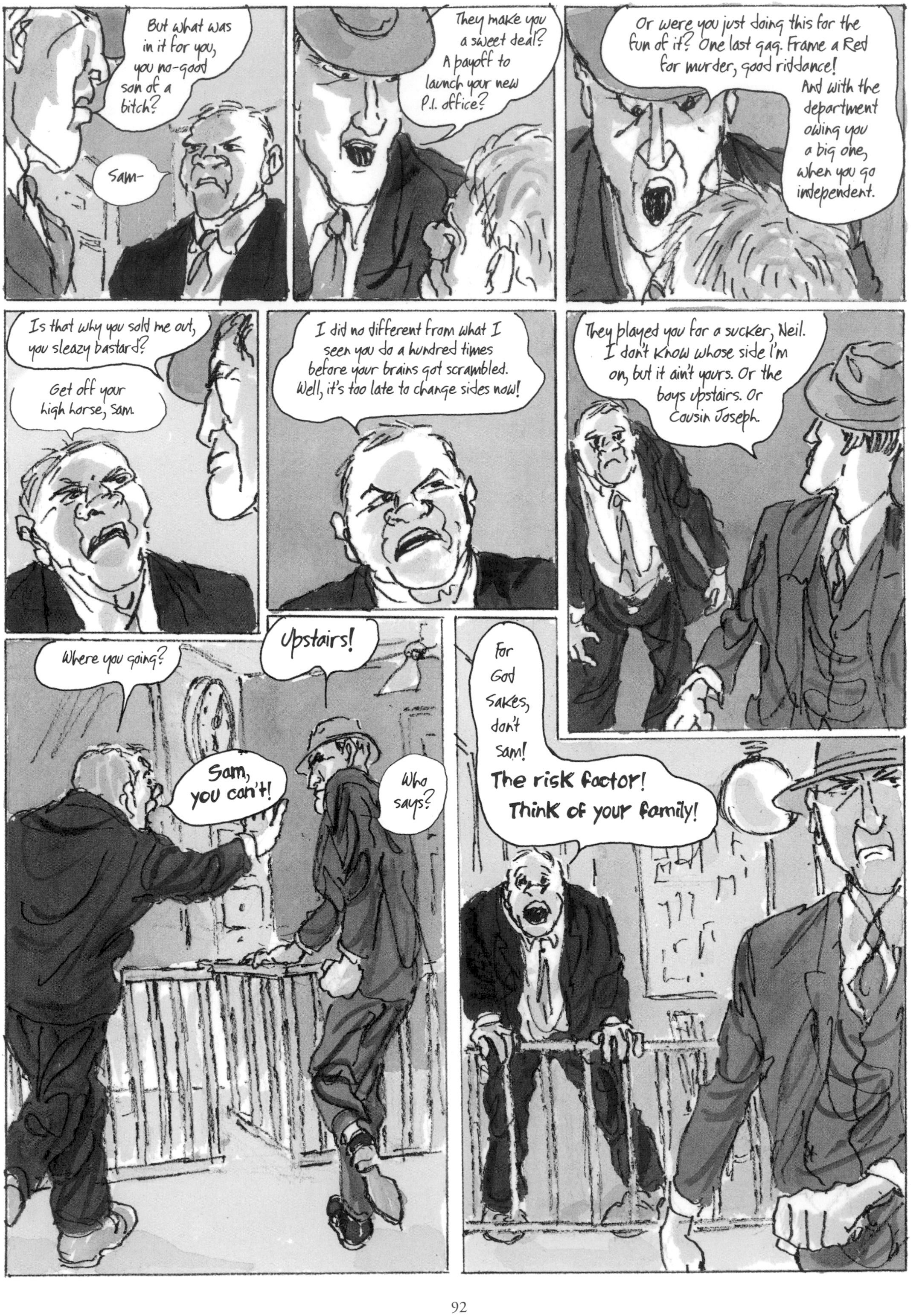
But what was in it for you, you no-good son of a bitch?
Sam-
They make you a sweet deal? A payoff to launch your new P.I. office?
Or were you just doing this for the fun of it? One last gag. Frame a Red for murder, good riddance!
And with the department owing you a big one, when you go independent.
Is that why you sold me out, you sleazy bastard?
Get off your high horse, Sam.
I did no different from what I seen you do a hundred times before your brains got scrambled. Well, it's too late to change sides now!
They played you for a sucker, Neil. I don't know whose side I'm on, but it ain't yours. Or the boys upstairs. Or Cousin Joseph.
Where you going?
Upstairs!
Sam, you can't!
Who says?
For God sakes, don't Sam!
The risk factor! Think of your family!

Chapter Thirty-Three: The Songs of Sam and Cissy

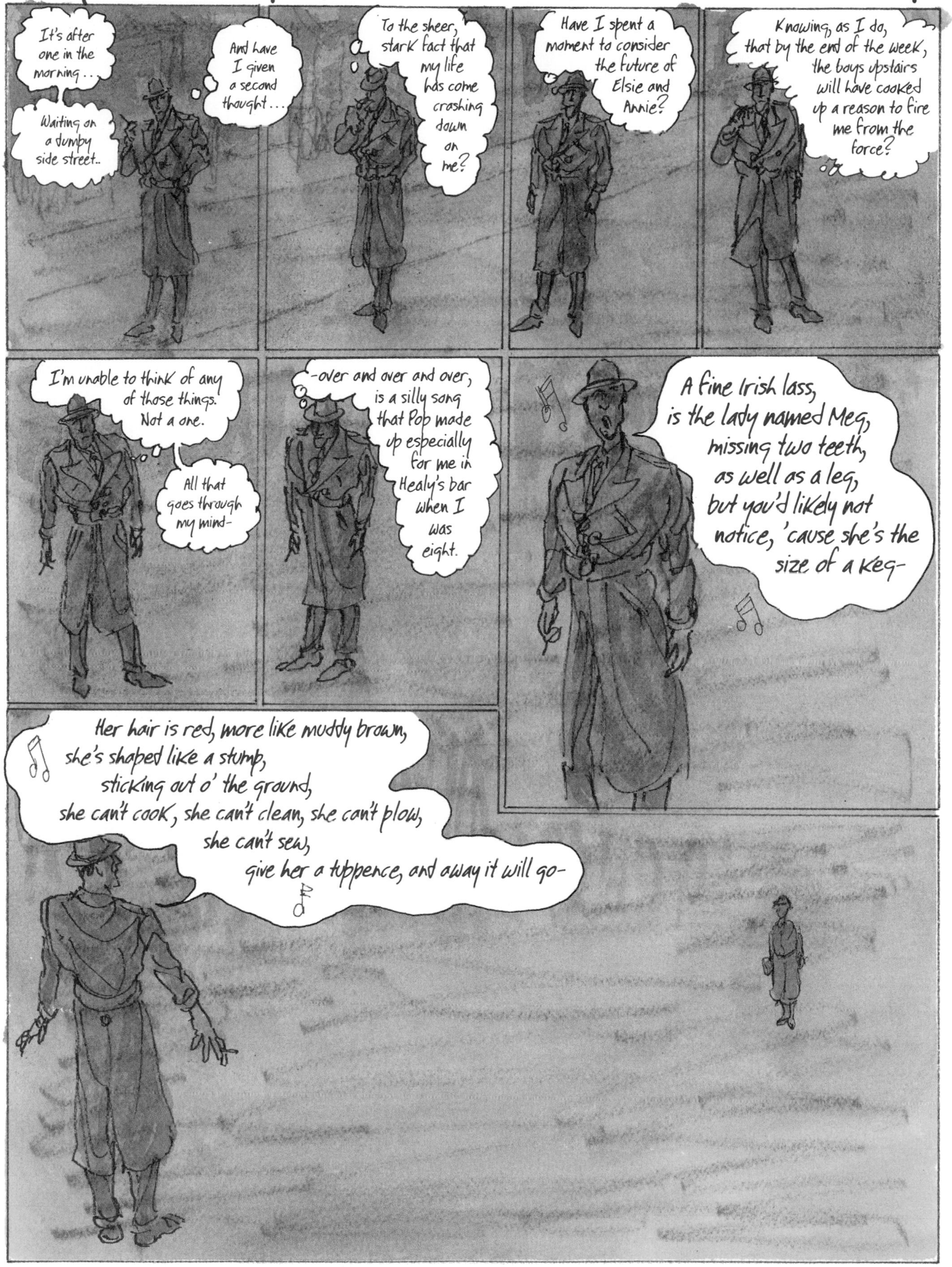

It's after one in the morning...
Waiting on a dumpy side street..
And have I given a second thought...
To the sheer, stark fact that my life has come crashing down on me?
Have I spent a moment to consider the future of Elsie and Annie?
Knowing, as I do, that by the end of the week, the boys upstairs will have cooked up a reason to fire me from the force?
I'm unable to think of any of those things. Not a one.
All that goes through my mind-
-over and over and over, is a silly song that Pop made up especially for me in Healy's bar when I was eight.
A fine Irish lass, is the lady named Meg, missing two teeth, as well as a leg, but you'd likely not notice, 'cause she's the size of a keg-
Her hair is red, more like muddy brown, she's shaped like a stump, sticking out o' the ground, she can't cook, she can't clean, she can't plow, she can't sew, give her a tuppence, and away it will go-

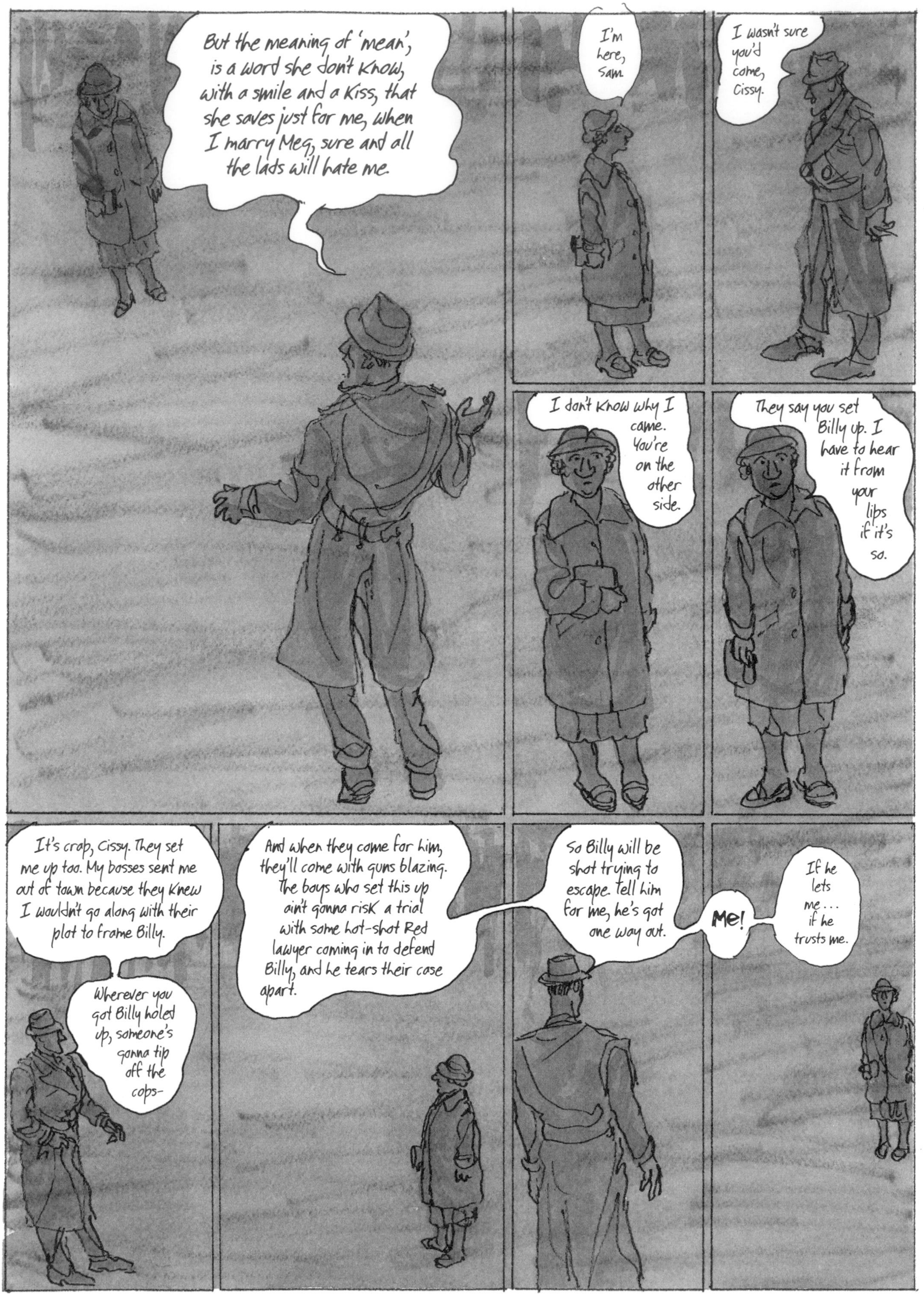

But the meaning of 'mean', is a word she don't know, with a smile and a kiss, that she saves just for me, when I marry Meg, sure and all the lads will hate me.
I'm here, Sam.
I wasn't sure you'd come, Cissy.
I don't know why I came. You're on the other side.
They say you set Billy up. I have to hear it from your lips if it's so.
It's crap, Cissy. They set me up too. My bosses sent me out of town because they knew I wouldn't go along with their plot to frame Billy.
Wherever you got Billy holed up, someone's gonna tip off the cops-
And when they come for him, they'll come with guns blazing. The boys who set this up ain't gonna risk a trial with some hot-shot Red lawyer coming in to defend Billy, and he tears their case apart.
So Billy will be shot trying to escape. Tell him for me, he's got one way out.
Me!
If he lets me... if he trusts me.

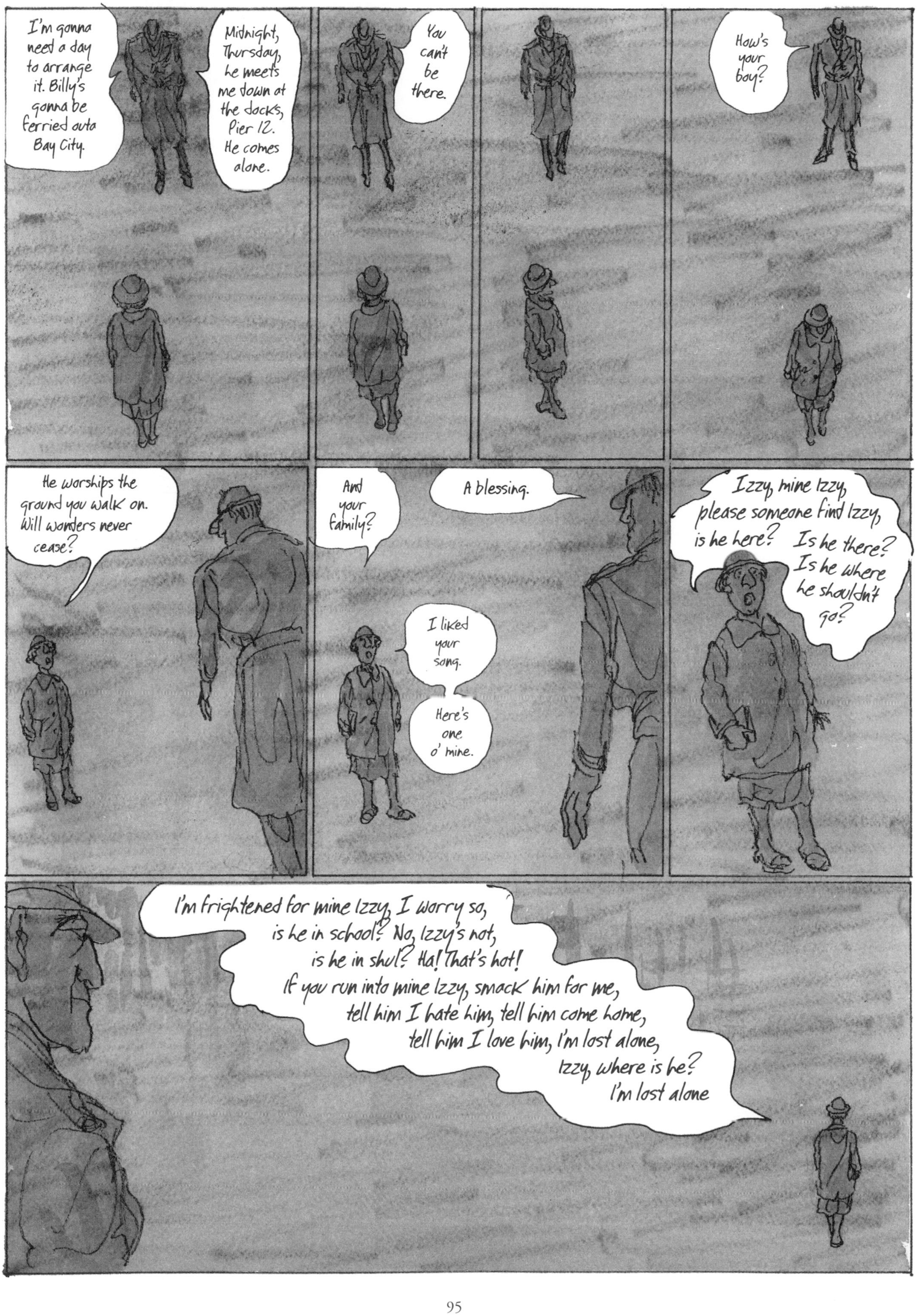
I'm gonna need a day to arrange it. Billy's gonna be ferried outa Bay City.
Midnight, Thursday, he meets me down at the docks, Pier 12. He comes alone.
You can't be there.
How's your boy?
He worships the ground you walk on. Will wonders never cease?
And your family?
A blessing.
I liked your song.
Here's one o' mine.
Izzy, mine Izzy, please someone find Izzy, is he here?
Is he there? Is he where he shouldn't go?
I'm frightened for mine Izzy, I worry so, is he in school? No, Izzy's not, is he in shul? Ha! That's hot! If you run into mine Izzy, smack him for me, tell him I hate him, tell him come home, tell him I love him, I'm lost alone, Izzy, where is he? I'm lost alone

Chapter Thirty-Four: Sam's Plan

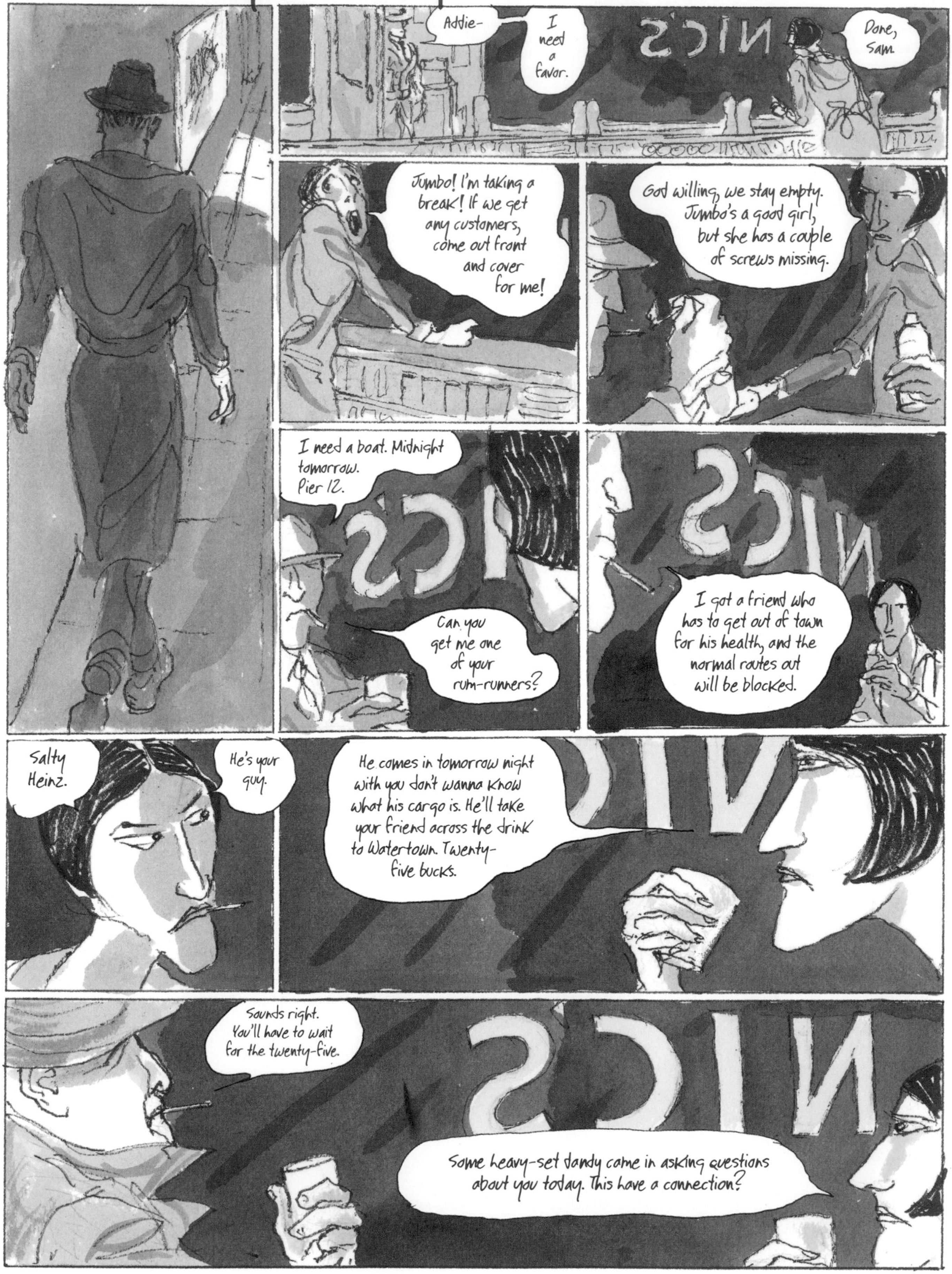

Addie-
I need a favor.
Done, Sam.
Jumbo! I'm taking a break! If we get any customers, come out front and cover for me!
God willing, we stay empty. Jumbo's a good girl, but she has a couple of screws missing.
I need a boat. Midnight tomorrow. Pier 12.
Can you get me one of your rum-runners?
I got a friend who has to get out of town for his health, and the normal routes out will be blocked.
Salty Heinz.
He's your guy.
He comes in tomorrow night with you don't wanna know what his cargo is. He'll take your friend across the drink to Watertown. Twenty-five bucks.
Sounds right. You'll have to wait for the twenty-five.
Some heavy-set dandy came in asking questions about you today. This have a connection?

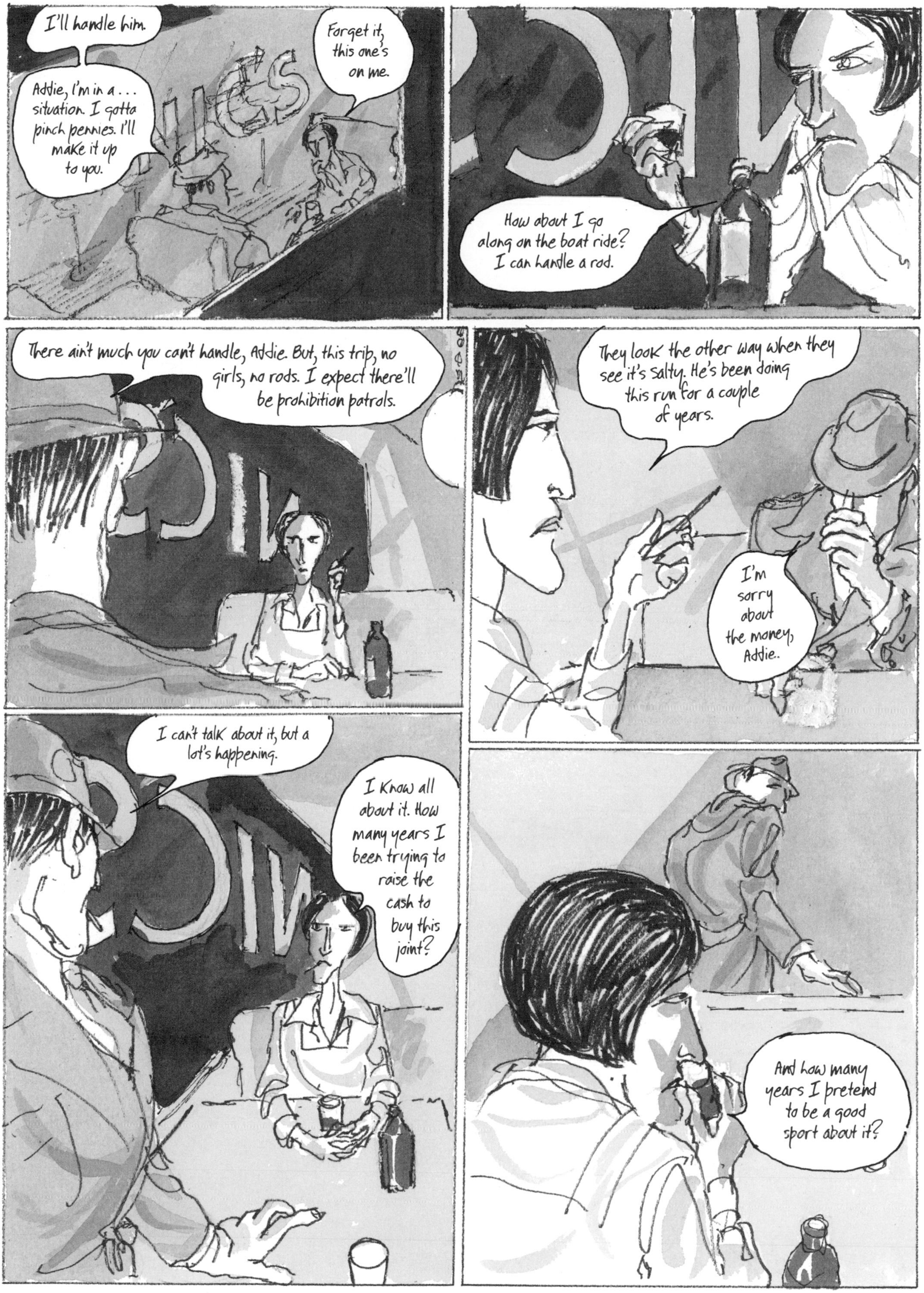
I'll handle him.
Addie, I'm in a . . . situation. I gotta pinch pennies. I'll make it up to you.
Forget it, this one's on me.
How about I go along on the boat ride? I can handle a rod.
There ain't much you can't handle, Addie. But, this trip, no girls, no rods. I expect there'll be prohibition patrols.
They look the other way when they see it's Salty. He's been doing this run for a couple of years.
I'm sorry about the money, Addie.
I can't talk about it, but a lot's happening.
I Know all about it. How many years I been trying to raise the cash to buy this joint?
And how many years I pretend to be a good sport about it?

Chapter Thirty-Five: SLAM!

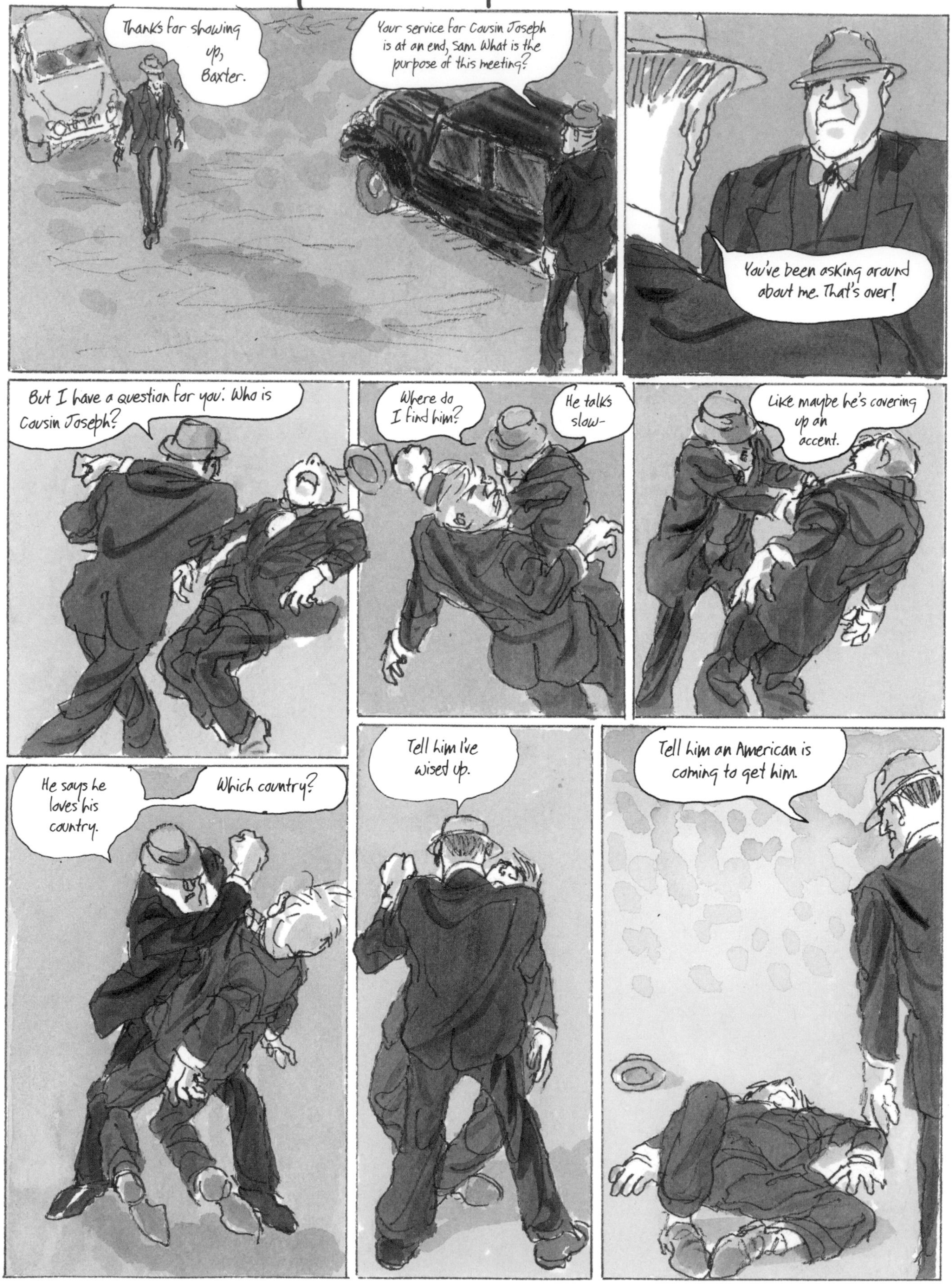
Thanks for showing up, Baxter.
Your service for Cousin Joseph is at an end, Sam. What is the purpose of this meeting?
You've been asking around about me. That's over!
But I have a question for you: Who is Cousin Joseph?
Where do I find him?
He talks slow-
Like maybe he's covering up an accent.
He says he loves his country.
Which country?
Tell him I've wised up.
Tell him an American is coming to get him.

Chapter Thirty-Six: Archie Goldman, Boy Detective

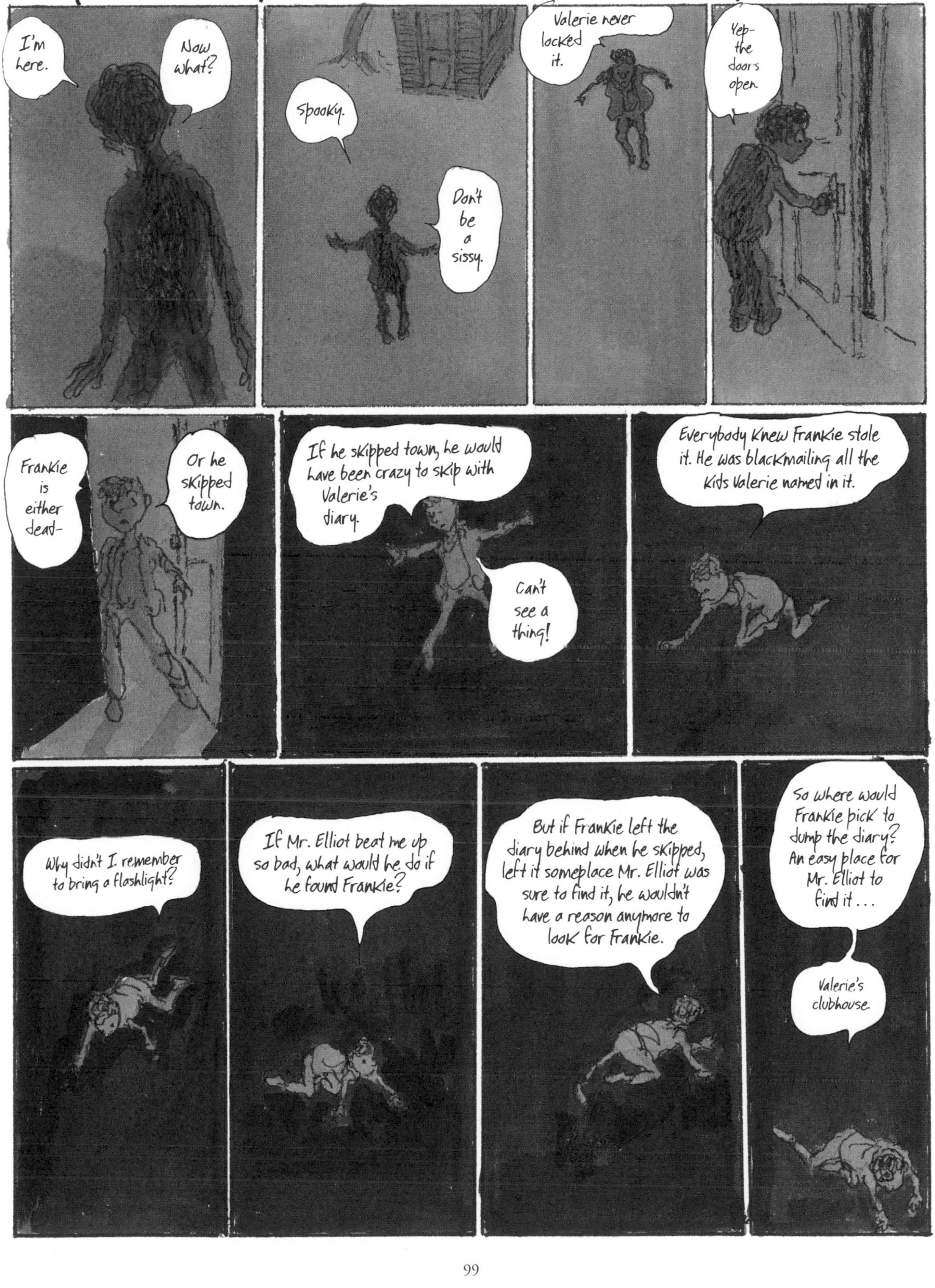
I'm here.
Now what?
Spooky.
Don't be a sissy.
Valerie never locked it.
Yep- the doors open.
Frankie is either dead-
Or he skipped town.
If he skipped town, he would have been crazy to skip with Valerie's diary.
Can't see a thing!
Everybody knew Frankie stole it. He was blackmailing all the kids Valerie named in it.
Why didn't I remember to bring a flashlight?
If Mr. Elliot beat me up so bad, what would he do if he found Frankie?
But if Frankie left the diary behind when he skipped, left it someplace Mr. Elliot was sure to find it, he wouldn't have a reason anymore to look for Frankie.
So where would Frankie pick to dump the diary? An easy place for Mr. Elliot to find it . . .
Valerie's clubhouse.

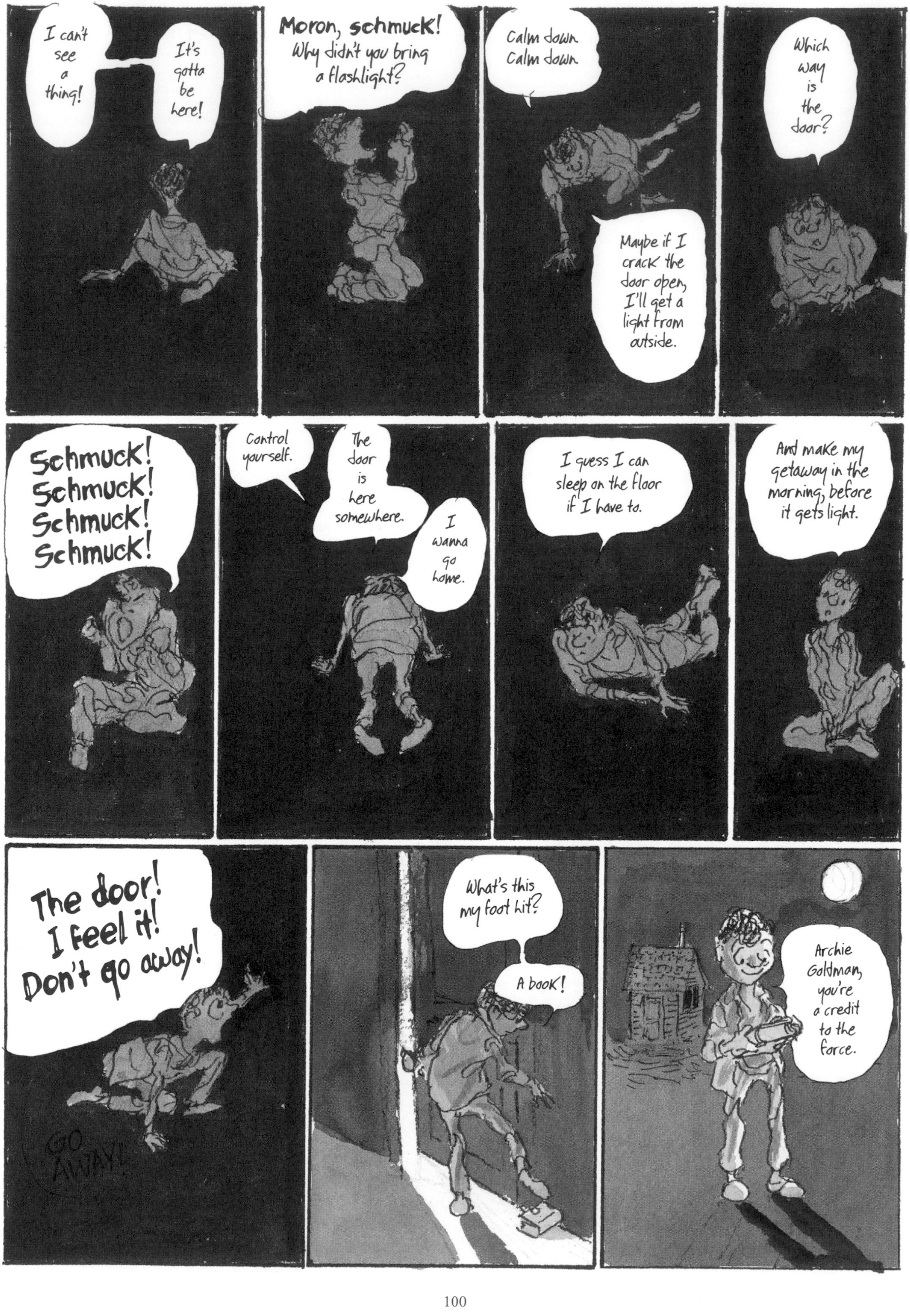

I can't see a thing!
It's gotta be here!
Moron, schmuck! Why didn't you bring a flashlight?
Calm down. Calm down.
Maybe if I crack the door open, I'll get a light from outside.
Which way is the door?
Schmuck! Schmuck! Schmuck! Schmuck!
Control yourself.
The door is here somewhere.
I wanna go home.
I guess I can sleep on the floor if I have to.
And make my getaway in the morning, before it gets light.
The door! I feel it! Don't go away!
GO AWAY!
What's this my foot hit?
A book!
Archie Goldman, you're a credit to the force.

Chapter Thirty-Seven: Oh, My God . . .

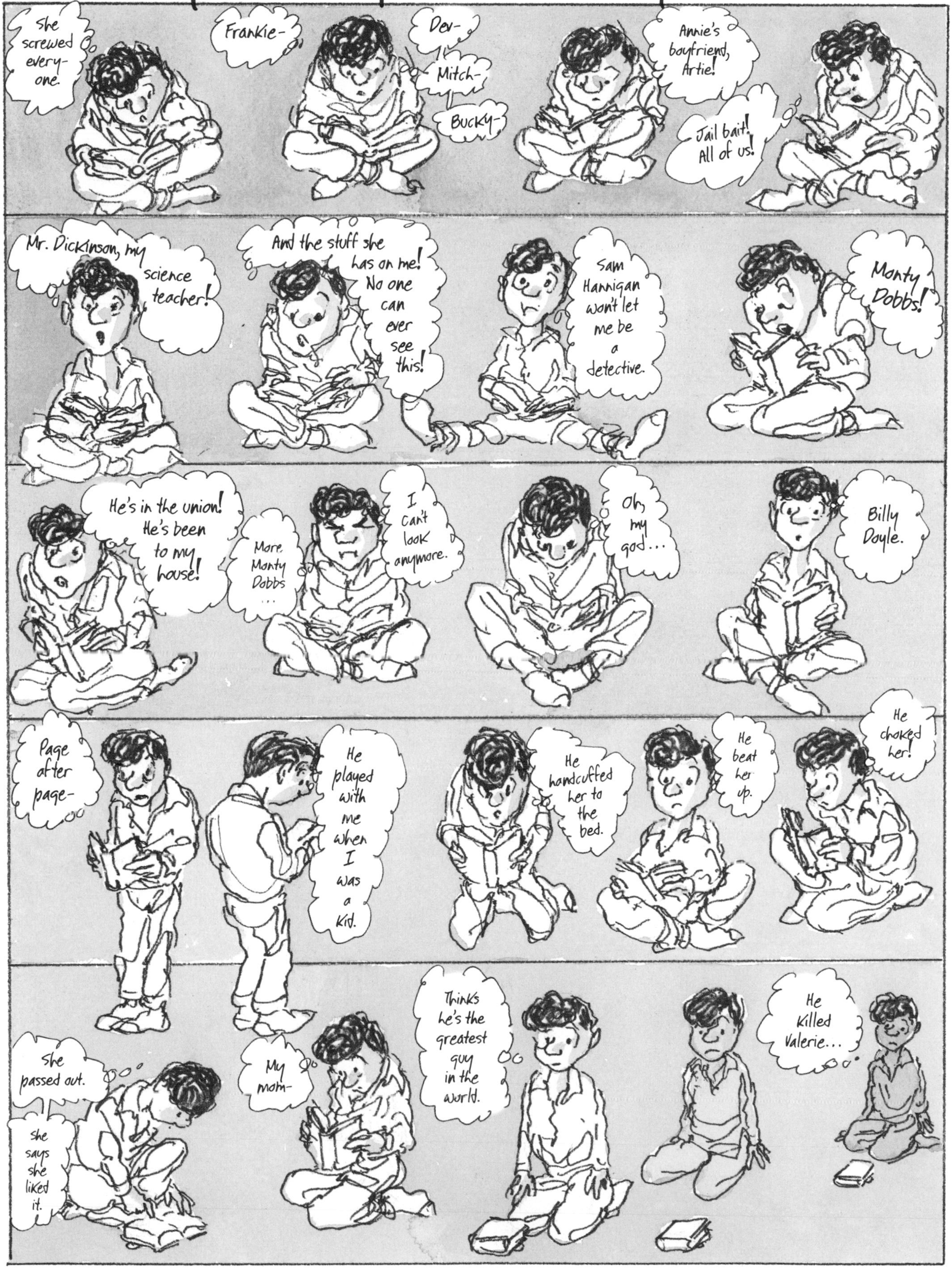
She screwed every-one.
Frankie-
Dev-
Mitch-
Bucky-
Annie's boyfriend, Artie!
Jail bait! All of us!
Mr. Dickinson, my science teacher!
And the stuff she has on me! No one can ever see this!
Sam Hannigan won't let me be a detective.
Monty Dobbs!
He's in the union! He's been to my house!
More Monty Dobbs . . .
I can't look anymore.
Oh, my god . . .
Billy Doyle.
Page after page-
He played with me when I was a kid.
He handcuffed her to the bed.
He beat her up.
He choked her!
She passed out.
She says she liked it.
My mom-
Thinks he's the greatest guy in the world.
He killed Valerie . . .

Chapter Thirty-Eight: How It Ends

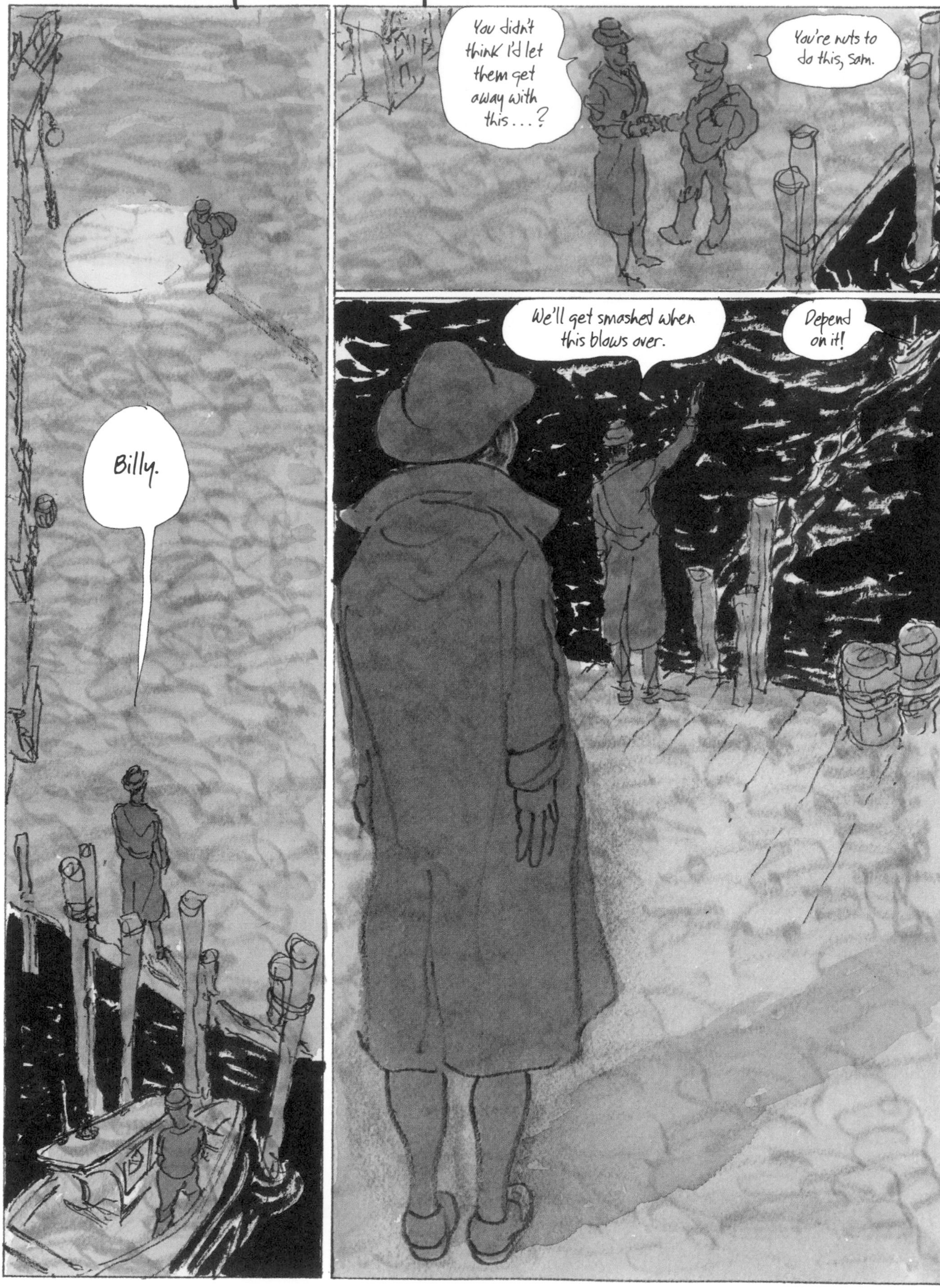
Billy.
You didn't think I'd let them get away with this...?
You're nuts to do this, Sam.
We'll get smashed when this blows over.
Depend on it!

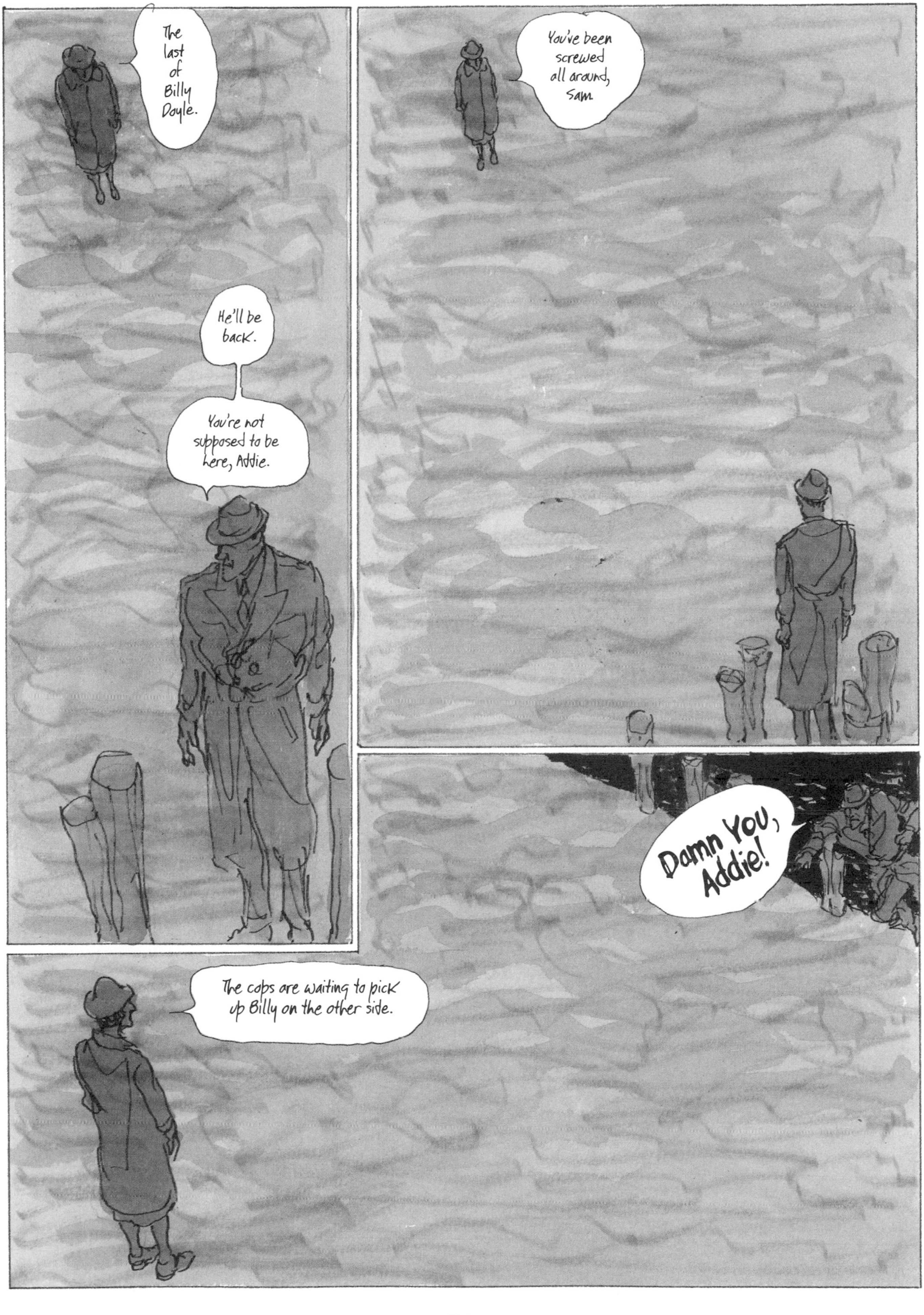
The last of Billy Doyle.
You've been screwed all around, Sam.
He'll be back.
You're not supposed to be here, Addie.
Damn You, Addie!
The cops are waiting to pick up Billy on the other side.

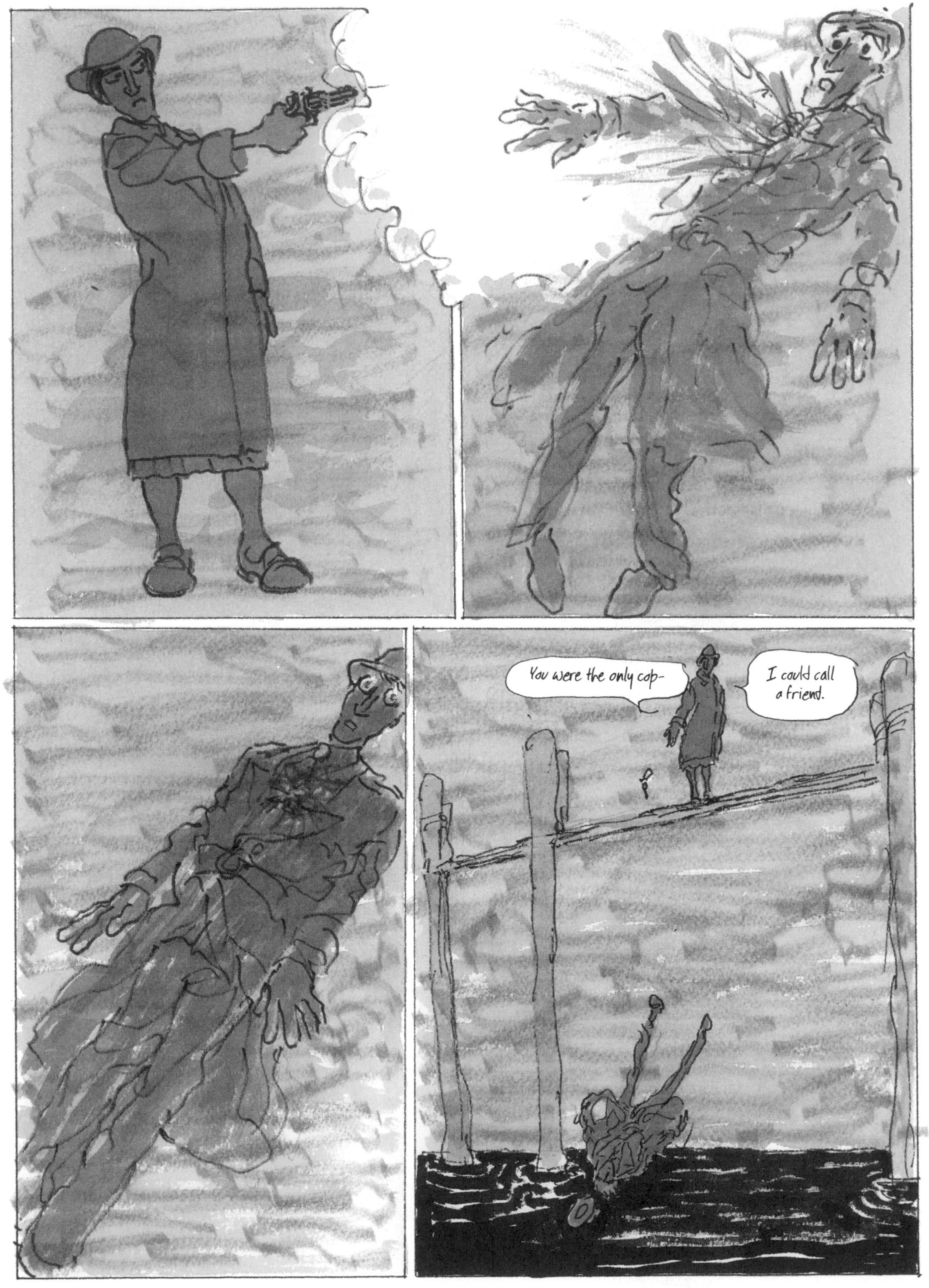
You were the only cop-
I could call a friend.

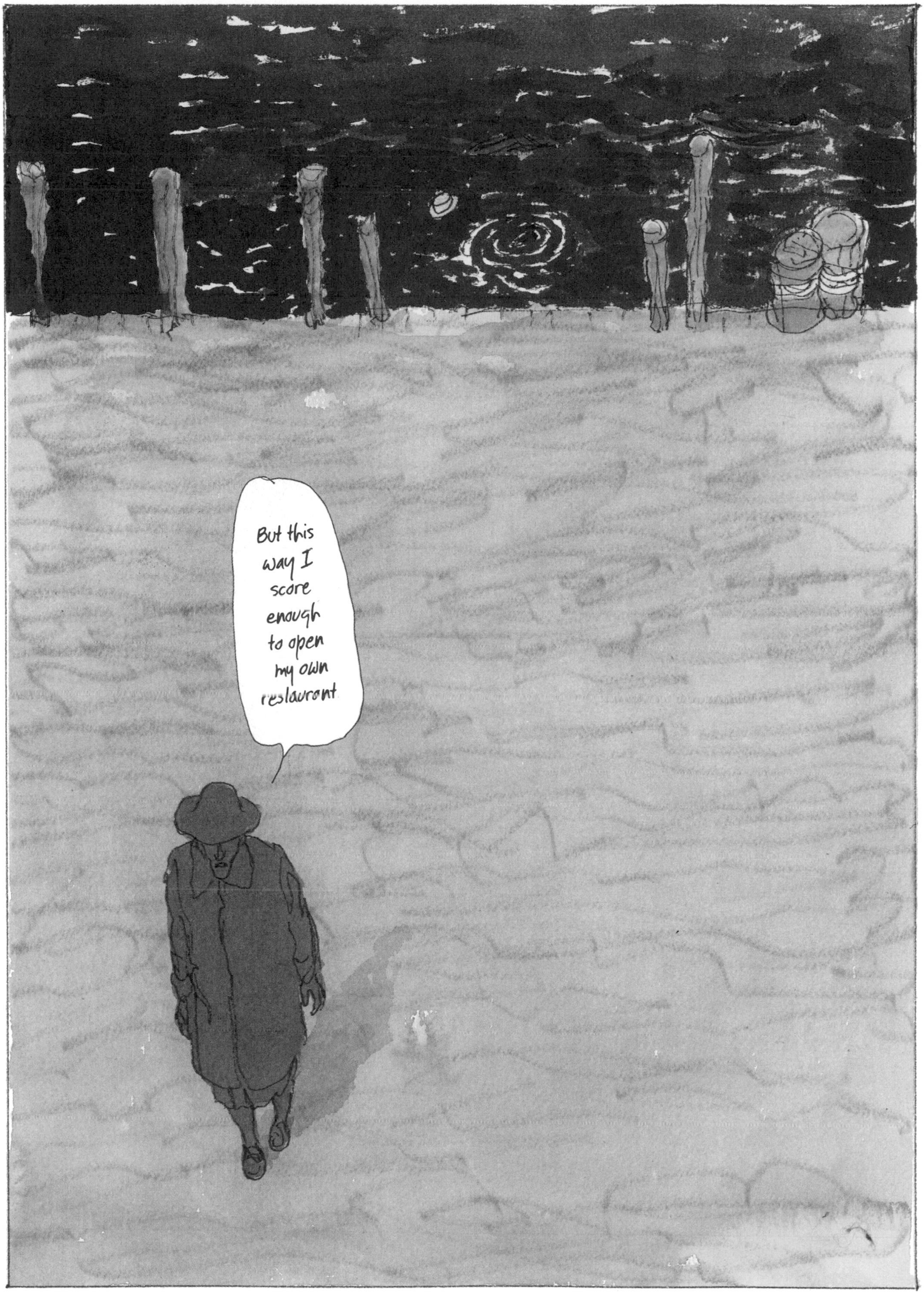
But this way I score enough to open my own restaurant.

Chapter Thirty-Nine: Bottoms Up

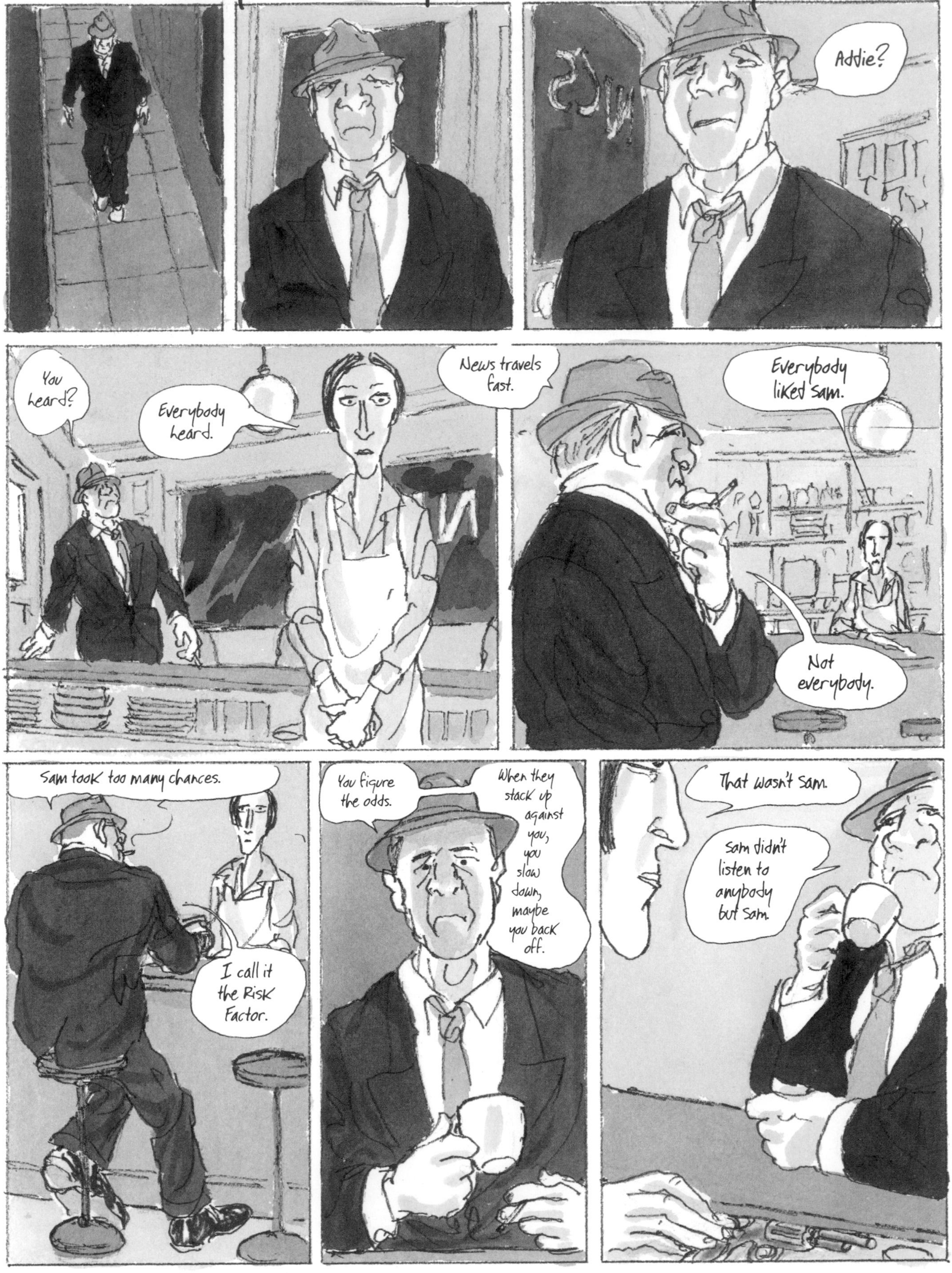
Addie?
You heard?
Everybody heard.
News travels fast.
Everybody liked Sam.
Not everybody.
Sam took too many chances.
I call it the Risk Factor.
You figure the odds.
When they stack up against you, you slow down, maybe you back off.
That wasn't Sam.
Sam didn't listen to anybody but Sam.

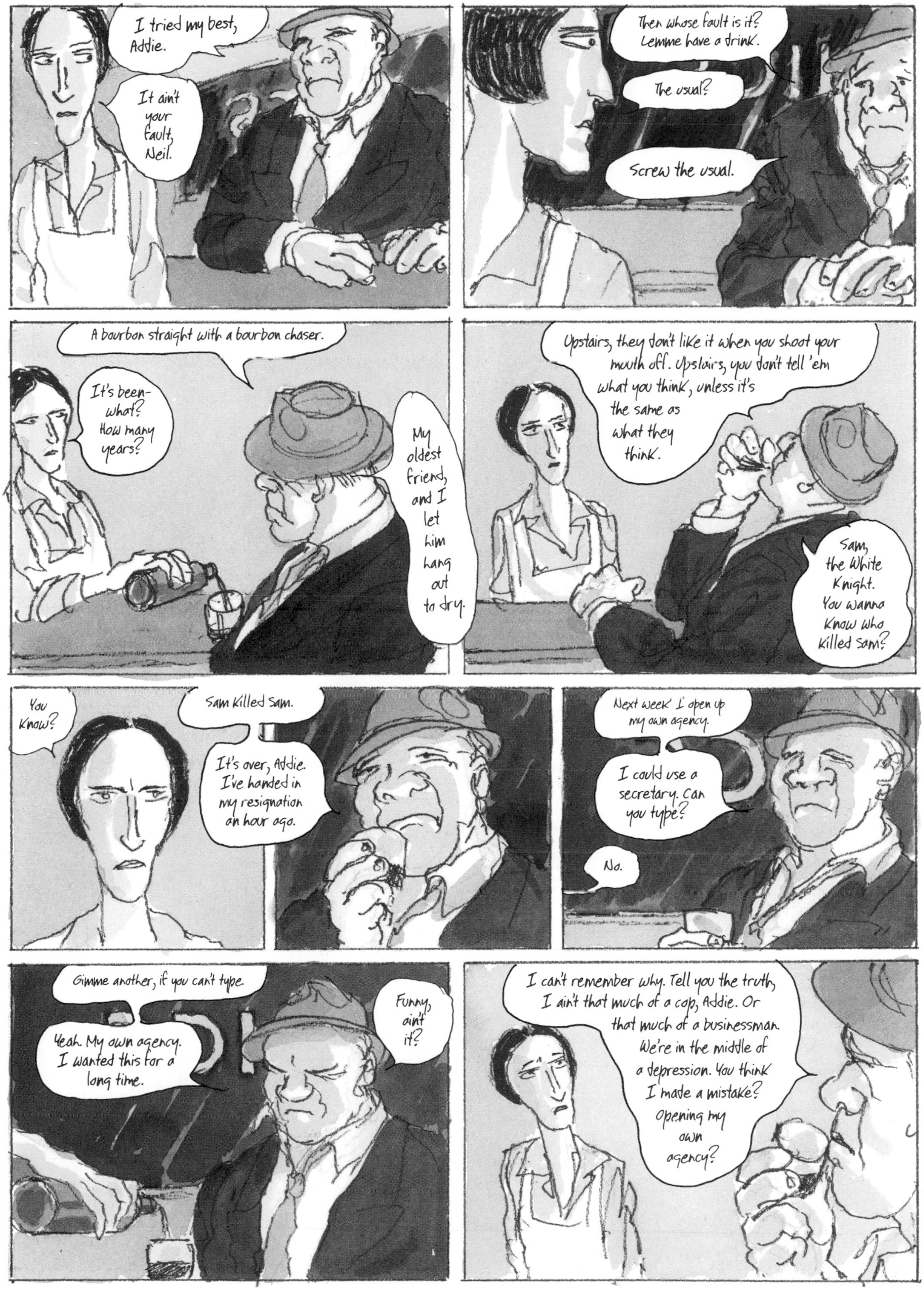
I tried my best, Addie.
It ain't your fault, Neil.
Then whose fault is it? Lemme have a drink.
The usual?
Screw the usual.
A bourbon straight with a bourbon chaser.
It's been— what? How many years?
My oldest friend, and I let him hang out to dry.
Upstairs, they don't like it when you shoot your mouth off. Upstairs, you don't tell 'em what you think, unless it's the same as what they think.
Sam, the White Knight. You wanna know who killed Sam?
You know?
Sam killed Sam.
It's over, Addie. I've handed in my resignation an hour ago.
Next week I' open up my own agency.
I could use a secretary. Can you type?
No.
Gimme another, if you can't type.
Yeah. My own agency. I wanted this for a long time.
Funny, ain't it?
I can't remember why. Tell you the truth, I ain't that much of a cop, Addie. Or that much of a businessman. We're in the middle of a depression. You think I made a mistake? Opening my own agency?

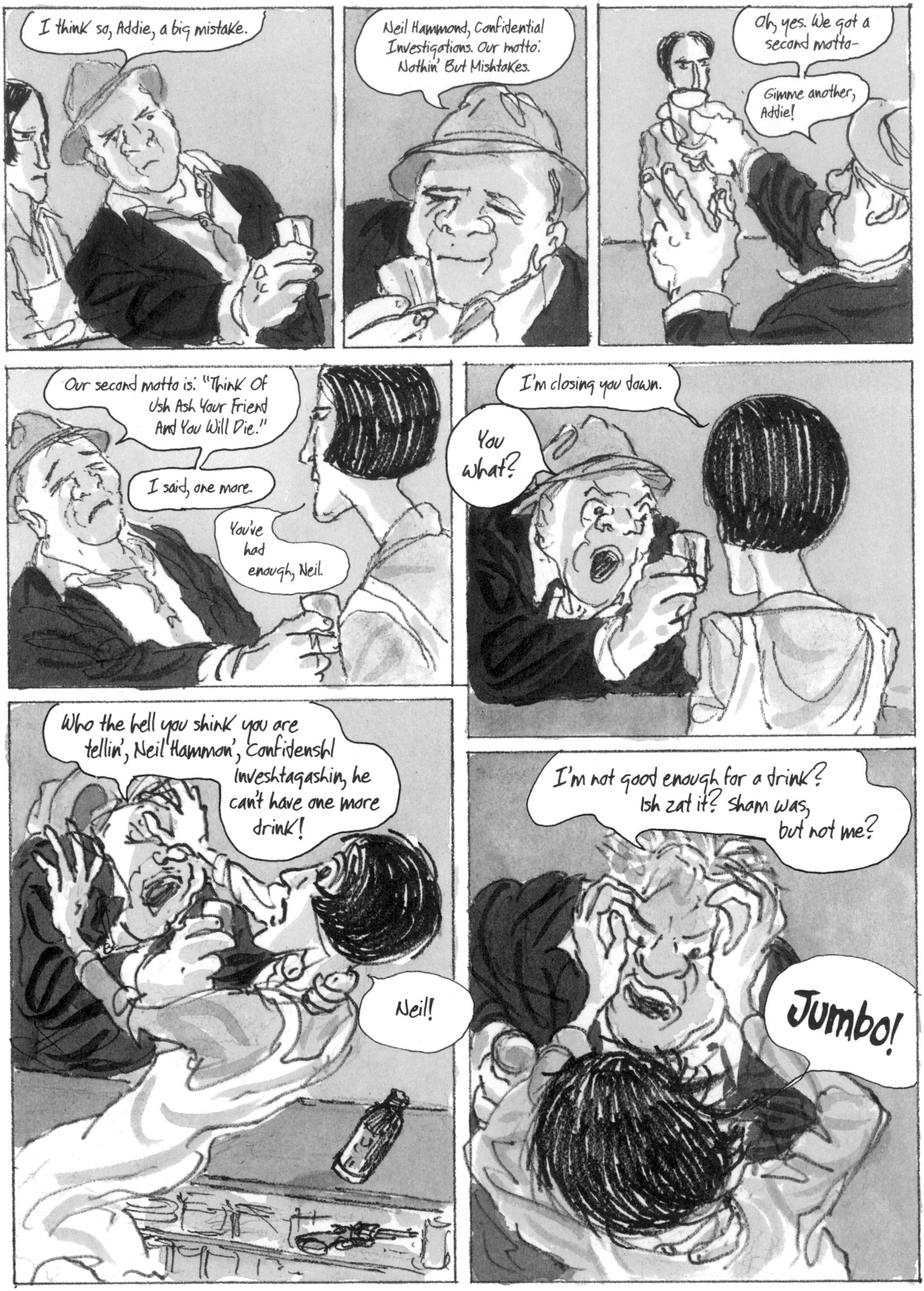
I think so, Addie, a big mistake.
Neil Hammond, Confidential Investigations. Our motto: Nothin' But Mishtakes.
Oh, yes. We got a second motto-
Gimme another, Addie!
Our second motto is: "Think Of Ush Ash Your Friend And You Will Die."
I said, one more.
You've had enough, Neil.
I'm closing you down.
You what?
Who the hell you shink you are tellin', Neil Hammon', Confidenshl Inveshtagashin, he can't have one more drink!
Neil!
I'm not good enough for a drink? Ish zat it? Sham was, but not me?
Jumbo!

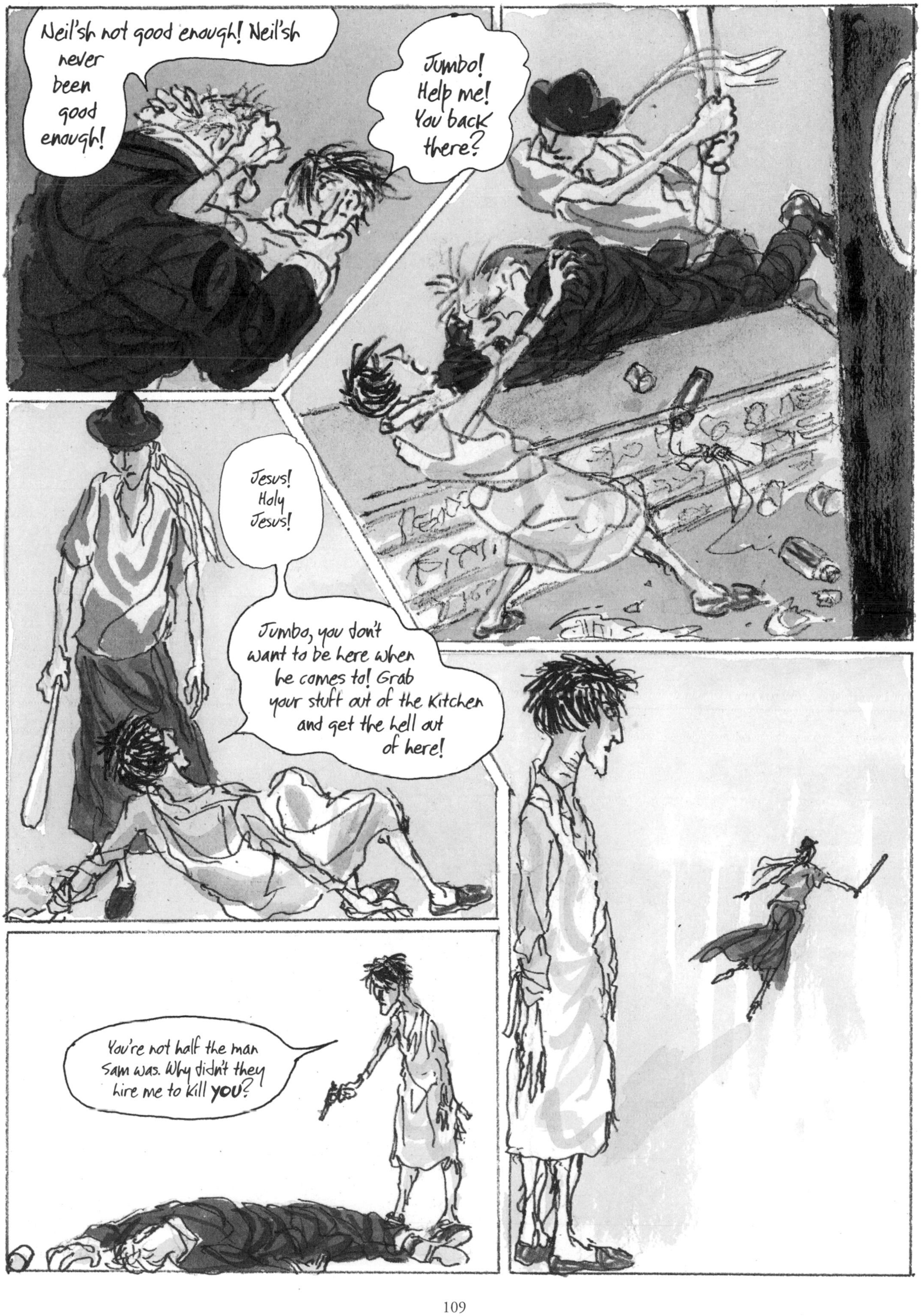
Neil'sh not good enough! Neil'sh never been good enough!
Jumbo! Help me! You back there?
Jesus! Holy Jesus!
Jumbo, you don't want to be here when he comes to! Grab your stuff out of the Kitchen and get the hell out of here!
You're not half the man Sam was. Why didn't they hire me to kill YOU?

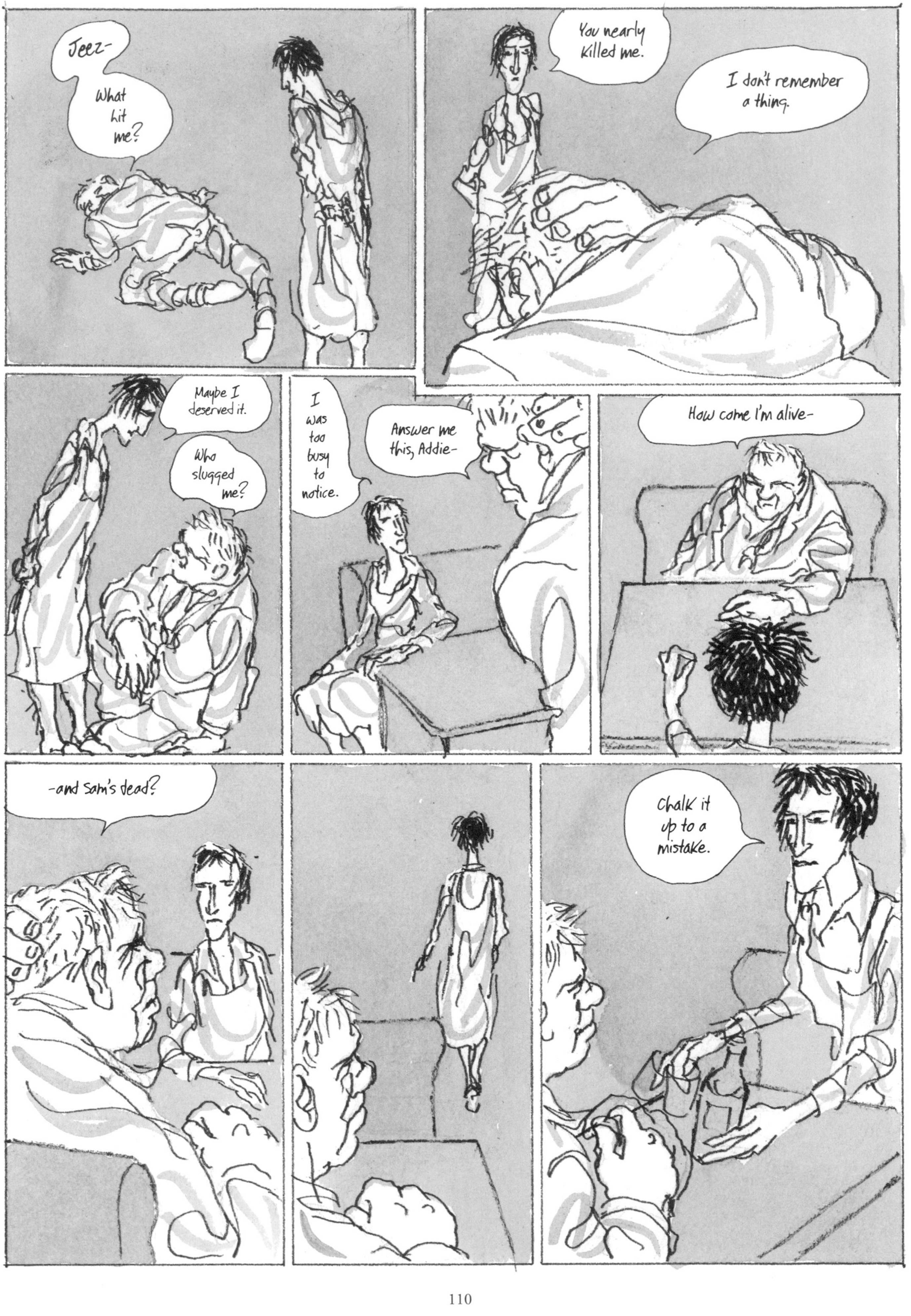

Jeez-
What hit me?
You nearly killed me.
I don't remember a thing.
Maybe I deserved it.
Who slugged me?
I was too busy to notice.
Answer me this, Addie-
How come I'm alive-
-and Sam's dead?
Chalk it up to a mistake.

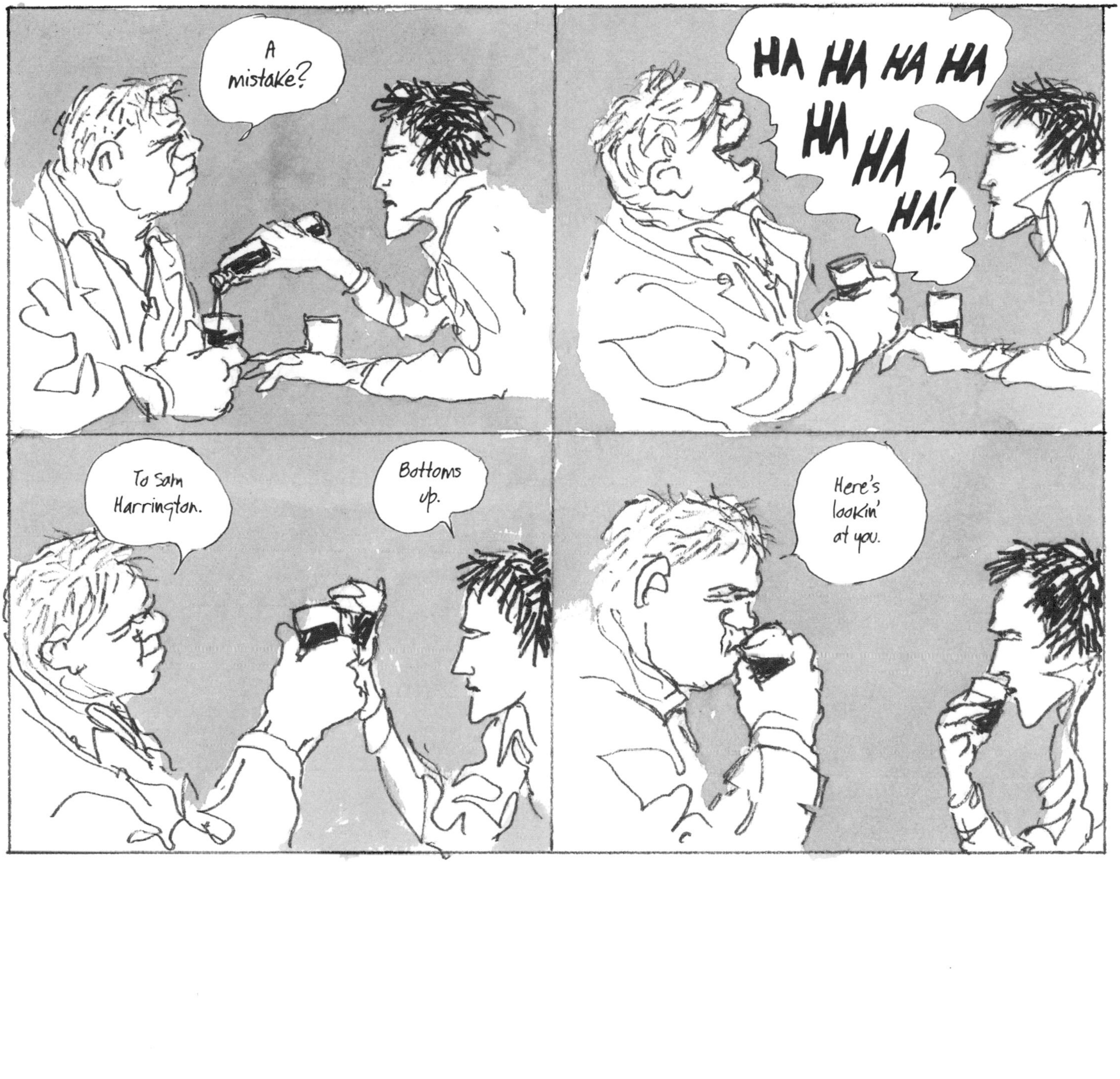
A mistake?
HA HA HA HA HA HA HA!
To Sam Harrington.
Bottoms up.
Here's lookin' at you.

To be concluded:

The Ghost Script

Acknowledgments

This accidental noir trilogy that began with *Kill My Mother* and will end with *The Ghost Script* could never have been conceived or illustrated were I still living out a life of quiet resignation in Manhattan. The fortuitous circumstances that led to my abandoning the city for the East End of Long Island, where I found a new life, new friends, and a new career as graphic novelist (no more than an extension of the adventure newspaper-strip cartoonist that I wanted to be as a boy), now brings me as much or more pure joy than at any time in my life.

To all those who count, and to my children and grandchild, who count on their own exalted level, I thank you many times over for this grand reprieve. You know who you are. Especially . . .